THE HUMAN Manifesto

WHAT HAPPENS WHEN ORGANIZATIONS ALLOW PEOPLE THE FREEDOM TO BE

 Jonathan Ledwidge

Morgan James Publishing • New York, NY

THE
HUMAN ASSET MANIFESTO

ISBN: 1-60037-041-1 (Hardcover)
ISBN: 1-60037-042-X (Paperback)
ISBN: 1-60037-043-8 (eBook)
ISBN: 1-60037-044-6 (Audio)

Published by:

MORGAN · JAMES
THE ENTREPRENEURIAL PUBLISHER™
www.morganjamespublishing.com

Morgan James Publishing, LLC
1225 Franklin Ave Ste 325
Garden City, NY 11530-1693
Toll Free 800-485-4943
www.MorganJamesPublishing.com

Habitat
for Humanity®
Peninsula
Building Partner

General Editor:
Heather Campbell

Cover & Interior Design by:
3 Dog Design
www.3dogdesign.net
chris@3dogdesign.net

CONTENTS

THE HUMAN ASSET MANIFESTO

FOREWORD

It touches me to think of human resources using their optical resources to extract the information resources from this page. Or, to put it another way, I like to think of people reading this foreword. And understanding the difference between those two statements is part of Jonathan's contribution in this book.

There are many books – and management courses – that deal with human beings as they would be if only they had been designed 'properly' as rational resources to fit smoothly into organizations. By contrast, this is a book by a human being, meant to be read by human beings, about human beings, as we know them.

Widespread assumptions about humans as mechanisms are set aside, and instead we are treated to a well read, intelligent, and witty view of an exciting emerging world of work and organization. More than that, this is one of those books that not only opens our eyes, but also makes very practical suggestions about how we might make use of new visions.

I am sure that many readers will not agree with everything this book says, or will feel that there are important areas that are not discussed, but those points are unimportant. This book makes you think and, if you wish, act. It is an exercise in thought leadership, which invites its readers in turn to come alive as leaders in new and effective forms of organization.

David Sims BA (CNAA), MA (Leeds), PhD (Bath)
Professor of Organizational Behavior, Associate Dean, and
Director, Centre for Leadership, Learning, and Change
Cass Business School
London
d.sims@city.ac.uk

THE HUMAN ASSET MANIFESTO

INTRODUCTION

The Human Asset Manifesto aims to transform the current socially dysfunctional approach to business, and liberate the energies and capabilities of people – energies and capabilities which organizations have become so proficient at suppressing.

The Human Asset Manifesto unreservedly asserts and unequivocally demonstrates that in the future only those organizations that lead social change will succeed.

The Human Asset Manifesto is a challenge to the established order – to look beyond the narrow confines of business and evaluate people in a total and more humanistic sense, and by so doing allow them to make the most of their capabilities, as well as greatly improving organizational performance.

There is a passion to this mission. That passion is derived from my sincere belief that every individual deserves the right and the opportunity to be the very best they can – to be the greatest asset for themselves, and whichever organization they choose to work with. It is born from an understanding of people that is based on who they are as real people – with ambitions, consumption patterns, families, and their own individuality. It is based partly on my experience and knowledge of business, but also on my lifelong vocation – the study of history, people, and cultures.

This synthesis of business, history, and culture is why The Human Asset Manifesto represents a new paradigm, a new business approach, and a new type of organization – The Human Asset Organization©.

If you are the average person who gets up in the morning to go to work, then this book is for you and about you – irrespective of age, gender, race, nationality or any other distinguishing factor. If you are a manager or executive, then it will be of even more relevance to you, given that your decisions directly affect the daily lives of others – it will help you improve your organization's performance beyond anything you may currently envisage.

Throughout the book, I will be offering you opportunities to participate in the mission of change and the development of a new order. At the end of each of the four main sections, there is a Statement of Affirmation, which allows you to express your support for the principles of The Human Asset Manifesto. Each statement invites you to visit the website at www.thamanifesto.com and register your endorsement. By so doing you will be telling the rest of the world that there is a community of individuals that believes there is a better way.

The philosophy behind The Human Asset Manifesto is that there can be no real understanding of businesses and organizations without an understanding of people in the most primal sense. This goes beyond the endless theories of management, leadership, and human resources, and focuses instead on history and social evolution – the things that determine who we are, why we are, and the very state of our existence.

The Human Asset Manifesto demands that we evaluate people in business as human beings – nothing more, nothing less. Nevertheless, within that context everything we examine will be directly and practically related to work, the business environment, and the evolution of whole industries both past and present.

This humanistic approach will facilitate a greater understanding of the true nature of business, and in the first main section, A FEUDAL EXISTENCE, it aptly defines and demonstrates why most people are less than enthused or motivated by today's working environment – why it is a pain for most people to get up and go to work in the morning.

Having established that people are less than fully engaged during most of their waking hours, we then take a human and social journey in the section REVOLUTION, EVOLUTION, ENLIGHTENMENT. Throughout that journey, you will see that since the time of the Industrial Revolution, organizations and industries achieve their greatest prosperity when they pay the greatest attention to human and social needs, both internally and externally. You will see that the success of mass production was only partially due to new production technologies, and greatly depended on an understanding of employee needs.

You will come to what is a very stark realization; that innovation, productivity, and competitive advantage have human and social roots, and that it is imperative that people, human assets, are placed at the forefront of every single business decision.

More intriguingly, we will also see that the opposite is also true – that throughout history, those organizations and industries that have failed to comprehend the impact of human and social evolution on their activities are the ones that placed themselves at greatest risk. You will see why the rise of Toyota and the gradual demise of GM are both grounded in their approach to their employees.

Throughout this journey, you will come to an understanding that people have always been far more important than technology. The section will lay the human and social foundations upon which we will proclaim a more enlightened view of the relationship between people, organizations, and their individual and collective prosperity.

Having thus succeeded, we are then suitably prepared to explore the section LIBERTY, EQUALITY, FRATERNITY, a systematic examination of the social myopia that afflicts modern management, and why that places organizations and whole industries in an invidious position. More specifically, it explores how and why the young, the mature, women, and minorities must be leveraged in very specific ways, if they are to survive and remain competitive.

In doing so, it rejects decisions based solely on "political correctness" as nothing more than a failure to understand the nature of both the opportunities and the risks associated with the diversity of human assets.

Having established the human and social imperative for change, it is only natural that we move from a position of acceptance to one of action. In the section RENAISSANCE, REFORMATION, LIBERATION, we create the new paradigm, new business approach, and a reformation that gives birth to a new type of organization.

THE HUMAN ASSET MANIFESTO

In so doing we liberate the human spirit, as well as that of the organization, such that together, they achieve far greater heights, improving not only their prosperity, but also that of the wider community. It is within this context that we define The Human Asset Organization© as one of shared values and objectives, and which optimizes its human assets by managing the human and social environment both internally and externally.

The section includes a comprehensive set of recommendations that establish a framework for achieving the status of The Human Asset Organization©, as well as a methodology for measuring progress in getting there. By definition, this methodology includes an assessment and evaluation of an organization's human assets.

Finally, we briefly discuss THE NEXT STEPS – the additional steps you might take to join the community of people who believe in principles espoused by The Human Asset Manifesto, and how you might contact me and learn more about my work.

However, we shall begin at the very beginning – with a cry for the liberation and freedom of the human spirit – THE HUMAN ASSET MANIFESTO.

Jonathan Ledwidge
April 2006

THE HUMAN ASSET MANIFESTO

People have always strived for freedom; it is the very essence of humanity

- *The freedom to be wholly human*
- *The freedom to enjoy our existence*
- *The freedom to engage our environment*
- *The freedom to define and shape the world around us*
- *The freedom to be our natural selves*
- *The freedom to consume*
- *The freedom to engage others*
- *The freedom to engage our wider communities*
- *The freedom to think*
- *The freedom to believe*
- *The freedom to articulate what we believe*
- *The freedom to be bold and ambitious*
- *The freedom to act*
- *The freedom to experiment*
- *The freedom to be creative*

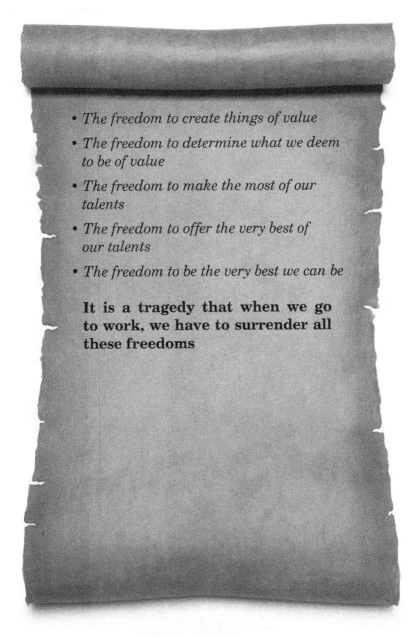

- *The freedom to create things of value*
- *The freedom to determine what we deem to be of value*
- *The freedom to make the most of our talents*
- *The freedom to offer the very best of our talents*
- *The freedom to be the very best we can be*

It is a tragedy that when we go to work, we have to surrender all these freedoms

THE HUMAN ASSET MANIFESTO

A FEUDAL EXISTENCE

THE HUMAN ASSET MANIFESTO

CHAPTER

1

THE CASE FOR THE PEOPLE

THE HUMAN ASSET MANIFESTO

THE CASE FOR THE PEOPLE

Organizations are socially dysfunctional because they have been singularly unable to understand the extent to which human and social changes within society are affecting their business. They have been unable to grapple with the wider evolution of society, as well as with the people factors that they need to leverage in order to optimize their business.

A large number of people, employees even, are genuinely not interested in work – they view it as an unfortunate but necessary intrusion into their lives.

A large number of people have come to believe, and maybe they always did, that there are more important things in life than working for an organization, for which the only long-term reward is the possibility of a small pension.

The dismal truth is that people spend most of their waking hours putting up or making do with something they do not really enjoy. Think about it. If you work a regular nine-to-five job, and you have a commute of an hour each way, you have a total of ten out of every twenty-four hours dedicated to work. If you manage to get eight hours of sleep, then it means that work takes up as much as 63% of your waking hours.

I suppose we should spare a thought for those who work longer hours, have a longer commute, and by definition get a lot less sleep. I have been there. It is not nice.

To most, work is something that pays the bills not somewhere to engage the mind, a fact that has been most brutally exposed by the human resources consultancy, Towers Perrin.

THE HUMAN ASSET MANIFESTO

In 2005, Towers Perrin performed a global survey encompassing 86,000 employees in order to ascertain their level of engagement. The results were in one sense amazing but they were also highly predictable. The survey showed that on average only 14% of employees were highly engaged in their jobs. Another 62% were only moderately engaged, and the remaining 24% were totally disengaged.

Industrialized nations such as Italy, The Netherlands, France, and Japan all had fewer than 10% of their workers fully engaged, with Japan having as many as 41% of its workers totally disengaged. The corresponding figures for the number of disengaged workers were India, 56% (watch that outsourcing!); the UK and France, 23%; Italy, 29%; and Spain, 23%. Germany and the US fared slightly better than many of the others with 16% and 15% of their respective workers being totally disengaged.

Julie Gaebar of Towers Perrin maintains that, *"If you have a significant portion of people disengaged, it may have an impact on quality and customer service."*

With all due respect to Ms Gaebar, that must rank as one of the greatest understatements of all time. More specifically, a Sunday Times 2006 survey of the 100 best companies to work for in the UK indicates that they outperformed those listed on the FTSE 100 share index by a factor of almost 2:1.

Towers Perrin also found that while pay was important, the opportunity to develop new skills was the No. 1 global driver of engagement. An organization's reputation and employee involvement in decision-making also ranked highly. Other positive influences on worker engagement included fairness, the ability to learn, and inspiring leadership.

The following extract from the FT of June 1, 2005 solidly supports what Towers Perrin has unearthed.

According to a study by the Conference Board, the business research organization, only half of Americans are satisfied with their jobs. A quarter said they were simply showing up to collect *their paycheck. Those earning more than US$50,000 were only slightly happier than those earning less than US$15,000.*

There is no question that organizations are out of touch with their people, and what is more it cuts right across the salary divide.

This should not be surprising. Organizations have a tendency to treat their people as if they were disposable diapers or nappies. They get used for a while and once it is believed that they have served their purpose, they are dispensed with.

The question we therefore should be asking is not why so many people are disengaged, but why so many people are engaged at all.

This conveniently brings us to a crucial juncture, an idea that begins to lay the foundations for our philosophy. You can only engage people if you deal with them as people.

To be a good leader you first have to be a human being – your understanding of people must move beyond the limited context of the organization to the wider context of their humanity.

There is no rocket science in this. There is nothing here that is difficult to comprehend. The fact that people are so less enamored of their work would have been highly predictable to anyone seriously concerned with the disposition of people, whom we refer to as human assets. It is part of a much wider trend, which is social and historical in context – one that is yet to be understood or acknowledged by many of today's business leaders.

People are consumers first and employees second.

This has a tremendous influence on and implications for productivity and competitive advantage. It is difficult to envisage a team or economic unit achieving optimal results when its principal members have conflicting objectives. People are increasingly defining their lives, and are being defined within society, not by their vocation, but by their lifestyles and what they consume.

THE HUMAN ASSET MANIFESTO

Their monthly pay is merely a means to an end.

As troublesome as this already appears, current and ongoing structural and generational changes in society will result in an ever-increasing divergence of corporate and personal objectives. The younger generation will challenge with new ways of thinking. The failure to treat women and mature workers with the respect and equality they deserve will also create major problems.

The above will be further exacerbated by the fact that organizations have never excelled in how they treat, manage, and reward individuals – you hear the horror stories every day. More generally, in recent years employees have had astonishingly regular and tremendous levels of change and organizational restructuring inflicted on them. Those who managed to remain sane throughout this ordeal might have begun to wonder whether or not it was all in pursuit of some hitherto unknown pleasure available only to managers and executives.

Without a rethink of the current strategies, corporate dysfunctionality will increase with the passage of time.

So what should organizations be doing? Few would argue that knowledge is the key to improving productivity and developing a sustainable competitive advantage. Unfortunately, many organizations fail to realize that people are the very essence of knowledge, including its acquisition, development, transformation, and delivery. All knowledge begins and ends with people.

In his book, *Intellectual Capital*, Tom Stewart maintains that the growth and management of knowledge has become the most important economic task of individuals, businesses, and nations.

Dawson, writing in *Developing Knowledge-Based Client Relationships*, maintains that if we want to develop sustainable competitive advantage we must embed greater specialist knowledge and expertise in products and services, develop closer and deeper client relationships, and improve the transfer of knowledge in our decision-making processes.

However, realizing that people are critical to the knowledge process is only the beginning. In a quote that defines everything we will explore in this book, **Drucker said, "You cannot hire a hand, the whole person comes with it."**

This is a fundamental principle that goes to the very heart of the practice of management. Managers and organizations often approach human and organizational development on a piecemeal basis, rather than in holistic terms. This piecemeal approach is not only grossly erroneous it is irrational.

If you want to develop your organization, you have to be concerned with the totality of the human experience. Contrary to what most managers and executives would like to think, people don't check in their personal needs and ambitions at the office door. Putting it another way, if they had an alternative they would not be coming to work at all.

In his book, *Beyond A Boundary*, CLR James thoroughly analyzed the origins and social evolution of the game of cricket in the Caribbean. James insisted that those who wanted to know the game had first to understand the human and social evolution that brought it about. He famously wrote, *"What do they know of cricket, who only cricket know."*

The same can be said of organizations, **"What do they know of organizations, who only organizations know."**

What organizations are and what they might become is grounded in the human and social evolution of societies, rather than in the nature of the business they conduct.

That is why much of what you will read in these pages is grounded in what for me has been a lifelong vocation – the study and understanding of peoples, their cultures, and their histories, in addition to whatever business knowledge and experience I might have gained over the past 26 years.

It is within this context that we are able to develop a more comprehensive understanding of what commercial activities actually represent, and re-evaluate our notions of progress.

The Industrial Revolution was successful not because of scientific breakthroughs, but because it made ordinary goods and services affordable to the vast majority of ordinary people. Soap, something previously exclusive to kings and queens, became available to the peasant.

Television redefined the idea of family entertainment. The car was never merely a product of man's ability to mass-produce but something that changed how people lived, where they lived, where they traveled, and how they connected. We could say similar things about the computer, the Internet, and the mobile telephone.

Every great product or technical innovation achieved its greatness because it changed the context, direction, and even the perception, of human life and social disposition.

Thus, to optimize knowledge we must first understand people in a holistic sense. We have to examine the whole person and their identity, not just the piece of them that we believe turns up to work. This requires an understanding of the wider human and social context within which knowledge in all its forms is derived, created, developed, and applied.

The Industrial Revolution is an extremely potent reference point for such an analysis, as it laid much of the foundations of both the modern corporation and the modern society. Using it as a reference point, this book will conclusively demonstrate that corporate/organizational success, both now and in the future, will be heavily dependent on their ability first to understand, and then to motivate and develop, their human assets.

The former cannot be underestimated, and without it, the latter will be impossible.

During the course of this book, we will examine and explore how, in the course of history, organizations have repeatedly made the same mistakes, simply because they have refused to recognize in principle the primacy of the human asset.

However, before we do anything else, it is imperative that we go beyond our empirical observations and better define just how important human assets really are, and why organizations are in desperate need of change.

THE HUMAN ASSET MANIFESTO

CHAPTER

2

PEOPLE REPRESENT AS MUCH AS 80% OF AN ORGANIZATION'S VALUE – WHAT ARE THEY DOING ABOUT IT?

THE HUMAN ASSET MANIFESTO

PEOPLE REPRESENT AS MUCH AS 80% OF AN ORGANIZATION'S VALUE – WHAT ARE THEY DOING ABOUT IT?

What is an organization?

An organization is nothing more than a collection of people comprising investors, managers, employees, suppliers, and customers. The efficiency and effectiveness with which an organization operates is wholly and solely based on the network of relationships that exists between these people, and that is why they are its assets.

Indeed, it could be said that organizations are of the people, for the people and by the people.

Given the old adage that a chain is only as strong as its weakest link, if on average only a mere 14% of employees are full engaged at any one time, it is difficult to envisage how or why most organizations should function at or even anywhere near their best.

Employees are the primary human assets, but an organization's human assets extend to all those who are involved in its business – including suppliers and customers. Taken together they constitute a single entity in which the actions of managers and employees are crucial in determining its overall economic health.

Organizations are living and breathing entities. The best way to realize this is to think of what happens when people leave their offices in the evening and go home. Despite the prevalence of automation in some industries, if employees do not return to their desks, then ultimately the organization ceases to exist.

THE HUMAN ASSET MANIFESTO

Studies on behalf of the World Bank and others by Levin indicate that two-thirds of an organization's financial performance is dependent on its employee strategies. Robert Grossman, a professor of management studies at Marist College in NY, places the value of the human assets still higher. Grossman reckons that checks by stock market analysts on the value of human resources plays at best a "bit part" even though **most experts agree that as much as 80% of a company's worth is tied to its human capital.**

For service organizations such as banks, insurance companies and software companies, one could argue that 80% is a conservative estimate – these organizations are entirely dependent on their people. We will later come to understand that manufacturing organizations are not immune to this level of dependency either.

It is not only professors of management and research consultants who recognize the importance of the human asset. Lee Kwan Yew, the architect of Singapore's economic transformation, was once asked to define the most important aspect of his country's development. His response was 'air-conditioning' – reflecting his belief in the importance of people's environments on their performance.

Given the importance of human assets, we would expect that managers would dedicate far more of their time and themselves to people issues. Wrong! Dead Wrong!

Organizations do not devote anywhere near 80% or even 67% of their time to people-oriented activities. People management has been outsourced to HR, which more often than not is kept as far away from the business as is humanly possible.

HR reminds me of another institution with the initials HR – the Holy Roman Empire. Napoleon had claimed that that empire was neither holy nor Roman (it was actually German). Similarly, HR is concerned with neither humans nor resources. Instead, it has become a byword for bureaucracy and interference.

This has nothing to do with the intrinsic quality of the people within HR, nor the importance of what they might have to offer. It is however due to the lack of alignment in terms of objectives and rewards between those who work in HR and the rest of the business. Fundamentally, it also reflects the extent to which the average manager either believes in or understands how precisely people development affects their business.

By adopting a systematic approach to human asset evaluation and assessment, we will be able to see the direct linkages between people development, organizational development, and strategic development.

A most intriguing aspect of HR is that while women are under-represented in most other areas of management, they are more often than not over-represented in HR. If you see a department on an evening out and it consists of one man and twenty women, it is probably HR. Not surprisingly, the man is usually the head of the department.

The fact that men tend not to view HR as a career proposition is indicative of the esteem in which the male-dominated business world views that department and the development of people. The day that men begin to see HR as a positive career move will signal a landmark change in their approach to that discipline and people development in general. In the interim, people will continue to be undervalued.

Several organizations are now attempting to improve the integration of HR into their business. The empirical evidence suggests that the results have been partially successful at best. Management exhibits great dexterity when it comes to calling something by a different name or changing job titles, only for things to remain precisely as they were before.

What often happens in such organizations is that HR is made "part of the business", but at meetings it is always the last item on the agenda – you might get to it, and if you do, it means that it will receive the minimum of attention. As we shall see in the next chapter, when actions are taken as part of a fad, rather than any fundamental change in the belief system, they are unlikely to be successful.

So much for that well-known maxim: weak generals think tactics, good generals think strategy, but great generals think logistics.

There is yet no evidence that most managers are convinced that focusing on human assets is the way to improve their organizations. They are yet to convert to the idea that optimizing human assets will optimize organizational performance.

Not only do managers not focus on people management skills, they tend not to recognize them. It also means that those who possess the greatest people management skills are almost never suitably recognized, rewarded, nor promoted. As such, placing importance on, and developing, those skills within the organization, is effectively discouraged and devalued.

The head of sales is usually the person with the best...well... sales – in financial terms that is. The person who is the best team leader and the one most capable of bringing out the best in other members of the team is usually ignored.

Unfortunately, an exaggerated emphasis on quantitative measures and standards, be they financial or technical, as against people or human asset standards, remains one of the main obstacles to organizational progress.

This obsession with all things quantitative has resulted in a practice of management that today is anything but open-minded and flexible. It is a key reason why organizations will remain socially dysfunctional, deterring progress and stifling productivity and competitive advantage.

Unbelievably, the modern organization has even greater troubles. The following extract is taken from the website www.prwatch.org. Its source was an article in the *New York Times* of January 9, 2005.

"More than ever, Americans do not trust business or the people who run it," reports Claudia H. Deutsch. "Pollsters, researchers, even many corporate chiefs themselves say that business is under attack by a majority of the public, which believes that executives are bent on destroying the environment, cooking the books, and

lining their own pockets." Deutsch cites polls from Roper and Harris, in which 72 percent of respondents feel that wrongdoing is widespread in industry, only 2 percent regard the executives of large companies as "very trustworthy," and 90 percent say big companies have too much influence on government.

What this tells us is that the very people who work for commercial organizations, and on whom those organizations rely to sustain their viability and competitiveness, neither trust nor believe in them. It is no wonder that people are not engaged.

This is a further explanation of why organizations are socially dysfunctional. They have become disengaged from the societies from which they draw their employees, and to whom they intend to market their products.

It is a most unenviable position.

As a result, people are far less likely to look to their jobs for any form of personal fulfillment. Fulfillment is something that for most people can only be achieved outside of work, even though they spend a large proportion of their waking hours engaged in work activities – this is another reason why they are consumers first and employees second. People are increasingly defining themselves more in terms of their lifestyles and beliefs, and less in terms of their work or vocation. This undoubtedly reinforces social dysfunctionality within organizations.

This completely justifies everything we have said so far about the need for organizations to understand and come to terms with their human and social environment. It reinforces the idea that progress requires a holistic approach that takes into account all aspects of the motivation and disposition of human assets.

So how do we move forward from here?

To begin with, we will have to critically analyze and deconstruct the very nature of modern management and how organizations operate. Then we will have to establish the basis on which they will need to optimize their human assets. It is obvious that the current foundations are too inadequate to build on.

We will have to construct a new paradigm, a new way of doing business, and a new way forward.

The new paradigm will have to focus on the human and social issues both inside and outside of organizations. It will have to be consistent with society's social evolution. Above all, it will have to be holistic in its approach because there are no partial solutions when it comes to human beings.

Thus, I invite you to journey with me on to the next chapter, where we will deconstruct modern management, and begin to lay the foundations for the new paradigm.

CHAPTER

3

THE
MAKE-BELIEVE
WORLD
OF THE
FADDISTS

THE HUMAN ASSET MANIFESTO

THE MAKE-BELIEVE WORLD OF THE FADDISTS

People are the constant factor in business. Yet, the modern practice of management is such that you would not believe that this is so.

Modern management has been reduced to a series of consultant-induced fads. It has become a series of timid maneuvers dictated by what consultants have to offer and what everyone else is perceived to be doing.

Each of these fads has a shelf life of about two years. There is a very good reason for that. It takes about two years for the average manager to realize that the panacea he paid good money for does not work. Conveniently, it also provides consultants with enough time to come up with the next bright new fad to ensnare the hearts and wallets of their intellectual hostages.

The cycle then repeats itself all over again.

The strangest thing about this two-step drill is that while the intended results are never achieved, managers can still hold their heads high and with a straight face declare they were merely following the popular practice of the day. It's like that old adage, no one was ever fired for buying IBM.

Unfortunately, once faddism sets in, there is no stopping it. I once heard a journalist from *The Economist* say that Corporate Social Responsibility, or CSR, may have been a good idea, but when he saw tobacco companies issuing CSR statements he changed his mind.

THE HUMAN ASSET MANIFESTO

The result of these face-saving and ass-covering petty maneuvers is that millions of employees all over the world operate in a state of flux. Employees are the true victims of faddism. As managers experiment with each new miracle remedy, employees find themselves having to come to terms with constant change. As ludicrous as it may sound, some managers even believe that constant change is good in that it keeps people on their toes! They call it mushroom management – keep them in the dark and feed them filth.

It should be of no great surprise that **a survey by Invisible Management indicates that more than 70% of people find they work better without management.**

My own experience has not been a whole lot different from that of most other people. **For almost two decades, I was based in the City of London, working for a number of major global banks. There was not a single year that I did not experience some major organizational change or some new initiative that happened to be the cause celebre of its time.** I am sure that you are quite familiar with many of them:

Business Process Re-engineering
Reorganization / Restructuring
Downsizing
Rightsizing
Just In Time (JIT)
Quality Standards
Delayering
Total Quality Management
Quality Circles
Outsourcing
Change Management
Knowledge Management

Now, I would be the first to admit that many of these tools and principles, when appropriately applied within the appropriate context, can produce good results. Therein lies the major problem – they are almost never adapted to the specific needs of the target organization.

This is further exacerbated by a propensity to embrace a single dimensional approach to implementation. In plain English, that means that all other considerations are usually thrown out of the window in a relentless drive to get right the theory of what they are supposed to be doing.

Finally, and most distressingly, **organizations have a marked tendency to emphasize systems over people.**

Take, for example, Knowledge Management – an excellent idea and one that I dearly loved. Tragically, it was turned into a large IT exercise that wasted so many billions that for many executives the term Knowledge Management became a nightmare. This was because in the rush to spend those billions on systems and computers, most failed to realize that all knowledge begins and ends with people. Had those organizations invested 10% of what they wasted on systems in people, the benefits would have been far greater.

Similarly, many companies relied on computers and technology to employ JIT techniques. Only to later find out when failures cost them dearly, that the concept as practiced by the likes of Toyota was based on the commitment of people to each other to always deliver, and not just a computer output that told them when stocks were running low. We will learn more about this in a later chapter. Typically, as in other instances of faddism, the people element was ignored during implementation.

Whether you employ TQM, Quality Circles, or Quality Standards, true quality can only come from within – it cannot be trained or reduced to a statistical exercise. Quality is a human and social experience both internally and externally.

Outsourcing is another favorite pastime that rarely delivers the previously envisaged benefits. Take the example of BA or British Airways.

BA had outsourced its catering staff to Gate Gourmet. No doubt they believed that the staff they got rid of had become someone else's problem. More importantly, the managers would have pointed out that Knowledge Management indicated that as catering was not a part of their core business, outsourcing was the way to go – make those people someone else's problem.

THE HUMAN ASSET MANIFESTO

A few days after BA had announced record quarterly profits in August of 2005, the prawn sandwich brigade got their revenge – the workers at Gate Gourmet went on strike. In doing so, they reminded BA – if you outsource it, you still own it.

The strike cost BA 700 cancelled flights, £40 million (US$70 million) in lost profits, and immeasurable ill will on the part of their customers. The fact that many believe that poor people skills on the part of the Gate Gourmet management was a primary cause of the strike further emphasizes the point.

In the rush to embrace faddism, techniques are slavishly followed and people are left behind.

Even from a financial perspective, such an approach makes no sense whatsoever.

Before the strike, when BA announced its quarterly results, its share price went up. That is quite natural you might say. After all, financial analysts and investors would have based their evaluation of BA on past results, market conditions, the price of oil – in fact everything but an assessment of its people. Had they employed techniques that evaluated people, and not just results and prices, they, and indeed the management of BA, might have been aware of the defects and inadequacies of their calculations.

Another organization that took the outsourcing route, neatly saddled with its Siamese twin, downsizing, was the giant oil company Shell. Unfortunately, in taking this route it also lost workers with the technical knowledge and operational competence to explore and maintain the value of its oil reserves.

Surprise, surprise – the market suffered a rude shock in 2004 when Shell reported very healthy profits, only to have its share price nosedive soon afterwards when it was discovered that they had vastly overstated their reserves.

Shell tried to pass off this mini-catastrophe as an accounting error. The truth was that a failure to manage human assets had resulted in a failure in financial performance – something that was never predicted by an army of investment banking analysts and their calculators. The following extract from www.financedirector.co.uk perfectly illustrates precisely what the obsession with reported results can do for an organization:

> *As Philip Nichol, global sector director for oil at investment bank ABN Amro says: "What we now discover is that, where we all thought Shell was a great company, the company has basically been in decline for a decade. Management have been focusing on profitability and allowing the reserves to wind down without that fact becoming visible to the market."*

The problem for analysts and the financial markets is that like management, they too have been obsessed with financial results. They unerringly echo management's quantitative focus, with an army of analysts, statisticians, economists, and accountants to back it up.

There is no question that this approach is inadequate.

Put another way, **any approach to evaluating organizations that is bereft of evaluating its people resources is almost certain to come unstuck.** As previously noted by Grossman, while people represent as much as 80% of the value of an organization, they never feature in the valuation techniques employed by analysts, bankers, and accountants.

As if to emphatically prove our point, study after study indicates that most mergers and acquisitions destroy value because they don't pay attention to people issues. The excessive focus on the rationalization of costs, markets, distribution channels, and revenue streams has repeatedly proved to be wholly inadequate.

In one study, Vestring, King, Rouse, and Critchlow writing in the *European Business Forum*, evaluated over 125 deals, each valued in excess of one billion US dollars. They concluded that it was the soft (a favored euphemism for describing undervalued ideas and themes) or people-related issues that matter most. Another body of research by *The Economist* notes that very few mergers, or one in six to be more precise, actually add value. The principal reason for this is again a failure to integrate people.

We will explore together how throughout history the failure to prioritize human assets is the single greatest weakness of organizations – they are slow learners.

One of the reasons for this is the confusion over what technology is and how it can best serve our needs. **It seems that we inhabit a world where people are made to serve technology, rather than one where technology is made to serve people.**

Somehow, the idea has developed that if you develop the appropriate technology, then people become mere props. Nothing epitomizes this phenomenon more than call centers – places with high staff turnover, endless menus of electronic messages, and relatively poor services that leave a host of their customers dissatisfied.

We have all been there and none of us has enjoyed the experience – but they call it progress.

In the words of Patrick O'Connor, modern management is still stuck in the Scientific Management Principles of the past, and is yet to recognize the social evolution that has taken place within our societies. This he maintains explains their inability to adopt the requisite human and social focus to their business activities.

Through these pages, we will develop a new paradigm that says that people development and paying attention to human and social issues are the way forward. We will learn how organizations that properly prioritize human assets above technology are today leaving their competitors in the shade.

What is most fascinating about all of this is that managers love to talk about the importance of people in business. "It's a people business" is one of the most abused phrases in the history of management. All the evidence suggests that most of the talk is just that – talk unmatched by relevant deeds.

In these pages, we explore how despite the best efforts of managers to ignore them, a focus on human assets can greatly improve performance, enhance productivity, and deliver quality results. The failure of organizations to consciously recognize and act on this is perhaps the greatest business mystery of all time.

My own theory is this – in the alpha male-dominated world of business, M&A, strategy and other high-minded pursuits, people are simply not sexy.

Leadership on the other hand appears to be both sexy and macho.

A cult of leadership and hero worship has been developed which is designed to promote the alpha male concept of what such leadership entails. It is a cult that pays homage to the likes of Alexander, Caesar, and Nelson. There are many other forms of leadership, some of which greatly contrast to this particular model. Yet, more often than not, they are overlooked. The fixation on this type of leadership has been so single-mindedly obtuse that its scholarship is extremely suspect.

So for example, there is no recognition that Alexander's successes owed much to the skill of the Macedonian phalanx, developed long before he was born. There is no recognition that Caesar's great conquest of the Gauls was due to the exceptional military training of the average Roman soldier – something that long preceded Caesar. One historian had described these soldiers thus, *"their drills were like bloody battles, and their battles bloody drills".*

In the case of Nelson, it is well known that victory at Trafalgar was possible because someone else had practiced British naval gunners to such an extent that their rate of fire exceeded that of Napoleon's fleet. Yet Nelson stands alone atop his column.

It is truly distressing that this constant focus on leadership is not matched by a similarly consistent and genuine focus on the led.

Unfortunately, it is not only the symbols of leadership that remain stuck in the past. The first corporations emerged in the latter part of the 17th century. In those days, due reverence was paid to popes, kings, archbishops, and the landed gentry – and regular employment was a fortunate circumstance. Since that time, human lifestyles have undergone a radical revolution. Leisure, conspicuous consumption, social activities, and even socio-political causes, now dominate people's lives. It seems incongruous that while societies have made these strides, the corporation as we know it remains unchanged, consisting as it does of investors, managers, and workers, in that definitive order of priority.

The idea that those who invest their money are superior in every way to those who provide their time, energy and services smacks of feudalism – it is entirely contrary to our socio-political evolution.

We should therefore not be surprised that corporate objectives are no longer coincident with their employees' personal objectives. It is not that they were coincident, but now more than ever, they increasingly diverge.

In an era when people continue to strive for social and political equality, organizations that do not fully comprehend this change in social dynamics will increase the extent to which they are socially dysfunctional.

In this book, we will see that the failure to address the human and social aspects of business, including issues of diversity such as age, ethnicity, and gender, is already costing organizations billions of dollars, euros and pounds. We will further examine how a failure to pay heed to these issues will threaten organizations' competitiveness and ultimately their very survival.

We will come to understand that those organizations that are prepared to lead human and social change, by redefining themselves in terms of their human assets, will improve their productivity, competitiveness, and overall performance.

While writing this book, I developed the intriguing idea that I wanted to make both Karl Marx and Nelson Rockefeller proud. Put another way, what I intend to prove, irrevocably, is that in

today's world, profits, productivity and business sustainability are all optimized when the human asset is optimized.

The process by which rewards and returns may be optimized has evolved and organizations have failed to evolve with it. The value of people is no longer in their subservience to diktat, but in their freedom to take action.

Left to logic alone, the task is not easy. There is more than a wealth of evidence to prove the case for the people, and you can be sure that much of that evidence will be included in the following pages. So much of it is patently obvious, hiding in plain sight, yet it appears as if it is being studiously ignored.

It is for this reason that what we seek is not merely to shine a light on the issue, but to raise it up to such an extent that we completely redefine the context within which organizations conduct their business.

However, before you move on to the next section please read the Statement of Affirmation on the next page. It represents a summary of the principles established in this section. I hope that you will also be moved to act on the suggestion that follows.

THE HUMAN ASSET MANIFESTO

The Human Asset Manifesto
Statement of Affirmation 1

- *I believe that an organization is a living entity*

- *I believe that people are truly an organization's greatest assets*

- *I believe that people deserve to be given every opportunity to be their very best*

- *I believe that the value of an organization is represented by the value of its people*

- *I believe that organizations should view people from a total human perspective*

You can evidence your support for this statement and by doing so help to send a strong message by going to www.thamanifesto.com

THE HUMAN ASSET MANIFESTO

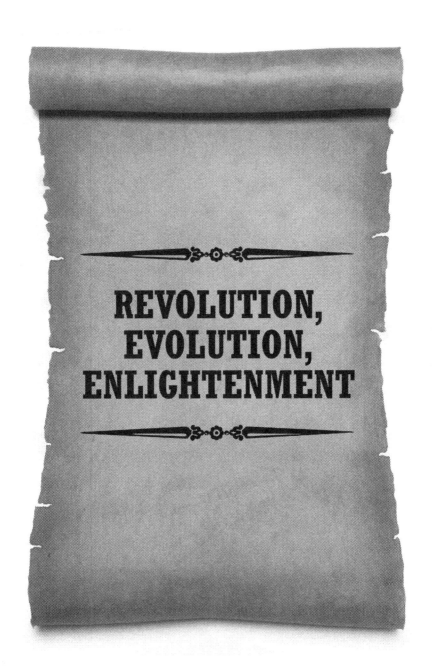

REVOLUTION,
EVOLUTION,
ENLIGHTENMENT

THE HUMAN ASSET MANIFESTO

CHAPTER
4

KNOWLEDGE IS OF THE PEOPLE, FOR THE PEOPLE, BY THE PEOPLE

THE HUMAN ASSET MANIFESTO

KNOWLEDGE IS OF THE PEOPLE, FOR THE PEOPLE, BY THE PEOPLE

The creation, acquisition, development, and application of knowledge are human and social processes. In this chapter, we will examine why this is, how it is, and what organizations must learn from it. As part of our analysis, we will come to see how the Industrial Revolution was primarily a human and social phenomenon, and why its lessons should be studied by organizations in order to improve their innovation and productivity.

Many would say that this is the Knowledge Age. They do so in an attempt to make a distinction between what transpired before we got to this stage. Thus, man's development is traced along a path that is divided into convenient little time capsules or historical eras. We have the Stone Age, Bronze Age, Iron Age, Agrarian Revolution, Industrial Revolution, Computer or Information Age, and now the Knowledge Age.

Although these eras might be historically correct in terms of how civilization has evolved, in one sense they are dangerously misleading. They would have us believe that the Knowledge Age coincides with the rise of computers and the Internet. Just as we cannot divorce man from his history, we cannot divorce current ideas and techniques from the historic evolution and exchange of ideas that brought them about.

The entire history of humans is a continuum of knowledge. We have always lived in the "Knowledge Age".

If the Arabs had not translated Greek manuscripts and if that knowledge had not reached Europe by way of the Crusades and the Arab conquest of Spain, then the Renaissance and the Industrial Revolution may not have happened as and when they did.

Where would European civilization be now without this input? Perhaps you are not yet convinced – let me provide you with another conundrum.

It is said that when the Great Library of Alexandria was destroyed, manuscripts describing the building of the pyramids, and many other secrets of the ancient world, were lost forever. Today there are hundreds, perhaps thousands, of scholars and Egyptologists devoted to resolving a 5,000-year-old riddle of how the pyramids were built. Today, we are no nearer to acquiring this knowledge since the destruction of the library around 2,000 years ago.

How would knowledge of Egyptian techniques have assisted modern architects and builders? What else do we not know? How would that additional knowledge have changed civilization as we know it? What could those thousands of scientists have otherwise achieved had their efforts been redirected elsewhere?

Let us take a more specific example – that of printing. Before printing, knowledge was spread by spoken word or hand-written manuscripts. This was laborious, prone to error, and severely limited access to knowledge to the fortunate few.

The Chinese first used stone tablets to print 2,000 years ago. Several hundred years later, they moved to wooden boards smeared with ink – known as block printing. The first book was available in China in 868 using paper, another Chinese invention – over 600 hundred years before it was used in Europe.

Block printing had its faults. A single mistake in the carving could ruin a whole block and the blocks were not reusable. In the 11th century, the Chinese graduated to reusable movable type made from baked clay. This technology found its way to Europe and eventually inspired Johann Gutenberg's movable metal type.

In the West, the fact that people today still say Gutenberg invented movable type is more than a simple inaccuracy. In the same way,

Europeans still claim that Columbus discovered the Americas, when in fact that land mass was well populated long before he got there.

This sort of failure to think beyond narrow social and cultural confines can often blind us to some very important ideas and principles that are fundamental to the creation, development, and utilization of knowledge.

The first principle is that knowledge is the result of a continuous evolution that has been taking place since the dawn of time. Every single development, and I specifically use the word development and not invention – we will come to the basis of that distinction later, is based on some prior knowledge. Computers and the Internet assist in absorbing, developing, and utilizing greater volumes and levels of knowledge in a much shorter timeframe – but they are not knowledge.

Consequently, one of the most important tasks of the modern organization is to ensure that the transfer of knowledge remains a constant and ongoing process. The better an organization is at creating the type of human and social environment that facilitates this, the more successful it may become.

The second principle underlies the first. **There is almost no such thing as an invention, or by implication, an inventor, i.e. someone who somehow creates knowledge or an application of knowledge where nothing existed before. Knowledge development and innovation are human and evolutionary in nature.**

The third fundamental principle is the most important. It may seem obvious but it happens to be the most overlooked aspect of knowledge and its development – it is that **all knowledge begins and ends with people.** Knowledge, knowledge development, technology, innovation – whatever you may want to call it – occurs only because of human interactions. Those who place their reliance on computers, like those who did so with Knowledge Management, are in for a rude shock.

The principles are easily demonstrated.

THE HUMAN ASSET MANIFESTO

It is often said that Thomas Edison invented the incandescent light bulb. This is not true. Edison's 'invention' simply improved on the work of others in developments that spanned the years 1841 to 1878.

The British would say that Watt invented the steam engine. This is more than stretching the truth. Watt's 'invention' was merely a next step refinement of Newcomen's in 1712, Savery's in 1698, Papin's in 1680 etc. etc. etc. Frankly, we could go all the way back to the first use of the wheel. Note the diverse nationalities involved here. Similarly, we could trace the development of the airplane from the Wright brothers to the work of many French inventors and perhaps ultimately all the way back to Daedalus and Icarus – man has always wanted to fly.

The fact is that knowledge develops cumulatively, until such time that there is a point where some effective application of that knowledge is determined or comes to fruition i.e. something that we as humans desire for our own purpose. Integral to every step in the knowledge process is the extent and the ability of a person or group of persons to improve, modify, or even develop new uses for knowledge, previously developed by others.

Given that knowledge is entirely human in its construct, it should be readily within our perception that its productivity and utility will be dependent on human strengths and fallibilities – hope, despair, motivation, failure, shortsightedness, and plain accidents.

When Edison was developing his improvement to the light bulb, one of his financial backers asked, "Tom, why don't you quit. Can't you see this idea of your is a failure?" **Edison replied, "Every time it did not work I got feedback on how to make it better. I have now eliminated 1,000 ways it did not work and I get closer and closer to success."**

History records that Edison was eventually successful much to the delight of those who had invested in his ventures, and GE, the company founded by Edison, is still with us today.

Failure is an integral component of the knowledge process – and there is no such thing as a guaranteed timeframe for success. It is therefore no wonder that man's development of knowledge was accelerated once he learned to cultivate and settle, giving him more time to think about what he wanted to do. It is a matter of historical record that the Industrial Revolution was preceded by the Agrarian Revolution.

This suggests that in general terms knowledge transfer, development and application are at their best in settled and secure environments – where people are actually allowed to experiment, get things wrong and evolve solutions.

As such, **constant downsizing, rightsizing, restructuring, and reorganization do not assist knowledge development. Organizations that engage in perpetual change destroy both knowledge and value.**

The exception to this is war. In development terms, nothing concentrates the mind more than war or something that threatens a people's very survival. So for example, aircraft and jet engine technology took a giant leap during forward during World War II. However, this only happens under certain conditions. Look at almost any country experiencing war and turmoil today and it is highly unlikely that they are at the forefront of innovation or intellectual capital development.

As such, we should not be surprised that many organizations only learn the error of their ways when they are faced with an extreme crisis.

Now we have some idea as to the kind of environment that facilitates knowledge development and innovation – how do we ensure that we fully exploit its outcomes?

When Watt devised his version of the steam engine, it was initially used as a water pump. However, other uses were quickly found for this valuable source of power. Therefore, steam engines were subsequently placed in cotton mills, trains, and ships. The important lesson is this – the application of new ideas and new technologies is limited only by the imagination – that is the extent to which humans can maximize the uses to which they can be put.

Back to Edison, a highly prolific innovator. When he developed the phonograph, he envisaged it being used to record, for posterity as well as legality, the final words of people on their deathbeds. He also wanted to use it to provide books for the blind. Then some other bright soul came along and used it to record and play music. Edison was outraged! This was a vulgarity, and for almost 20 years he refused to accept that this was a legitimate use of his beloved creation. He finally gave in when its commercial success could not be denied.

The next example of a failure to optimize the human and social applications of new technology was a far greater disaster.

AT&T, once the sole telecom operator in the US until it was broken up, developed wireless telephony in what was then one of the greatest research laboratories in the world – their own Bell Labs. **In 1984, McKinsey told AT&T that wireless telephony was worthless and that by the year 2000, there would only be one million users. According to** *The Economist***, by the year 2000 there were 740 million users!** That number has probably doubled since then.

It would be easy to blame McKinsey for being wrong by a factor of 740. However, the failure is that of AT&T. In his book, The Practice of Management, Peter Drucker states that the first purpose of a business is to create customers, or a market for its goods. AT&T had one of the greatest developments of modern times in its exclusive possession and blew it. It failed to articulate, develop, and exploit a social purpose for its groundbreaking innovation.

The old AT&T no longer exists – it has since been bought by SBC Communications who has renamed itself AT&T. If IBM had made a gaffe in allowing Microsoft to license its operating system to all and sundry, what would you say about AT&T's blunder?

The fact is that this phenomenon has been repeated over and over again. The Graphical User Interface or GUI, and many other features of the modern PC, were first developed by Xerox. However, the company failed to take advantage of their development and watched helplessly as Microsoft and Apple exploited their ideas.

It proves that customers and indeed potential customers are human assets with human and social needs that organizations must approach from a human and social perspective – regardless of their scientific capabilities. **Today, most of us can hardly imagine life without our mobile phones. AT&T's problem was that it could not imagine our lives with one.**

Human purpose, human needs, and human desires are what define markets and therefore the utilization of knowledge. If you are convinced that the continued growth and development of knowledge is important, it also means that you need to be similarly convinced of the need for the growth and development of how that knowledge might be applied.

Successful people processes and understanding of the human and social environment both inside and outside of an organization are absolute prerequisites for knowledge creation and application.

Jared Diamond, the author of the book, Guns, Germs And Steel, describes in various ways how the evolution of technology was born out of man's necessity as well as the nature of his environment. The wider human and social context has a significant impact on what organizations may or may not accomplish. The development and transformation of 19th and early 20th century Japanese society provides a very good example of this.

By the early 1600s, the Samurai in Japan were so fearful of Christianity disrupting their established social order that they completely closed the country to all outside influences for the next 250 years. That was until Commodore Perry and the US Pacific Fleet turned up in 1853 and forced them to change their ways.

How was Commodore Perry able to do this?

The answer is simple. Perry had the modern guns of the age and the Japanese did not. Samurai policy had not only alienated Japan from new developments in weapons technology, it had expressly forbidden the manufacture of guns – theirs was an order of the sword and guns were viewed as a dishonorable method of warfare.

THE HUMAN ASSET MANIFESTO

This imbalance in knowledge capabilities, applications, and resources meant that Japan was unable to resist the power of the American invasion.

The same of course happens to organizations that are too focused within.

This particular knowledge lesson was not lost on the Japanese. Now acutely aware of their technical and scientific disadvantages, the country launched a most ambitious attempt at modernization. We know it as the Meiji Restoration. By the turn of the 20th century, Japan had become a major industrial power. When their advances in military technology resulted in the defeat of the Russian naval fleet in 1905, it sent shock waves throughout the world.

The following extract from an article by Maria Christensen provides us with a very interesting insight into how the Japanese were able to effect such a change, once they had been rudely awakened by the arrival of the Americans:

> *The first step was to foster a sense of nationalism and unity...*
>
> *The old class system of Japan was abandoned. With astounding speed, universities were founded, telegraph, and railroad lines cross-crossed the country and a national postal system was set up. The shipping and textile industries took off, as shown by the facts that "by the end of the Meiji period, more than a third of the world's supply of silk came from Japan" and the percentage of exports carried on Japanese built and owned ships rose from 7% in 1893 to 52% by 1913. How was such progress at such a rate possible? The answer lies in the Japanese traits of flexibility and adaptability. Simply put, they borrowed the best of the West and molded it to fit Japan's needs.*

Christensen then goes on to demonstrate how the Japanese, determined to accelerate the process of learning and make up for the centuries of "lost knowledge", effectively reversed the mistakes made by the Samurai. They decided that the world had moved so far forward that rather than trying to reinvent the wheel, they were going to absorb as much knowledge as they could from everyone else and adapt it to their needs.

Many characterize what Japan did at this time as "rational shopping." They borrowed technology, social systems, infrastructure, and educational methods from countries around the world, adapted, and fitted them to their own needs and culture. They used what worked and abandoned what did not. To do this, the Meiji oligarchs set off on an around the world junket in 1871 known as the Iwakura Mission, named for the head of the delegation, Iwakura Tomomi. They spent several months each in the United States, England, and Europe, and studied everything they encountered from banking systems to zoos. They brought home anything that might be useful to Japan, in one form or another, including a police system modeled somewhat on the French system, an educational system influenced by both America and Prussia, and new forms of agriculture.

The Japanese modernized their economy by human interaction and exchange on a grand global scale. Their success came about because they did not rely on osmosis, the natural passage of time or history – they went out and became actively engaged in those interactions. Increasing the frequency, directness, and level of human interaction, and learning as much as they could from the experience of others, greatly accelerated their development.

The fate of those who resisted change in Japan, the old Samurai order who feared the rapid decline in their power, is summed up in the Hollywood movie The Last Samurai, a stylized depiction of what happens when swords clash with gunpowder. Events are brought to a rapid and brutal climax – unless of course you have a light-saber like that of Luke Skywalker or Obi-Wan-Kenobi.

If you have not already guessed it, the other message here is quite clear; **humans, the greatest purveyors of knowledge, can also be the greatest obstacle to its application and development.**

There is a well-known story about Henry Ford. The man became so obsessed with the marvels of mass production of which he was the leading light that he refused to countenance any introduction in model variation. When asked about offering customers different colors he reputedly proclaimed, "They can have any color they want, as long as it is black."

In the end, Ford nearly wrecked the company and had to be forcibly removed to maintain its survival in the face of the competitive onslaught from GM – a manufacturer that was not afraid to offer variety.

In contrast to the Japanese, Europeans were always at war with each other. Its nations were a hotbed of religious, national, and ethnic conflict. This constant state of warfare produced extraordinary advances in war, weapons technology, and ships, as each country in turn tried to gain the upper hand.

The urgency with which one needs to survive or counter extreme threats may indeed spur innovation. The opposite is also true – a benign environment may lead to a slowdown in, or even an absence of, knowledge development, innovation, and application.

Good competitors and demanding customers are important to knowledge development and it is imperative that an organization learns from both. Customers in particular are invaluable sources of knowledge. The better an organization is at incorporating customer ideas and needs into their products the more likely they are to be successful. At the same time, those who fail to learn from their competitors are asking for trouble.

The Soviets could compete with, although not surpass, the Americans in military hardware and space exploration. For example, they developed the classic teardrop shape that all submarines now adopt. Both sides spied on each other to learn as much as they possibly could about their competitors' latest advance in technology.

However, in terms of consumer goods the Soviets were hopelessly outclassed. Soviet consumer goods came from the same state factories as their military counterparts. The stark difference in quality was due to the stark difference in the competition or lack thereof in the market for Soviet consumer goods.

The failure of the Soviets in the development and manufacture of consumer goods was also a reflection of the socio-political ethos. Soviet citizens were not in any way supposed to differentiate themselves from each other. That is hardly the kind of environment to foster consumer product development and innovation. In addition, the country was stuck in a kind of time warp. Economic power was measured by the volume of coal and steel production because that was how British and German industrial power was measured for much of the 19th and early 20th centuries. The Soviets had failed to realize that behind those production numbers were the measurable benefits that industrialization had brought to the citizens of those countries.

We now move from a predominantly classless society to one that was practically driven by class and to some extent geography, Britain.

Being an island nation of no particular great size, Britain's survival was critically dependent on its ability to trade – Napoleon once described it as a nation of shopkeepers. The country became a great seafaring nation due to the power of its navy and merchant marine. Yet social class played a crucial role in its development.

Social elitism in Britain meant that in the height of its industrial transformation, the country trained relatively few scientists and engineers, especially in comparison to Germany. In time, German industrial production rapidly outpaced that of the UK, even though the latter had had a significant head start.

Just as important in Britain's later manufacturing decline was the nature of its customers. Britain's colonial empire largely consisted of captive and relatively unsophisticated consumers. Even when the products were not strictly required, they created a market for them. They taxed Indian textiles exorbitantly to ensure there was a market for inferior British textiles – it kept the Lancashire mills going. They even exported cotton vests to the Caribbean – a climate that hardly needs them, but whose inhabitants were socialized into wearing them.

British manufactured goods generally never reached the standard of excellence required for more competitive First World markets.

As countries obtained their independence and improved their ability to diversify their imports, British producers had to find new markets. Unfortunately, their cutting edge had been dulled by the quality of their customers, and British manufacturing fell into a rapid decline – one from which it never properly recovered.

When Japanese cars were first introduced into western markets, many belittled them, even calling them "Jap Crap". As the Japanese learned from their new customer base, suddenly the joke was no longer funny – their vehicles were dominating global markets and Toyota, the leader of the pack, is this year poised to replace GM as the world's largest manufacturer.

The ability to learn from customers is one of the key aspects of innovation and knowledge development. More fundamentally, companies are only partially a product of their managers and employees. The human and social environment, war, peace, customer quality, politics, and misadventure all play a crucial role in their development.

That is why we can safely repeat the mantra, what do they know of business, who only business know.

This brings us to a greater understanding of the Industrial Revolution, and why it started in Britain; at its core, it was a human and social phenomenon, not a scientific one.

The Industrial Revolution was made possible because Britain's enforceable patent, copyright, and property laws ensured that a person would reap a just reward for the results of their endeavors. When it started, Britain was no more or only marginally more technically advanced than many other nations. In fact, many British 'inventions', including the steam engine, owed much to work previously performed on the continent.

To understand how this significant episode in modern civilization was at its core a human and social revolution, I have reproduced the following extracts from a paper entitled *The Industrial Revolution, The Myths, and Realities* by Peter Landry. Landry's major source is Johnson, *The Birth of the Modern.*

> *There existed in England during these times a Free Trade in Ability, it was, indeed, more important than, Free Trade in Commodities. "In early industrial Britain, qualifications, degrees, certificates, professional rules and trade conventions were swept aside by masters and men who were anxious to get on. ... The universities, as opposed to the grammar schools and Dissenting Academies, had little to do with it, and the government, nothing at all." Men sprang from nowhere to take the lead.*

The extract further explains that **the people who made the Industrial Revolution were ordinary people in pursuit of their dreams.** It backs it up by providing background details on the humble background of a host of major contributors.

> *"George Stephenson [the inventor of the steam locomotive] began as a cowherd; Telford, a shepherd's son, as a stonemason. Alexander Naysmith started as an apprentice coach painter. ...Joseph Bramah, the machine-tool inventor, creator of the first patent lock, the hydraulic press, the beer pump, the modern fire engine, the fountain pen, and the first modern water closet, started as a carpenter's apprentice and got his essential learning, and experience from the local blacksmith's forge. Henry Maudsley, perhaps the ablest of all machine-tool inventors, who created the first industrial assembly line for Brunel's block-making factory in Portsmouth, began work at 12 as a powder monkey in a cartridge works and graduated in the smithy [sic]. Joseph Clement learned nothing at school except to read and write and began helping his father, a humble handloom weaver; he too was a forge graduate. So was the great engine designer and manufacturer Matthew Murray of Leeds, who shared with James Fox of Derby the honor of inventing the first planning machines (1814). Fox began as a kitchen boy and butler. The Welshman Richard Roberts, another brilliant inventor of machine tools and power looms, including the Self-Acting Mule - described by Smiles as "one of the most elaborate and beautiful pieces*

of machinery ever contrived" - was a shoemaker's son, had literally no education, and began work as quarry laborer. William Fairbairn who designed and built the second generation of machinery for the textile industry in the 1820's, was the son of a Kelso gardener, who left school at age 10 to work as a farm laborer. John Kennedy, Fairbairn's partner in this second Industrial Revolution and the first great builder of iron ships, was another poor Scot, who received no schooling except in summer and, like Bramah, started as a carpenter's boy.

The social and class structure of the British society played a highly important if very unexpected role in this revolution. British universities and royal institutes of science and technology were filled with the upper classes. These gentlemen did not have the same motivation and urge to innovate as their poorer countrymen. That is not to say that scientific inventions never emanated from these august bodies – they were simply not the leaders in one of the greatest periods of innovation and technological advance. Landry explains:

"The English universities might be comatose and the government indifferent to industry, but the law left the entrepreneur and the self-advancing artisan free to pursue their genius. Moreover, it was the only country with an effective patent system."

There is a huge lesson in this for the modern organization. First, motivated employees are the key to technological advancement. Second, **do not leave innovation and advances in productivity to white-coated scientists locked away in labs or any other separate group of researchers. Innovation and productivity are the result of human and social processes.** These processes are best replicated when the men in white coats find a human and social application for their knowledge.

One extremely important innovation neatly combines both class and entrepreneurship. John Harrison, a humble carpenter's son, solved the problem of longitude by the development of a clock that could work at sea and maintain its accuracy. It made maritime navigation and trading a far easier prospect. He had succeeded where others such as Galileo, Cassini, and Newton had failed. The Royal Society of

Horologists for a long time refused to believe him and even refused to reward him for his troubles – delaying the introduction of his device for much too long. To the Establishment, John Harrison was of the wrong class and as such could not possibly solve one of the great problems of the day.

Yet, he did, and grudgingly the honored gentlemen awarded him his prize after the intervention of the King.

Prejudices of any sort are only good for one thing – ignorance. As with the examples of Columbus and Chinese block printing, social and cultural narrow-mindedness often blind us to the truth.

Similarly, for many years, the British could not understand why proud Oxbridge produced Nobel laureates by the dozen, and yet Japanese consumer goods manufacturers were far outstripping their British equivalents. They failed to realize that the Japanese were not trying to solve the secrets of science, but to make products that people could use.

This confusion between technological excellence and customer focus has caused many an organization to stumble. I am reminded of the introduction of satellite TV in the UK in the late 1980s.

Rupert Murdoch's Sky TV was first out of the blocks. Access to Sky's channels was via a regular 60cm or 90cm dish that allowed viewing of not only the Sky channels, but any free-to-air channels that were broadcasting from a similar orbit. Murdoch had cleverly positioned his broadcasting satellite close to everybody else's.

Murdoch's competitors, BSB, scoffed at his approach. They endeavored to introduce the British public to a high technology 'squarial'. The squarial would be locked into a particular position in order to receive a specially developed package of channels – this automatically precluded the viewer from seeing other free-to-air channels. Eventually, when BSB was launched, they made no bones about the fact that their technology was clearly superior to that of Sky.

Sadly, it did not take long for BSB's technology-driven vision to crumble, leaving Murdoch's Sky to dominate the market. Eventually, they folded BSB into Sky's operations and Murdoch has dominated the market ever since.

A socially-driven vision will far more often than not, triumph over a technology-driven vision. We will see this repeated over and over again. This assertion is vigorously reinforced by the personal experience of a good friend and colleague of mine who read an early version of my manuscript, and responded thus:

Hi Jonathan

I am liking this book more and more. I just read the chapter on knowledge and wanted to add an observation with regard to IBM and Microsoft.

I got into the computer business in 1966 working for GE (in Canada) who was making mainframes and outside of the US government was the second biggest user of computers. They used them for project management and all of the scientific uses associated with making electrical and military equipment. GE was, to the best of my knowledge, the leader in quality computers although Sperry Univac, RCA, Honeywell, Burroughs were close. Around about that time, IBM introduced the 360 series, which was not a success in terms of engineering, but they got them installed at big companies and worked out the bugs later while people like GE focused on product improvement, much like the story you told.

To me, the interesting thing is that IBM understood that you had to have customers while GE and the others felt you needed a high quality product before you could sell it.

IBM (Big Blue) is still around while the seven dwarves are not very big players in the home computing business. Even Digital (which I also worked for) has disappeared.

Back to Landry – his extracts leave us in no doubt that for best results knowledge must be aligned with opportunity and motivation. Britain's stock of knowledge was greatly increased by foreigners who were motivated by opportunity and the certainty of reward. They played a significant role in the Industrial Revolution.

> *It was the same story with clever immigrants. Frederick Koenig, who built the first steam presses in London, was the son of a Saxon peasant and began as a printer's devil. Charles Bianconi, who created the first successful passenger transport system, in the remote west of Ireland of all places, was a packman from Lake Como.*

> *Such clever and enterprising men came to the British Isles because of the opportunities provided by its great wealth and, still more, by its free economic climate.*

The final point I want to make is absolutely critical. It reflects Edison's thinking; without the ability to experiment, knowledge development is stunted. It is a singularly important message for those organizations that not only disallow experimentation but also punish failure. The relevant passage reads as follows:

> *No one invention came suddenly into bloom; all was trial and error. For an advance in one field required the paralleled advance in another. The whole process that brought on the great inventions of the Industrial Revolution was evolutionary with all the necessary factors being integrated. It happened without any central direction; it happened by each man pursuing his own particular interests; it happened because men were motivated by profit. It could not have happened through some mortal and designing mind; it could not have happened with altruistic motives singularly in mind; it could not have happened if men, each on account of their own unique contribution, did not see the likelihood of some personal advantage or benefit for their actions.*

We now know precisely the human and social factors that in their various combinations are the essential ingredients of knowledge creation, acquisition, development, and application. Motivation, initiative, personal reward, personal ingenuity, teamwork and unity, entrepreneurship, experimentation, history, training, socio-political structure, social diversity, ordinary people, an unstructured environment, freedom of action, opportunity, collective learning – these

human factors spawned the Industrial Revolution. We can add to these having the right customers and a competitive environment.
Just in case you are left in any doubt as to human and social dynamics of the development and evolution of knowledge, I hope the following anecdote, one that I find as illuminating as it is highly amusing, will finally put the matter to rest. It is taken from an extract from Adam Smith's *The Wealth of Nations* – the seminal work in modern economics.

> *Whoever has been much accustomed to visit such manufactures must frequently have been shown very pretty machines, which were the inventions of such workmen in order to facilitate and quicken their particular part of the work. In the first fire engines, a boy was constantly employed to open and shut alternately the communication between the boiler and the cylinder, according as the piston either ascended or descended. One of those boys, who loved to play with his companions, observed that, by tying a string from the handle of the valve which opened this communication to another part of the machine, the valve would open and shut without his assistance, and leave him at liberty to divert himself with his playfellows. One of the greatest improvements that has been made upon this machine, since it was first invented, was in this manner the discovery of a boy who wanted to save his own labor.*

The history of knowledge is the history of human evolution and human endeavor. Wars, the rise and fall of empires, seismic shifts in global affairs, the exchange of ideas and technological innovation have all been determined by human and social conditions and the extent to which those conditions facilitated, motivated, or even impeded the development of knowledge.

There is only one way to develop knowledge in order to improve productivity and gain competitive advantage – that is to focus exclusively on people – both inside as well as outside an organization. Further, organizations must be completely irreverent as to the possible sources and applications of knowledge. An open mind must be kept at all times.

Organizations that understand the social and human purpose of their activities have been critical in shaping our times.

It was this understanding that contributed greatly to the spread of personal computers and ultimately the Internet and the world we now inhabit. While IBM became more concerned with technical standards, forgetting what had originally made them successful, Bill Gates wanted to place a computer on every single desk and in every single home. It is that social purpose, the human aspect of development that resulted in IBM almost going to the wall while Microsoft was busy becoming the dominant firm in the computer industry.

IBM has since reverted to its original principles by focusing on the serving its customers' needs, and less on technology.

It was the human and social recognition of the use and application of technology that sparked the ICT Revolution of the past 25 years. In that regard, nothing has changed since the time of the Industrial Revolution – after all, people are still people. We might further add that, as noted earlier, the great products are the ones that have had the greatest impact on our society.

This also explains the competitive dynamics of companies as well that of the nations that spawned them.

The Dutch are best at building dykes and sea barriers because their land had to be claimed from the sea – things might have been different in New Orleans after Katrina if the Americans had bothered to learn those lessons. The Scandinavians, with companies such as Ericsson and Nokia, have been at the vanguard of mobile telephony – their sizeable but thinly populated lands with its long winters were no doubt a huge motivating factor. Alternatively, high population density and relatively cramped living conditions have made the Japanese geniuses at minimizing any and everything they can lay their hands on.

Brazilians with their vast cane fields are pioneers in ethanol-based fuels. Last year, for the first time, the country produced more flex-fuel cars – cars that operate on any combination of ethanol and petrol – than conventional petrol-only cars. The US has many of the world's most competitive banks because of the size of its domestic market, a competitive capability that it has been able to leverage into other countries.

These are factors worth considering for any major organization. They can even make the much-abused practice of outsourcing a sensible option. Boeing, for example is using Russian scientists with expertise in titanium to reduce the weight of their aircraft and make them more fuel-efficient. For the same reason, because of its large and diverse population with its human and social challenges, many Pharmaceutical companies are using India as a research, development, and clinical testing base for new drugs.

Our conclusions; knowledge is of the people, for the people and by the people. Exploiting it requires a thorough understanding of the human asset and the human and social context within which it exists.

I hope you have found the evidence presented here mightily transparent and compelling. Unfortunately, organizations have been extremely slow to learn from it.

CHAPTER

5

KNOWLEDGE IS IMPORTANT BUT CORPORATIONS HAVE BEEN SLOW LEARNERS

THE HUMAN ASSET MANIFESTO

KNOWLEDGE IS IMPORTANT BUT CORPORATIONS HAVE BEEN SLOW LEARNERS

Businesses and corporations have consistently failed to take advantage of human ingenuity.

History shows that productivity consistently lags behind innovation, and today's organizations have done little to alter that equation. This is primarily because they have been slow to understand the human and social imperative at the heart of knowledge development, innovation, productivity, and technology.

For long periods in history, most large-scale and organized forms of work were executed by the military. These tended to be structural such as roads, bridges, and dams. The Roman army was one of the greatest builders in history. Later, in the 15th century, the shipbuilders of Venice developed a mass production assembly line. During these times, consumer goods and utility items were made by craftsmen working from home or in small, specialized units adjacent to their home e.g. a blacksmith. Craftsmen produced goods to a high specification but the problem was that few people could afford their output.

Then two things happened to change the world of work. The Agrarian Revolution meant that fewer people were required to work the land, and in a relentless process that in many countries persists even today, people left the land and congregated in cities.

The surplus labor by-product of the Agrarian Revolution was immediately utilized by the Industrial Revolution. However, despite the technological innovations of the time, factories were almost non-existent – much work was subcontracted to people at home. Cottage industries developed.

Many early companies were initially incorporated to meet specific nation-state or Government needs, such as managing overseas colonies e.g. East India and West India companies. They were yet to turn their attention to the consumer – except insofar as their overseas produce made it into the domestic market.

Factories began to emerge when it was realized that pooling labor resources into one place was a more efficient way of working and taking advantage of the technical innovations of the times. However, this pooling was only possible if capital was pooled not only to pay wages but also to make the necessary investment in buildings, plant, and machinery. The need to pool capital was one of the driving forces behind the emergence of the early corporations.

Then there was a most extraordinary phenomenon. With all the innovations that were taking place, productivity in the new industrial economy remained low. The quality and quantity of output remained irregular at best. The fact was that many businesses took a long time to make the transition from sub-contracted cottage industries to factory work. The advantages of steam engines as a new source of power were not being fully utilized, and even when they were introduced, overall productivity remained low.

In effect, people were more productive when they were working at home for themselves, unsupervised by managers. Productivity fell when sub-contraction ceased, and workers were forced to obtain regular employment in factories.

To begin with, people did not like the idea of having to work regular hours in a highly controlled environment with someone constantly watching over them. Acts of sabotage were not unknown. It is said that the word sabotage has French origins – a sabot was the wooden shoe thrown into machinery to 'sabotage' operations. Whether or not this is the actual origin of the word, it provides an interesting insight into early manufacturing problems.

Factory work required co-ordination but the workers did not like it. It took time for managers to understand how best to organize their workforce and supervise them for best results.

Economists describe this phenomenon as the S-Curve – when a new process is introduced, productivity decreases, makes minor improvements, and ultimately increases. **It took over 50 years for the Industrial Revolution, regarded by many as one of the most creative and innovative periods in human history, to bring about significant improvements in productivity.**

Most of those gains were achieved towards the very end of the period, after much trial and error. Managers and owners formed associations where they could share information on how best to optimize their combination of physical and human resources. As the complexity of the production and the manufacturing process grew, management began to understand the nature of the challenges facing them, and began to see training and exchange of knowledge as important to their success.

However, the reality is that it took more than two generations before the Industrial Revolution could reap the promise of its technological innovations. This represented a failure to understand and adapt to the human and social factors of the manufacturing production process. Unfortunately, this was repeated when electricity arrived in the latter part of the 19th century. It was several decades and another two generations before full advantage was taken of electricity's potential.

This proves yet again that **the Industrial Revolution was at its heart a human and social revolution, which achieved its best results when it learned to optimize human assets and effect a new paradigm in people management.**

One may be forgiven for thinking that these lessons would have been fully absorbed in an effort to avoid the failures of the past. That is wishful thinking. The record shows that to this very day, the same mistake have been repeated over and over again.

We can begin the exploration of this topic by moving on to the next great event in industrial history – mass production.

Henry Ford introduced mass production to the auto industry in the early 20th century. It was based on a simple principle – the ability to interchange parts by manufacturing everything to a standard gauge. It meant that the exact same bolt could go into the exact same position on every single car of a specific model. The principles were broadly the same as those used in Venice in the 15th century. It had taken man half a millennium to adopt them – again emphasizing the importance of knowledge discovery and transmission.

What was different about the mass production approach of Ford was the moving assembly line, developed entirely by accident. It forced workers to adopt a more regularized approach to their work.

Ford wanted to integrate man and machine into a single unit and forced his workers to adapt to the new pace of work and he "often wondered why workers brought their heads to work when all he really needed was their hands and feet" (Losey, 1998).

This created problems. Although Ford made some initial progress, his attempts floundered. Workers committed acts of sabotage or simply left in droves. In an aptly titled article, *Slouching Towards Utopia: The Economic History of the Twentieth Century*, J. Bradford DeLong of the University of California, Berkley noted that:

> *In one year, 1913, Ford had an average annual labor force of 13,600 and yet 50,400 people quit or were fired...*

Ford believed in his mission – the Model-T, so designated because it was the 20th design. His motivation for developing the Model-T was to make the motor car available to the ordinary man. This is highly significant. The average car of the day was not only expensive it was prone to breakdown. If you owned a car, you also had to be mechanic or have sufficient means to hire one. It was not just the price that eventually made the Model-T attractive – its construction was simple, and as such, so was its maintenance.

Ford clearly understood and was motivated by the human and social needs of his prospective customers. Therefore, he was undeterred. He kept going until he found the right tactic. As DeLong noted:

> *Ford's solution was a massive increase in wages: to US$5.00 a day for unskilled workers whose family circumstances and*

deportment satisfied Ford. By 1915, annual turnover was down to 16%, from 370% before the raise. Many to whom Ford jobs had not been worth keeping at US$1.75 a day found the assembly line more-than-bearable for US$5.00 a day.

The higher wages were a complete antithesis to the accepted norm of the time but Ford wanted to meet the needs of his employees. Crucially, he also wanted them to be able to afford the price of a Model-T. The greater incentive, employee stability, and greater learning that resulted gave an extraordinary boost to both quality and productivity.

The era of mass production was truly born. The massive increase in output for a given input of the factors of production meant that what was once considered a luxury for the few suddenly became affordable for the many. It was the start of the era of keeping up with the Joneses.

Most history or business books will tell you that the miracle of mass production was due to engineering and technical achievements, but that does not really explain what happened. **In truth, the success of mass production owes much to the fact that Henry Ford eventually had to pay attention to the requirements of both his internal and external human assets.**

The mass production of cars was the great social revolution of its time in many ways. Ford's wages provided a route whereby relatively large numbers of ordinary working-class men could climb into the middle classes. To Americans it was a social revolution almost akin to the affordability of the Model-T itself. It also explains why vehicle manufacturing became part of the very fabric of American life.

Ford did have his detractors. His assembly line work was considered belittling of skilled craftsmen and that it forced workers to do simple, repetitive, and demeaning tasks.

Mass production was not as successful in the UK. Rather than flat hourly rates for all workers, the British, who still believed in individual craftsmanship, created a myriad of wage and piece rates for every single activity. This set the foundation for ongoing battles between management and unions over pay, conditions, and responsibilities. Skilled workers revolted, the assembly line, so important to Ford, remained unpowered for 20 years, and Americans and their methods were for some reason unpopular.

This culture of differences, in job descriptions and worker categories, was merely a reflection of the class distinctions that existed within the wider British society. So too were the constant disputes between management on the one hand, and staff and their unions on the other. Again, this was grounded in class differences – no doubt contributing to the fact that many unions were leftwing and militant.

British car manufacturers were engaged in class wars that went way beyond their compound.

I am sure there were other issues, but human and social factors ultimately led to the failure of British-style mass-production. Organizations that fail to understand fully the social and human context within which their organizations operate eventually pay the price.

Meanwhile, back in the US, the idea of using mass production to optimize the investment in plant and machinery was rapidly taking hold. Theodore Vail, President of AT&T in 1908, argued:

> *"Net revenue can be produced in two ways: by a large percentage of profit on a small business, or a small percentage of profit on a large business. And in America the second was best..."*

This placed a premium on productivity and it was on this basis that corporate owners and managers embraced Frederick W Taylor's work on Scientific Management.

The logic behind Taylor's work was brutally simplistic – employees are lazy, unmotivated and have no reason whatsoever to maximize their output. Scientific Management improved productivity by improving the effectiveness and efficiency of worker in relation to machine. It laid the groundwork for what became known as Industrial or Production Engineering.

Scientific Management essentially ignored social and human issues. However, it critically linked employee output to their remuneration and rewards, just as Ford had done, and made possible ever-larger economies of scale, and improved access to basic goods and services.

Later, US and Allied successes in World War II were attributed to the fact that the US had relentlessly applied Taylor's principles to both military and industrial production – not then realizing the extent to which war played a role in ramping up production.

Nevertheless, as products and production methods became more complex, the need for employee interaction increased. Thus, simply rewarding workers on an individual productivity or work basis would become less appropriate. There was also the fact that the service sector began to play an increasingly significant role in developed economies and Scientific Management principles could not be readily applied.

From as early as the late 1920s, The Hawthorne Studies showed conclusively that workers were motivated by a variety of different factors. As such, Scientific Management alone could not be relied upon to provide sustainable improvements in productivity. Later work by Gregory, Maslow (which we shall come to later) and a host of others provided a sound basis for focusing on personal factors as a means of improving productivity.

Other developments indicated that Scientific Management on its own was not enough. In 1869, Siemens developed the first industrial laboratory, recognizing that electronics could and should be studied as a separate discipline in order to improve innovation and the application of new technologies. Siemens was quickly followed by the German chemicals industry and by the turn of the 20th century, Germany, with its superior application of knowledge to production, had overtaken Britain in terms of both output and productivity.

After World War II, pharmaceutical companies in particular, as well as IBM and AT&T, all started their own research labs. The assumption was that each industry had its unique technology. The expectation was that all the knowledge an organization needed, and all the applications of their research would be respectively developed and utilized if not within their own organizations, then certainly within their own industry.

They were in for a nasty surprise.

Computers and electronics transformed the motor industry. Digital technology and optical fibers transformed the telephone industry. The pharmaceutical industry is being transformed by work in genetics and molecular biology.

More spectacularly, AT&T's Bell Labs, the same organization that later failed to make optimum use of its development of wireless telephony, had earlier developed the transistor. Unable to find any "application" for the product related to telephones or telecommunications, the lab virtually gave its discovery away by licensing it for US$ 25,000 to anyone who wanted it.

That was another goldmine, or in this case, we should say diamond mine, squandered on the failure to expand the social horizons and applications of newly-developed knowledge. Transistors are now used in every computer, television, and mobile phone – and that's just the beginning. This extract from Wikipedia suitably illustrates the full extent of AT&T's debacle:

> *The transistor is considered by many to be one of the greatest inventions in modern history, ranking in importance with inventions such as the <u>printing press</u>, the <u>automobile</u>, and the <u>telephone</u>. It is the key active component in practically all modern <u>electronics</u>.*

Even at the height of Scientific Management, the competitive strategies of whole industries were being transformed not only by the ability to develop new knowledge, but also by the ability to discern its social purpose.

Nothing emphasized the human and social imperatives at the very core of business more than IBM's domination of the computer industry in the 1950s and 1960s. As illustrated in the extract below by Ted Egan, IBM was not the technology leader of its time – it was its emphasis on maximizing the usefulness of technology that made it the industry leader.

In the 1950s IBM rose to dominance in the new market for electronic computers by combining a critical focus on marketing—developing and advertising new uses for computers—along with a number of software innovations, which lowered the cost, and expanded the range, of computer use (Bashe et al., 1981). IBM's computers were rarely more powerful than competitors', but one major way the company developed a competitive advantage was by investing in software (operating systems, programming languages, and general-purpose database management systems), and in relationship-building with the programmers in large corporate data processing, such as General Motors. These connections to customers, and IBM's focus on maximizing the usefulness of technology, always gave it more time than competitors to meet current technological standards. In fact, I would argue that strategies which expand the potential applications associated with a computer technology—through investment in system software, training, and marketing—has always been, and continues to be, the primary determinant of the success of the technology company: raw computer power diffuses far too rapidly to serve as a basis for market control over an extended period of time2.

The second major method of obtaining and consolidating market power, which IBM pioneered in the 1960s, was the manipulation of compatibility and customer lock-in, which solidified their "installed base" of computer rentals and sales (DeLamarter, 1986). The IBM 360 series was the first line of computers, of different costs and abilities, which would easily permit the exchange of data and software code among themselves. Central to this innovation was a major system software innovation, the OS/360. Software written for a small member of the series would only need to be re-complied, and not re-written, to be run on a larger machine. IBM's 360 series then saved customers money over competitors' systems that had no such compatibility, which it then could extract in the form of customer loyalty and/or higher prices. IBM built these two strategies: focusing on maximizing the value of IBM technology for customers, and shepherding customers into a long-term reliance on IBM by building a closed universe of compatible products—into world leadership in the computer industry.

You might recall that this is also consistent with the experience of my friend noted in the previous chapter.

Things got even more interesting when the US Justice Department intervened in the 1970s, forcing IBM to unbundle hardware and software. This led to the rise of Microsoft, which ironically was able to lock customers in even more securely than IBM, by establishing relationships further down the human and social chain – as Kagan further elaborates:

The new and old orders of computing came into open conflict during the 1980s, as IBM legitimized the microcomputer for business use in 1981 with its IBM PC. IBM had intended the PC to disseminate processing power to line departments in corporations, while strengthening EDP software developers' application monopolies and corporate dependence upon mainframe computers, its high-margin line. Apple Computer, however, was demonstrating success in non-corporate markets with its easy-to-use microcomputers, which permitted information processing to take place out of EDP the loop. This strategy of establishing lock-in with end-users, as opposed to EDP departments, was to become the dominant source of market power in the 1980s and 1990s. When Microsoft, IBM's chief PC software partner, adopted this strategy in the late 1980s, it quickly became the world's largest software company, benefiting from Apple's strategy and IBM's customer base. When Microsoft's Windows 3.0 product overwhelmingly defeated IBM's own OS/2 in the early 1990s, the new organization of the software industry was further cemented, perhaps permanently.

This places us into a position to develop a more comprehensive understanding of the dramatic change in ICT that brought about the revolution of the last 25 years. The change from a predominantly IBM ecosystem to a Microsoft ecosystem is that Gates' vision of a PC on every desk extended the boundaries of a social revolution started by IBM several decades earlier.

An ancillary lesson in all of this is **if you are not supplying goods and services to the ultimate user, then you must think very carefully about how your customer is going to use your product.** The 'Intel-inside' campaign is one based on the idea of reaching out to the ultimate consumer.

The computer has been around for over half a century. Intel developed the microprocessor in 1971 and PCs have been around since the mid-1970s. Yet only in the past decade has productivity shown signs of being significantly impacted by the new digital technologies.

It was as if we were back to the Industrial Revolution – it has taken a generation, and in some cases more than a generation, to take best advantage of the new technologies. Organizations continue to make the same mistakes of relying on organizational goals, concepts, and structures. The many companies that have tried to take advantage of global markets best illustrate these mistakes.

By 1980, ITT was the second largest supplier of communications equipment in the world. However, it had one major problem – its worldwide operations were a series of local fiefdoms. While local autonomy produced a multitude of different ideas, they were never effectively utilized on the global level. Each national organization wanted to undertake their own R&D. This failure to manage the human and social conflicts within the organization translated into a failure to integrate technology and standards that caused significant waste. Eventually ITT was no longer in the telecommunications equipment business.

The Dutch electronics giant Philips had a similar problem – it was a national company everywhere but could not harness global scales of efficiency.

Alternatively, Philips's Japanese competitor, Matsushita, developed centralized global scalability in R&D and production and established leadership in the global consumer electronics business. However, Matsushita's success came about because it had a few more tricks up its sleeve. Just as Microsoft licensed its software to all PC manufacturers, Matsushita licensed its development of its VHS Video format to other major manufacturers such as Hitachi and Sharp. Additionally, it developed global marketing and distribution capabilities that improved its responsiveness to different local country conditions.

Sony had brought out its Betamax video product two years before Matsushita's VHS and Philips's V2000 was considered the technically superior product. Yet Matsushita triumphed – because its acquisition and application of knowledge, both in the company through local market intelligence, and outside of the company through licensing of its technology, was superior to its competitors.

Matsushita capitalized on its human assets in every dimension – employees, potential competitors, and clients.

In their book, *Management Across Borders*, Bartlett and Ghosal highlighted the organizational dilemma faced by many companies, the global efficiency of centralization as against the innovation and local responsiveness of decentralization. In attempting to benefit from the best of both worlds, many companies adopted matrix management structures. Inevitably this was followed by successive and numerous reorganizations.

Bartlett and Ghosal maintain that constant reorganizations are a very firm indication that the answers are not to be found in the organizational structure. Having read the book *Barbarians At The Gates*, that is what Ross Johnson, head of RJR Nabisco, would have called a BGO – a blinding glimpse of the obvious.

Sadly, this is not so obvious to many of today's organizations.

Bartlett and Ghosal argue that formal organizational structures and hierarchies are static while the environments within which corporates operate are complex and dynamic. In order to develop what they call multi-dimensional strategic capabilities, they assert that organizations need better and more integrated informal structures and organizational flexibility. These can only be brought about by greater communications, personal relationships, training, and people development.

In other words, the key to developing a sustainable and responsive competitive advantage is to harness, nurture, and integrate human and social assets. Bartlett and Ghosal designate as 'Transnationals' companies that can effect this change. Table 1 summarizes the different organizational types and how they each cope with the demands of a dynamic environment.

TABLE 1
THE CHALLENGE OF DIFFERENT ORGANIZATION STRUCTURES

Organizational Characteristics	Multinational	Global	International	Transnational
Configuration of Assets and Capabilities	Decentralized and nationally self-sufficient	Centralized and globally scaled	Core skills centralized, others decentralized	Dispersed, interdependent and specialized
Role of Overseas Operations	Sensing and exploiting local opportunities	Implementing parent company strategies	Adapting and leveraging parent competencies	Differentiated contributions by national units, integrated global operations
Development and Diffusion of Knowledge	Knowledge developed and retained within each unit	Knowledge developed and retained at the centre	Knowledge developed centrally, utilized globally	Knowledge developed jointly and shared globally
Problems	Globally Inefficient Poor Knowledge Transfer	Globally Efficient Slow to adapt to local conditions	Moderate efficiency and globally responsiveness	Maintaining integrated vision, learning, communication

Source: Management Across Borders, Bartlett and Ghosal

THE HUMAN ASSET MANIFESTO

In an FT article on January 6, 2006, Ben King provides with a very good example as to why future innovation and technological progress will continue to be dependent on human and social values, and the extent to which organizations can promote collaboration. The title of the article, *Managing Change: When systems converge but people don't*, provides an insight into why technology initiatives aimed at the convergence of IT and telephones have until recently, proved to be less than successful.

The convergence of these two platforms means that instead of running separate IT and communications networks, organizations that effectively manage their integration can save themselves a lot of money by using a single network, as well as take advantage of lower Internet phone charges. As the following extract demonstrates, that has not always been easy:

> *Getting facilities and IT staff to work towards a single goal can be arduous...*

> *"Voice and data are usually handled by separate teams, who don't always work together," says Steve Blood, vice president of Gartner, the research group. "Earlier technology initiatives that bridged the voice-data divide, like unified messaging, failed because they couldn't get enough cooperation.*

In the last fifteen years, in addition to matrix management and constant reorganizations, we have seen Downsizing, Rightsizing, Quality Standards, Change Management, Business Process Reengineering, and Outsourcing. They all pay homage to the traditions of Scientific Management. They are all primarily focused on Scientific Management principles and organizational goals. Hence the need to continue changing their structure and reorganize – constantly failing to recognize they are focused on completely the wrong objectives.

Too little emphasis is being placed on the human and social factors of organizational development. The argument firmly supports what we explored in the chapter, *The Make Believe World Of The Faddists*. It also provides a further framework and context within which we might understand such behavior – organizations are still stuck with the principles of Scientific Management.

Nowhere is this more obvious than in the PC industry. The winners in that industry are Microsoft and Intel, two knowledge-focused organizations, and Dell, through its innovation of the social interface with the customer. Likewise, IBM now makes twice as much from services as it does from building computers because it changed its focus from building machines to devising customer solutions.

It is highly instructive that in the early 1990s when IBM nearly collapsed, it was able to refashion itself and focus on customer needs by appointing a CEO who was a former customer. Louis Gerstner had worked for American Express, a major IBM customer. When he took over at IBM he focused on what he wanted the company to do for him when he was a client – the integration of systems and technology and advice on how to use it, not just the technology itself.

The last 30 years have seen the proliferation of service industries – financial, leisure, software, and IT, and the relative decline of manufacturing in the more advanced economies. This means that, more than ever, the delivery of products and services is dependent on social and human factors – the direct interface between human assets in all spheres, inside and outside the organization. Yet many organizations are still making century's old mistakes.

Incredibly, some organizations in the UK have recently introduced electronic tagging of workers. The following is an extract from a Guardian article entitled *Firms tag workers to improve efficiency, and is dated June 7, 2005.*

> *Workers in warehouses across Britain are being "electronically tagged" by being asked to wear small computers to cut costs and increase the efficient delivery of goods and food to supermarkets, a report revealed yesterday.*

> *New US satellite- and radio-based computer technology is turning some workplaces into "battery farms" and creating conditions similar to "prison surveillance," according to a report*

from Michael Blakemore, professor of geography at Durham University.

The technology, introduced six months ago, is spreading rapidly, with up to 10,000 employees using it to supply household names such as Tesco, Sainsbury's, Asda, Boots and Marks & Spencer.

Others in the US have increased electronic surveillance in the belief that monitoring employee movements will improve productivity!

Some firms are even going one-step further. They are using GPS enabled mobile phones to pinpoint precisely the location of those employees who work outside the office. While this technology does have genuine logistic applications, such as improved scheduling of loading and delivery times for lorries, it is increasingly being used as a surveillance tool to track employees.

Unbelievable, but true, there are organizations today that are doing precisely the same things as their predecessors in the early part of the Industrial Revolution. Is there any doubt that it will have the same negative effect? The following article from www.management-issues.com on June 22, 2005, entitled *Ever get the feeling you're being watched?* highlights the futility of these big-brother practices:

Surveillance also has its flip side. Studies have shown that monitored workers suffered more work dissatisfaction, depression, extreme anxiety, exhaustion, strain injuries and neck problems than unmonitored workers.

A recent report from the London School of Economics also argued that the sort of scrutiny and micromanagement that results from supply chain technologies developed for monitoring goods being applied to individuals undermines the productivity benefits of the technology-driven economy.

There are better ways of moving forward.

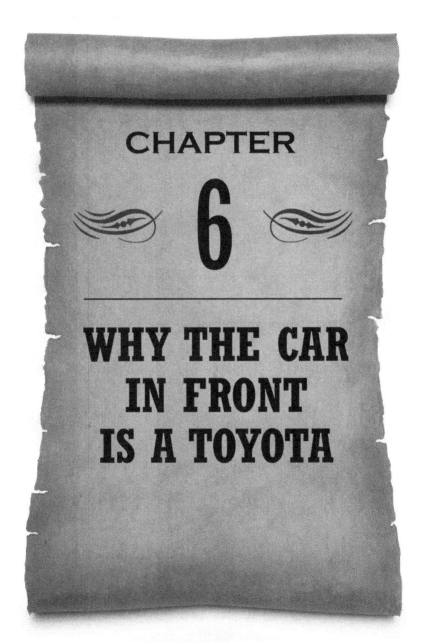

CHAPTER

6

WHY THE CAR IN FRONT IS A TOYOTA

THE HUMAN ASSET MANIFESTO

WHY THE CAR IN FRONT IS A TOYOTA

The making of automobiles is still the world's largest manufacturing activity, with over 50 million new vehicles assembled each year. That alone would make it worth studying – but it gets even better. The very nature of its evolution provides very pertinent lessons.

Ford perfected not only the interchangeable part, but also the interchangeable worker – at one time 50 different languages were spoken on his assembly line. Mass production was the foundation of American global dominance for several decades. It took over 20 years for others to even begin to catch up. World War II was to accelerate this process as representatives of the devastated European and Japanese economies visited the US to learn more about the industrial power and dynamism of the economy that had won the war.

Amongst those visiting the US, Detroit in particular, were Eiji Toyoda and Taiichi Ohno of the Toyota Motor Company. Like everybody else, they hoped to return home inspired and infused with ideas. Instead, they were dispirited – the realities of the two markets were so different.

Japanese clients required small numbers of a wide range of vehicles and only flexible production methods could provide that. Detroit was very good at mass-producing large quantities of similar items. Changing production models required a complete change in the machine tools for stamping body parts. These changes could take several months to execute and had to be performed by specialists. A modicum of production flexibility could be accomplished if one had the resources to purchase large numbers of these stamping machines, or dies as they were known, as well as the vast factory space required to store them.

Unfortunately, in war-shattered Japan, Toyota did not have the resources for that kind of investment. That was just the beginning of their problems. In addition to capital scarcity:

1. The unions were militant

2. Japan did not have a relatively cheap and/or immigrant labor pool like their competitors in Germany, the UK, the US and France (respectively Turks, West Indians, Africans, African Americans)

3. Japanese workers did not want to be treated as interchangeable parts

4. American occupiers introduced laws so that workers could not be easily hired and fired

5. A combination of the additional new legislation and pressure from the unions meant that there was no longer any distinction between white and blue collar workers

The final point is of vital importance. In the previous chapter, we explored how the British class system negatively affected mass production. In Japan, the elimination of class distinctions resulted in the elimination of worker categories and rifts between management and staff. This human and social revolution laid the initial foundations for Lean Production.

At a time when the rest of the world was rushing to embrace mass production, Toyoda and Ohno decided that it would never work in Japan. Thus, they began the development of the Toyota Production System or TPS – now commonly known as Lean Production.

Toyoda and Ohno recognized that many of their problems were human and social in origin, and these were precisely the issues they first addressed by negotiating a tough union deal:

Toyota Union Compromise

1. A quarter of the workforce were fired

2. The remainder of the workforce were guaranteed lifetime employment

3. There was to be flexibility in work assignments

4. Steep pay progression by seniority (in terms of experience) rather than function, with bonuses tied to profitability

5. Employees active in initiating improvements rather than simply reporting problems

6. Employees granted full access to Toyota facilities (housing, recreation etc.)

In effect, employees were made and recognized as the primary assets of the organization, and the foundation on which it would achieve its success. They would start working for the organization between the ages of 18 and 22 and retire at 60. Thus, it made sense to continuously develop and harness these human assets in the form of continuous learning and development, and that is precisely what Toyota did.

Toyota placed people before technology. In contrast, western assembly plant workers were treated with little regard and managers often told them that it was just a matter of time before their jobs were automated.

Toyota decided to organize workers into teams with a team leader rather than a foreman. If anyone was absent on the day, the team leader would take over his role. Hierarchies and specialists were largely eliminated and their responsibilities devolved to the average worker.

Toyoda and Ohno had noticed a large amount of downtime in Detroit that resulted from workers waiting for specialists to fix things. They believed that with a little more training the workers could do much of this work themselves. Toyota also made teams responsible for their own quality control and gave every assembly line worker the authority to stop the line whenever they believed such action was required. In Detroit, only shift managers had such authority.

Finally, each team was allowed time to reflect, explore and suggest ways of continuously improving the work in which they were engaged. This process of continuous improvement or kaizen was done in conjunction with engineers – rather than by engineers. The people at Toyota recognized fully that everyone involved in the process was perfectly capable of adding value. As far as the possible sources and applications of knowledge were concerned, they were supremely irreverent. This is entirely consistent with the findings of Towers Perrin which we came across in the very first chapter; more than anything else employees want to be engaged.

The Toyota Production System, TPS is at its heart a social and human construct, and this is confirmed by Jeffrey Liker in his book, The Toyota Way:

> *The more I have studied TPS and the Toyota Way, the more I understand that it is a system designed to provide the tools for people to continually improve their work. The Toyota system means more dependence on people not less. It is a culture, even more than a set of efficiency and improvement techniques. You depend on your workers to reduce inventory, identify hidden problems, and fix them. The workers have s sense of urgency, purpose, and teamwork because if they don't fix it there will be an inventory outage. On a daily basis, engineers, skilled workers, quality specialists, vendors, team leaders, and – most importantly – operators are all involved in continuous problem solving and improvement, which in time, trains everyone to become better solvers.*

While affecting their new social order, the company turned its attention to the manufacturing process and, in particular, the problem of dies – the machines that stamp or mould sheets of metal into desired shapes. After much experimentation and development, the need for large numbers of dies was rendered unnecessary. They accomplished such a dramatic simplification in the die changing process that the work could now be devolved to workers on the assembly line. The benefits that accrued from their achievement were tremendous in that they:

1. Reduced the levels of capital investment necessary for conducting business

2. Reduced the amount of factory space required for production

3. Reduced the worker downtime that was a constant feature of mass production

4. Significantly reduced the amount of waste previously associated with the process

5. Eliminated completely the specialist workers required to effect die changes

6. Improved the job satisfaction of the assembly line worker who was now made responsible for a task previously done by specialists

7. Vastly improved manufacturing flexibility and productivity

As with all the great developments in history, Lean Production was made possible by the simple application of the human mind to a problem. It is also quite apparent how the nomenclature Lean Production came about – compared to mass-production it requires:

1. Less human effort in the factory

2. Less manufacturing space

3. Less investment tools

4. Less engineering tools

5. Less time to develop new products

The following extract from Liker's, *The Toyota Way* demonstrates the precise nature and extent of Toyota's achievements, as well as their commercial and competitive value.

1980s the Japanese got caught out by reduction in oil prices. Fuel-efficient cars were no longer the rage. Manufacturers were tooled up for 4-stroke cylinder engines and changing to 6-stroke would have been very expensive and time consuming. The answer, the lean production development went into high gear and came up with the results; fuel injection rather than carburetors, four valves per cylinder rather than two, turbochargers and overall engine performance.

Lean production meant that design and manufacturability of these complex changes were efficiently and effectively effected and the Japanese all of a sudden looked high-tech. The fact of the matter was that western firms did have these technologies

*as they were already in some high quality cars – what they did
not have was lean manufacturing and production that could
effect them – in their eyes they were too complex to implement.
Often when such changes were suggested, management vetoed
them as being too expensive and too complex to implement.*

*It took GM four years to bring in similar changes; albeit in a
limited range with performance issues.*

We should be amazed at the nature of GM's current problems. Its production is geared for gas-guzzling SUVs at a time when petrol prices
have soared, and it does not have the production flexibility to switch
quickly to more fuel-efficient models. GM's production technology is
less capable than Toyota's of 30 years ago – incredible but true.
Toyota introduced its TPS in the 1950s and GM still has not caught
up. They still do not understand that TPS or Lean Production is
a social system. Motor industry commentators point to what they
believe to be a significant part of the problem. For some reason North
American and other motor manufacturers have not realized that
Lean Production is not just a production issue – it must be embedded
throughout the whole organization for best results.

**At Toyota, TPS did not stop at the production floor – it was
extended to every facet of the organization. Teamwork, trust,
job partnership, communication, efficient use of resources and
continuous improvement were extended to research, design,
supplier relationships, and buyer relationships.**

"The real difference between Toyota and other vehicle manufacturers
is not the Toyota Production System, it is the Toyota Product Development System," claims Kokako Yamada, Chief Engineer of Toyota's
Lexus line. Toyota's development times are amazingly short because
of the team ethos at the heart of their methodology. The shusa or
Chief Engineer responsible for developing a new product is given
complete autonomy – it is the most desirable job within the organization. There is absolutely no interference from senior management.

**At Toyota, staff are assigned to the team, not as representa-
tives of their departments but as fully committed members**

who sign a binding contract at the outset. As such, remuneration and promotion are dependent on performance within the team, and are determined by the head of the team.

Witness how many of today's organizations believe that they have formed a team when they manage to throw together any arbitrary group of people.

At Toyota, the team is cross-functional, autonomous, collaborative, and self-managed. Such an arrangement means that the team has the freedom to operate independent of management and make their own decisions. Its cross-functional nature facilitates the use of a wide range of skill sets on the part of the individual employee, thus challenging them to make the most of their capabilities. This is entirely consistent with the optimization of human assets.

Precisely this format was used to make Lexus, at a time when many said it was impossible to create a luxury marque to challenge the likes of Mercedes and BMW. It is not surprising that Lexus has surpassed many if not all of its North American and European counterparts in terms of quality and reliability. However, even lower range Toyotas are more reliable than many of their counterparts' luxury models.

Lean Production was spawned by human and social factors, and was developed by focusing on human and social factors. It is superior to mass production in terms of customization, quantity, and quality.

This is an extremely important differentiation. Craftwork was supposed to be superior to mass production in terms of customization. Mass production was superior to craftwork in terms of quantity. Lean Production combines the best of these traditions and outperforms them both in all areas.

Suppliers and buyers are integral to Lean Production. It is said that the first step in the *kanban*, the efficient inventory system, occurs when a client orders a new car.

Similarly, Dell's ability to copy precisely such characteristics while enriching the customer experience has distinguished it from other PC makers.

These are prime examples of the principle that an organization's human assets are both internal and external.
It is true that today more customers are ordering items, including cars, which are built to their specification. In its own way, Toyota has been incorporating its customer human assets to improve its product for many years now.

In the early 1990s, while I was on a business trip in Tokyo, a westerner told me a remarkable story. He had just bought a second-hand car for his wife. The car must have been about four years old. While relaxing at home on a Saturday morning, the doorbell rang. He and his wife were slightly taken aback as they were not expecting any visitors at that time. They opened the door and there was a representative from the car company asking them if there was anything he could do to help them with their purchase.

It is said that the only way to escape your Japanese car salesperson is to emigrate.

The relationship with suppliers is at least as interesting. **Suppliers are not given detailed specifications; they are given performance standards – essentially allowing them to come up with solutions that allow the best use of their intuition, know-how and technical capabilities.** Suppliers do not compete amongst themselves on price; they actually cooperate and share knowledge to come up with the best solutions. Finally, suppliers are included and fully integrated into all development and design teams within the organization – they don't come in after the fact, they are part of the business.

The most critical factor in all these relationships is that the customer, the employee and the supplier all know best. Lean Production explicitly recognizes that the person engaged in the activity is the greatest source of knowledge and innovation. This directly facilitates the well-known and highly valuable dictum, the most important knowledge you will ever receive is what you didn't know that you didn't know. It is for these specific reasons that promotion within Toyota is based on leadership and teamwork.

At Toyota, the ability to leverage and harness the knowledge of those around you is more valued than individual technical capabilities.

Table 1 summarizes the differences between Lean Production and mass production.

TABLE 1
LEAN PRODUCTION VS
MASS PRODUCTION

Mass Production Characteristics	Lean Production Characteristics
Even when organized in teams, commitment and responsibility less than complete	Work based around committed teams that are given total responsibility for their work
Relatively lower skilled, less motivated with variable levels of remuneration	Highly skilled, highly motivated and highly remunerated employees
The supervisor or manager knows best	The person doing the work knows best
Quality based on standards	Quality based on continuous improvements
Research and innovation done by specialists scientists and engineers removed from the production process – apart from GM's catalytic converter, not highly successful	Engineers and scientists all start on the production floor, then into marketing, engineering, and development teams – then given job assignment after two years
Many different categories of workers	Essentially two categories of workers, assemblers and technicians
Large numbers of middle managers	Low levels of middle management
Management skills are technical	Management skills are social and organizational
Communications and commitments not as easy and explicit	Team kept in one place, pledges are signed and there is a strong commitment to keep open communications and resolve conflicts

THE HUMAN ASSET MANIFESTO

Sequential development	Simultaneous and integrated development
Poor on mass customization	Facilitates mass customization
Quality control performed at the end of the production	Quality control performed continuously by teams on the line
Everything designed by industrial engineers –tools, work practices, quality standards	Greater involvement of teams in design and development of tools, machinery and working practices
Luxury vehicles produced by craftsmen – problems with quality…Quality and productivity inversely related	Luxury vehicles subject to the same lean production techniques producing very high quality e.g. Lexus
New designs have low manufacturability and have a long lead time before introduction	Ease of manufacturing, design, delivery are integral to and natural a part of the system
Information guarded by managers	Continuous and open communications of plant conditions, status, production etc
Promotions based on technical capabilities within hierarchical framework	Promotion and rewards based on teamwork and leadership
Competitive supplier network – given design specifications which must be met at cost	Cooperative supplier network and partnership – suppliers part of design process
JIT manufacturing subject to labor agitation Slower to respond to flexibility	JIT is a social construct – highly successful Focus on flexible production engineering, facilitated by flexible working, produced an ability to mass customize
Attempts at JIT inventory management often thwarted by labor disputes	Integrate dealer and buyer into the product development process – dealer is the first step into the kanban, supplier first step in JIT

GM's woes and Rover's recent demise have made us all aware of the success of Japanese car companies relative to their western counterparts – 'Jap Crap' is not so funny any more. Actually, it ceased being funny a long time ago. The following extract, written in April 2005 by Leonard Karpen an independent commentator, highlights the extent of Toyota's success in the US. It also provides insights into where its competitors are going wrong i.e. they are still stuck with elements of mass production – they focus on process but not enough on people:

Toyota's productivity and profitability reflects the commitment not only of management but of the entire organization; something U.S. and European automakers must understand to survive...

With productivity growth that is 2x that of Detroit, a profit margin of close to 7% in a 2-3% world, and market capitalization exceeding that of GM, it is no wonder analysts have taken notice of Toyota's success. To the man in the street, especially in the U.S., however, these statistics come as not surprise -- just look at how many cars next to you, ahead of you, and in your ass-view mirror has the Toyota insignia on them. And that's the point really, isn't it? Cars on the road rather than on the lot, customer retention, and new sales of product that moves upscale as customers earn more. Innovation is in there too of course -- who would not want a Prius in an environmentally conscious world. So what of this incredible success in an industry wracked with pain?

In Europe and the U.S. management is constantly at odds with its workforce. The Europeans try to appease, Detroit tries to cajole but the end result is a sense of division. Maybe the Japanese culture allows for a more unified approach to making things -- better philosophers than I have written volumes on this -- but the results are clear -- just look at Toyota. In the U.S. everyone has become jaded; Detroit tried kaizen and couldn't sustain it. Hollywood made funny movies about Japanese management (remember "Gung Ho") and to talk about it again would just be blasé'. This type of scoffing is deep seated in U.S. business today -- partly because U.S. companies don't really care about their workers; they've shown it over the course of the last 15 years in the downsizing, rightsizing, outsourcing, etc. And workers know it and thus are reluctant to be loyal and embrace any new ideas that management tries on them. The whole system is bereft of the spirit of cooperation that makes Toyota exemplary.

Downsizing, Rightsizing and Outsourcing – sound familiar?

The productivity of Toyota and other Japanese vehicle manufacturers relative to their European counterparts was highlighted by World Market Research in 2003.

> *The average productivity of the four Japanese plants - Honda Swindon, Toyota Burnaston (UK), Toyota Valenciennes and Nissan Sunderland (UK) - was 87.5 units per employee in 2002, a very impressive record far exceeding the European average of 61 units per employee.*

What is even more interesting is that Japanese car manufacturers are not rushing to build factories in low-wage countries. This was the prediction of many industry observers who, like western manufacturers, have been unable to comprehend that Lean Production is a human and social phenomenon. Instead, Toyota and Honda are building cars in the UK and the US.

It also explains why South Korean manufacturer Hyundai is at last emerging as a competitor. The earlier low wage, mass production efforts of Hyundai and Kia were a disaster. Hyundai has now converted to Lean Production and it too is building factories in the US, not lower-wage South Korea.

We now know why countries like Brazil and Mexico have not emerged as low-wage champions in vehicle manufacture. Lean Production is about people and their skills – not low wages and outsourcing.

Critically, Lean Production is also about the mission. Table 2 sets out the contrast in Mission Statements, effectively reflecting the core value of the respective organizations:

TABLE 2
SPOT THE DIFFERENCE

Toyota Motor Manufacturing North America	Ford Motor Company
1. As an American company, contribute to the economic growth of the community and the United States 2. As an independent company, contribute to the stability and well being of team members 3. As a Toyota group company, contribute to the overall growth of Toyota by adding value to our customers	1. Ford is a worldwide leader in automotive and automotive-related products and services as well as newer industries such as aerospace, communications, and financial services 2. Our mission is to improve continually our products and services to meet our customer's needs, allowing us to prosper as a business and to provide a reasonable return to our stockholders, the owners of our business

Source: *The Toyota Way*, Jeffrey K. Liker

Lean Production values are not manufacturing values; they are human and social values that extend to the human assets both inside and outside the organization.

Internally, Toyota has constructed a social order that facilitates people making the most of their capabilities, while giving them the freedom to continuously innovate and make important decisions. Within this social order, employees, suppliers, and vendors are equal and active participants. The quality, responsiveness, and customization made possible by such a system is precisely what enhances its value to customers. It is a system that utilizes all human assets to the best of their capabilities.

Further, we should also note that Toyota and Honda factories in the UK and the US have proved just as productive as those based in Japan, invalidating the myth that the triumph of Lean Production is due to inherently Japanese cultural values.

One of the most dramatic examples of the human and social roots of quality and innovation is the "5-Why Analysis" Toyota uses in problem-solving, set out in Table 3.

TABLE 3
THE GASKET PROBLEM

A method to pursue the deeper, systematic causes of a problem to find correspondingly deeper countermeasures

Analysis	Level of Problem	Countermeasure
What is the problem	There is a puddle of oil on the shop floor	Clean up the oil
Why?	Because the machine is leaking oil	Fix the machine
Why?	Because the gasket has deteriorated	Replace the gasket
Why?	Because we bought gaskets made of inferior materials	Change gasket specification
Why?	Because we got a good deal on those gaskets	Change purchasing policies
Why?	Because the purchasing agent gets evaluated on short-term cost savings	Change the evaluation policy for purchasing agents

Source: *The Toyota Way*, Jeffrey K. Liker

Technical development and innovation accomplished without a computer in sight. This type of analysis can be applied in any scenario. Table 4 illustrates a type of "Why Analysis" of email problems encountered by the Toyota Technical Centre in Michigan.

TABLE 4
PRACTICAL PROBLEMS –
WHY ANALYSIS

Analysis	Level of Problem
What is the problem	Employees are frustrated and complaining about the new email system
Why?	Employees do not know how to use the functions of the system
Why?	The employees did not receive adequate training on the new system, a manual they can use, and didn't give input on their needs for the new functions
Why?	The IT manager had a poor planning process: didn't ask employees about their needs on system functions, didn't plan for training upfront, didn't notify employees using multiple communication channels; didn't review the manual with employees (pilot group)
Why?	The manager didn't get direction and support from his boss, or receive planning process training
Why?	The company as a whole does not have effective internal processes in place, nor is it disciplined in using good process
Why?	Senior management hasn't worked to create a work culture that encourages and reinforces effective internal processes

Source: Toyota

Not only was I greatly impressed with the power of this analysis, I was prompted to recall a personal experience. The Global Head of Institutional Sales in an investment banking institution asked me why employee productivity was so low. If I had used a Why Analysis, my complete answer would have been as indicated in Table 5.

TABLE 5
WHY ANALYSIS –
A PERSONAL EXPERIENCE IN
INVESTMENT BANKING

Analysis	Level of Problem
What is the problem	Employee productivity is low – they are not executing enough value-added business with clients
Why?	We are not providing portfolio management and other high value advisory services to our clients
Why?	Our clients do not consider us as advisors because we don't have the level of client relationships necessary to provide such services
Why?	We don't have the tools and technology that facilitate providing such high value services; in addition many staff have not been on the appropriate training courses
Why?	Management does not understand that there is a direct relationship between knowledge inputs and achieving sustainable competitive advantage and value added results
Why?	Management is not focused on people as the primary determinant of results but on continuous reorganizations and cost cuts to achieve profit targets

Maybe you can put together a similar analysis for yourself.

When Toyoda and Ohno set out on their journey, they estimated that it would take them 20 years to achieve their goals. Their story is a triumph of human ingenuity and social values. We should be bewildered as to why after over 50 years much of the rest of the world is still struggling to catch up. We should be confounded that US manufacturers in particular are making exactly the same mistakes they did 30 years ago and are in a no better position to remedy them. Need I remind you that these are the same mistakes that were made some 300 years ago during the Industrial Revolution?

Then again, we should be reminded of what we said in the previous chapter – organizations are slow learners.

It is not that western manufacturers have not tried implementing Lean Production – the problem is that when they do so, they forget or have been unable to realize that it is at its core a human and social construct. Take Just in Time Inventory or JIT. GM and Ford tried to implement JIT, but without the commitment both to and from employees that makes the system work so well at Toyota. As such, labor disruptions now result in production bottlenecks far more perverse and destructive than before.

Detroit and others have implemented the mechanics of Lean Production– but forgotten its soul. Without shared values, shared objectives, and shared beliefs, and without everyone believing in the importance of contribution and commitment to the entire enterprise, no amount of technology will make an organization more efficient.

For those who are still scared of empowering their employees, I have news for you. In Detroit, where only senior staff have the authority to stop the production line, it is a regular occurrence. At Toyota, where everyone has the authority to halt the production line, it very rarely occurs.

Still mass production is not all bad. In the early 1960s one man got so bored working on Ford's production line in Detroit that he gave it up to form his own company. That man's name was Berry Gordy and the name of the company was Motown – and as a result, we had Supremes, Miracles, and Temptations! Sure enough, they had soul!

Unfortunately, a lack of soul and an obsession with standards is at the heart of many of today's organizations. In the following chapter, we will see how this has blinded them to what they should be doing. However, before we depart this chapter I would like to share with you two highly instructive tales. Although quite different in scale, they are highly instructive of the need to place people before machines.

THE HUMAN ASSET MANIFESTO

In 2005, the Johnson Diversey Company won a competition for best manufacturer in the UK just five years after it almost closed. During that time, they had tripled production and achieved enormous improvements in productivity. How did they do it?

They did it by focusing on their employees as human assets. They encouraged employees to think more about the manufacturing process, without requiring the company to spend large amounts on capital investment. They also involved staff and encouraged them to come up with ideas to improve processes and avoid the problems in the first place.

Pixar is another example of an organization that has not lost the soul of its objectives or subjugated their human assets to technology, and greatly benefited as a result. The company is known for its amazing animated movies such as Toy Story, A Bug's Life, and The Incredibles, is one of the most successful movie studios of our time. Yet, it is at pains to stress that it is not the technology, as this extract from the Guardian Unlimited online demonstrates.

> *Pixar's quasi-religious focus on characters and story leaves its army of computer scientists in a curious position. Their technological expertise is emphatically relegated to second place. Instead, the importance of traditional drawing techniques is impressed upon everybody - even the workers in the accounts and human resources departments - thanks to Pixar University, an in-house animation school presided over by Nelson, at which all employees are allowed to spend several hours a week.*

> *"When we made Toy Story, almost all the reviews only had one line about the fact that it was the first ever computer-animated film," says Ed Catmull, the soft-spoken computer scientist who founded the studio in 1986 with Steve Jobs, who at the time was in exile from Apple and desperate for a major new success. "And the technical people here were immensely proud of that."*

Pixar's performance is truly impressive. It is a beacon to floundering competitors who believe that technological excellence is the way forward. In promoting and developing its internal human assets, Pixar has ensured that it remains in sync and is aligned with its external human assets, the cinema-going public, and has reaped the corresponding rewards.

It is this triumph of traditional human values, despite the presence of advanced technology, that is the reason for Disney paying US$7.4 million for the studio.

It is a pity that more organizations have not followed the example of Johnson Diversey and Pixar. We can only speculate as to what it might cost them.

THE HUMAN ASSET MANIFESTO

CHAPTER

7

DIRTY
ROTTEN
STANDARDS

THE HUMAN ASSET MANIFESTO

DIRTY ROTTEN STANDARDS

It is important that we follow up the study on Lean Production with an examination of the preferred alternatives – standards-based regimes, and why they don't work.

Having standards is not entirely a negative thing. In many instances, it is important that minimum standards are adopted. The can prove particularly useful in the initial adoption of new techniques and technologies.

Standards themselves are thus not the problem, but rather how they arise and how they evolve. If they are developed by those who have to use them, and they are constantly being reappraised in the normal course of work, then they can be excellent. **Alternatively, if standards are imposed from above, rigidly applied, and involve the constant ticking of little boxes, then they will hamper rather than improve quality and productivity.**

ISO 9000 is such a standard.

ISO 9000 was first brought in to establish quality control procedures during World War II. It was sparked literally, by bombs going off in weapons factories, causing much tragedy and mayhem.

Since those early days, ISO 9000 has been implemented by tens of thousands of organizations in over 150 countries globally. The Japanese largely ignored it, and even those that had registered stopped using it.

ISO 9000's core principles rest on rigid monitoring, oversight, enforced adherence and bureaucratic control. Such a system leaves little scope for human discretion and innovation. It is the antithesis of everything we have come to understand about optimizing human assets, and, in particular, what we encountered in the previous chapter on Lean Production.

One of ISO 9000's fiercest critics is John Seddon. After receiving many complaints and much feedback on its ineffectiveness, Seddon codified and summarized his criticisms of the system. The following extracts are taken from his work, The Case Against ISO 9000. It eloquently summarizes the pitfall and inadequacies of standards based operations – or more generally, those that put controls, systems, and technology before people. At the end, he also explains why people-based systems are far superior.

The Case Against ISO 9000, John Seddon

In 1993, I conducted the first major opinion study of ISO 9000. Six hundred and forty seven organizations were represented. The results were, to say the least, disturbing. Less than fifteen percent of the people who responded claimed their organizations had achieved all of the benefits attributed to ISO 9000 in the literature of its promoters. There were problems of interpretation, value for money, understanding of quality, and so on. The general conclusion was that we had significant problems with ISO 9000 and the next obvious step was to visit those who had claimed to achieve benefits, to learn how this minority had taken a more productive approach. So my research team visited them. What we found was shocking. In every case, we found evidence of things put in place to comply with the Standard that sub-optimized performance. And in every case, we found things that could have been done to improve performance that were not done because ISO 9000 had led them to a worse alternative. These organizations were worse off, not better off. These claimants had, to be kind to them, rationalized their experience...

There are ten arguments in the case against ISO 9000:

1. ISO 9000 encourages organizations to act in ways that make things worse for their customers...

My printer announced that he could no longer supply me with quotations over the telephone. He had become registered to ISO 9000 and this meant that paperwork had to go between us. Even using the fax, I found that quotations now took days rather than hours. I changed printers.

The printer argued he was now a better quality company. I (his customer) thought his quality was worse.

2. Quality by inspection is not quality

Inspection increases errors, adds to costs and decreases morale...

3. ISO 9000 starts from the flawed presumption that work is best controlled by specifying and controlling procedures...

The following E-mail was sent to me by a government employee who was frustrated by the damage ISO 9000 had done to his organization:

"Twelve months ago over 'two feet' of procedures arrived on my desk with the instructions that they are to be implemented immediately. Implementing those procedures increased our workload by, I would guess, 10 to 15 per cent. This was the start to ISO 9000.

We found that everything was beautifully detailed. There were sub-tasks for each procedure, with a person responsible for each. But nobody was actually responsible for ensuring the overall activity was achieved. Innovation was totally stifled; the only way to do it was by the procedure. We had implemented some computerized bring-forward systems, more efficient but not in accordance with the procedures, so we had to go back to a manual paper system. Many procedures had been written by people who didn't understand the work. In some cases, the procedure was absurd in its impracticality.

Twelve months later the amendments to the procedures are flying around at a furious rate to try and correct for the fact that people cannot (or, I have to admit in some cases, will not) follow all the procedures. The total cost of this exercise is circa £800,000 (excluding time spent learning procedures).

We got ISO 9000. Was it worth it? In my opinion, no. Talking to several major industrial companies, they will not implement ISO 9000 except where they are customer facing and need it for public relations purposes. Comments like 'just a paper chase' are frequent. I work in a government department, so the natural Civil Service way of working may have made things worse.

Nice to see someone else admitting that the emperor has no clothes. Criticizing 'quality' is like criticizing the Queen Mum."

4. The typical method of implementation is bound to cause sub-optimization of performance

It does not start with performance; it starts with a view of the organization compared to a set of requirements. It is of course assumed that the requirements will, when properly interpreted, have a beneficial impact on performance. But this is not proven; nor, I argue, is it theoretically sound.

5. The Standard relies too much on people's and, in particular, assessors' interpretations of quality

6. The standard promotes, encourages and explicitly demands actions which cause sub-optimization

Dictating how customers should be treated and over-bureaucratic documentation are two ubiquitous examples. The requirements for control and inspection are more pernicious forms of sub-optimization. The consequential de-motivation is, in large part, a natural response to being controlled. And ISO 9000 starts, a priori, from an attitude of control.

7. When people are subjected to external controls, they

will be inclined to pay attention only to those things that are affected by the controls

Following the war, Deming's ideas were ignored by US industry. A growing market tolerated the waste of inefficient production, because organizations could pass their costs onto the customer. Indeed, Deming used to joke "let's make toast the American way: I'll burn - you scrape!" Approaching quality through inspection results in scraping toast. Managing through understanding variation is the foundation for learning and improvement, which leads to my eighth contention in the case against ISO 9000:

8. ISO 9000 has discouraged managers from learning about the theory of variation

Deming eschewed inspection as a means to quality. The Japanese were the first to understand him. They set out to manage their organizations as systems, using measures to establish capability and improving performance through learning from variation. They out-achieved his expectations in five years. In contrast, we have had BS 5750/ISO 9000 since 1979. It is no surprise that ISO 9000 cannot compare with the success of Deming's methods in Japan, for the two are based on entirely different philosophies.

9. ISO 9000 has failed to foster good customer-supplier relations:

When I was doing research for my book I met a man in Birmingham who told me the following story:

"We supply British and Japanese motor manufacturers. The British want to know that we are registered to ISO 9000 before we can become a supplier. Then they only pay attention to us when things go wrong. The Japanese don't care about ISO 9000 registration, but on the day of becoming a supplier, they are in our processes, working on what we do and how it affects what they do."

10. As an intervention, ISO 9000 has not encouraged managers to think differently

ISO 9000 has taught managers little or nothing about the most important subject on the management curriculum - quality - and it has probably made many of them averse to the subject. Some managers, and certainly the majority of assessors, believe an organization has 'done quality' through having registered to ISO 9000, when nothing could be further from the truth.

ISO 9000 represents further reinforcement of the idea that work is divided into management and worker roles. I believe it was the fundamental mistake of twentieth-century management, for ISO 9000 continues the tradition that 'managers decide' and 'workers do'. This tradition has led to means of control - through adherence to procedures, budgets, targets, and standards – all of which cause sub-optimization. It is a way of thinking about management that began in mass-production systems and, throughout most of this century, has been the starting point for defining the purpose of management.

I call this 'command and control' thinking. Changing our thinking about management is the key to performance improvement. ISO 9000 does no more than encourage managers to follow a recipe that, because of its antecedents, reinforces the wrong thinking. The better way starts with understanding the organization as a system. It implies a completely different management philosophy.

The Japanese companies that adopted this philosophy have achieved remarkable results. When we woke up to the 'Japanese phenomenon' (in the 1970s) and sent managers to look at what they were doing, those managers copied the things they could see, for example quality circles and suggestion schemes. They did not see the thinking behind what was happening. As a result, the things they copied failed - they were incompatible with the surrounding system. You cannot 'do quality' in a 'command and control' system.

John Seddon has very kindly consented to the use of this material. John runs Vanguard, www.lean-service.com/home.asp, an organization that specializes in applying lean production techniques to service organizations. In closing, I will add a few brief comments.

The fact that ISO 9000 has been linked to things such as TQM is proof positive that things are not headed in the right direction. The Big Three US automakers Ford, GM, and Chrysler imposed their own version of ISO 9000, QS-9000, on their suppliers – we can clearly see where that has led.

Quality is not a destination, it is a journey. That journey is best undertaken by those human assets engaged in the work, not some external body that tells them whether they have passed or failed.

Rigid standards are totally contrary to the principle of optimizing human assets and organizations that rely on them should definitely reconsider.

THE HUMAN ASSET MANIFESTO

CHAPTER

8

"YOU CANNOT HIRE A HAND, THE WHOLE PERSON COMES WITH IT." — DRUCKER

THE HUMAN ASSET MANIFESTO

CHAPTER

8

"YOU CANNOT HIRE A HAND, THE WHOLE PERSON COMES WITH IT." – DRUCKER

Our journey so far has left us in no doubt that organizations must value their human assets above all else. We have also looked at some of the conditions that might facilitate the development of knowledge. In this chapter, we take it down to a personal level. We will examine how and why people can be motivated and engaged to give of their best. We will also briefly occupy ourselves with why managers might be motivated to act irrationally, and counter to their organization's best interests.

In my considered opinion, the best place to start is with the work of Abraham Maslow.

In the general scheme of things, Maslow was a highly rational man – especially when you consider the subject matter he was studying. **Darwin, Freud and others expressed their opinions on human motivation and behavior by observing animals or humans with a psychological imbalance.** Maslow thought that this approach was rather peculiar to say the least and decided that he would adopt a more elementary approach.

Maslow examined and based his studies on normal healthy individuals.

Maslow's seminal work, *Motivation and Personality,* was first published in 1954 and it is as least as relevant today as it was then. In many aspects, it is even more relevant. What is particularly striking about Maslow's work is that it resonates with one's intuition – it makes plain sense. The best way to describe Maslow's approach is with a quote from

THE HUMAN ASSET MANIFESTO

Mort Myerson, former head of EDS. **Myerson said, "If we do not deal with the whole employee or the life of the employee, then we are dealing only with part of the power or creativity of the person."**

Maslow's most famous legacy and one that is firmly grounded within his concept of the whole person is his Hierarchy of Needs. They are as follows:

1. Physiological – Food, Drink, Sex
2. Security and Safety – Home, Stability, Security, Job Security, Protection
3. Social – Belonging and Love
4. Respect and Self Esteem – Achievement Adequacy, Competence, Reputation, Prestige
5. Self Actualization – The fulfillment of individual potential

Maslow maintained that people needed to have each of these needs gratified starting with the first, the most basic, and so on until they reached a state of self-actualization. Self-actualization is desirable because it is the state of being where employees are able to maximize their contribution.

In the ordinary course of things, the sequence may not be strictly observed; different people will have different needs at different times. However, we may still assume that self-actualization can only be attained if all the other needs are gratified.

The working environment has a direct impact on items 2, 4, and 5 and has implications for the first two aspects of item 1. Most people reading this document will not be concerned as to whether or not their wages cover the cost of their food and shelter. Nevertheless, we must recognize that this is a very real issue for large numbers of people on this planet and without question it influences their performance at work. **This explicitly supports Maslow's proposition that you cannot divorce the human being from his environment or personal circumstance.**

Nevertheless, those organizations that outsource their operations to parts of the world where health, strength and daily bread cannot be taken for granted definitely need to take these issues into account.

We will also exclude the final part of item 1 and all of item 3, and thereby exclude the very thorny issue of office romances. Of course, if anyone would like to advise how this may have helped or hindered their performance I would be interested! However, it is back to items 2 and 4.

Item 2, the need for security and safety, means that job insecurity is not good. The constant reorganization, outsourcing, rightsizing, downsizing, and BPR, so common in today's workplace, are highly counterproductive. Employees will only be concerned with the longer-term goals of an organization if they believe the organization is concerned with their long-term goals. Quite apart from that, our earlier lessons in history inform us that a sense of stability is essential for promoting creativity.

Item 4, the need for respect and self-esteem, is one that goes to the very heart of the relationship between an organization and its employees. That relationship is very much dependent on the degree of trust, responsibility, and autonomy with which employees are allowed to operate. Maslow, along with a contemporary Douglas McGregor suggested that the creation of such an environment was entirely dependent on management's assumptions about people. In order to determine the nature of these assumptions they formulated the following questions:

1. Do you believe that people are trustworthy?
2. Do you believe that people seek responsibility and account ability?
3. Do you believe that people seek meaning in their work?
4. Do you believe that people naturally want to learn?
5. Do you believe that people don't resist change but they resist being changed?
6. Do you believe that people prefer work to being idle?

Maslow and McGregor reasoned that the answers to these questions influence every aspect of management's approach to their employees – and by definition employees' response to management and the organization. An unequivocal yes to all of them would imply that the organization is practicing what they describe as Enlightened Economics. A definition of it can be found in the book *Maslow on Management*; **Enlightened Economics is the assumption that everyone prefers to be a prime mover rather than a passive helper, a tool, a cork tossed about on the waves.**

Alas, they also reasoned that **most executives do not take the time out to analyze assumptions about people and are therefore not even in a position to answer these questions, let alone shape the nature of their organization.** Consequently, management secrecy, lack of transparency, censorship of information, poor communications, and a perceived lack of employee freedom, all negatively affect corporate performance.

It obviously follows that these taken together effectively reduce the value of human assets.

If an organization is creating the environment where its employees are attaining self-actualization, then the benefits are considerable. Maslow describes self-actualization as that state of being where, in the normal course of things, all the other basic needs are satisfied. It facilitates rationality, objectivity, and spontaneity, as well as an ability to take fresh perspectives. It imbues confidence and facilitates the formation of positive relationships. It accepts rather than merely criticizes the failure of others.

The following are relevant extracts from Maslow's book, *Motivation and Personality*, describe self-actualization, who self-actualized express themselves, and the how and why of why such people are inherently more creative.

> *Even if all these (basic) needs are satisfied, we may still often (if not always) expect a new discontent and restlessness will soon develop, unless the individual is doing what he or she is individually, is fitted for. Musicians must make music, artists must*

paint, poets must write if they are to be ultimately at peace with themselves. What humans can be they must be. They must be true to their own nature. This need we call self-actualization...

It refers to people's desire for self-fulfillment, namely, the tendency for them to become self-actualized in what they are potentially. This tendency might be phrased as the desire to become more and more what one idiosyncratically is, to become everything that one is capable of becoming...

All my subjects were relatively more spontaneous and expressive. They were able to be more natural and less controlled and inhibited in their behavior; it seemed to be able to flow out more easily and freely with less blocking and self-criticism. This ability to express ideas and impulses without strangulation and without fear of ridicule from others turned out to be a very essential aspect of self-actualizing creativeness. Rogers has used the excellent phrase "fully functioning person" to describe this aspect of health...

Another observation was that creativeness in self-actualized people was in many respects like the creativeness of all happy and secure children. It was spontaneous, effortless, innocent, easy, a kind of freedom from stereotypes and clichés...

In any case, this all sounds as if we are dealing with a fundamental characteristic, inherent in human nature, a potentiality given to all or most human beings at birth, which most often is lost or buried or inhibited as the person gets enculturated.

We should not be surprised that people are at their most motivated, most vibrant, and most creative when they are self-actualized.

One of the most important aspects of this state of self-actualization is that since by definition the other basic needs are fulfilled, it allows a person to become motivated for higher purposes and to move beyond selfish requirements. We achieve far more when we are unencumbered by selfish motives, or when we are simply doing something that we love. It is for this reason that people find voluntary work so fulfilling.

The greater an organization's ability to create an environment conducive to self-actualization, the more productive and creative the output of their employees. Self-actualization improves the value of human assets.

In the course of his work, Maslow studied the Blackfoot Tribes who he describes as the most synergistic of human societies. His findings, summarized below, perfectly illustrate the principles of Enlightened Economics – an organization based on responsibility and respect, where people act in harmony to achieve their common goals. The key attributes of the Blackfoot included:

1. Emphasis on generosity – giving highly prized

2. Weaknesses not highlighted and ostracized, but accepted as part of human nature – removes self-doubt and self-consciousness more prevalent in competitive societies

3. Strong emphasis on personal responsibility – within a supportive environment

4. Consistency between the needs and goals of the tribe, and the needs and consistency of the individual

5. Different leaders for different functions – the right man for the job

An enlightened approach to management is critical to the development of self-actualized employees and optimizing productivity. The lessons provided by the Blackfoot indicate that there must be room for experimentation, and that genuine mistakes should not result in sanctions. This is of course entirely consistent with the development of knowledge, and reflects the circumstances we encountered in the earlier chapter on that subject.

While on a consultancy assignment, Drucker once asked the Board of the company that had hired him to raise their hands if they thought that there was too much deadwood within their organization. They all raised their hands. He then asked the Board to raise their hands if they believed that all these people were deadwood when they were hired. This time none of the Board members raised their hands.

Management is responsible for the environment in which employees operate and the extent to which they are able to express their creativity. As such, **rather than asking why employees are not more creative, the true question is what management should do to make them more creative.** Studies by Levin on behalf of the Alfred Sloan Foundation, and in conjunction with Columbia University, Carnegie Mellon University, and the World Bank provide powerful insights into the strategies that need to be adopted. They also provide unequivocal support for the work of Maslow and McGregor.

The Relationship Between Human Resource Practices and Economic Indicators

1. Companies that share profits and gains with employees have significantly better financial performance than those that don't.
2. Companies that share information broadly and that have broad programs of employee involvement (the researchers define involvement as areas of intellectual participation) perform significantly better than companies that are run autocratically.
3. Flexible work design (flexible hours, rotation, and job enlargement) is significantly related to financial success.
4. Training and development have a positive effect on business financial performance.
5. Two-thirds of the bottom line impact was due to the combined effect of group economic participation, intellectual participation, flexible job design, and training and development.

The findings are extraordinary. The last point in particular is entirely consistent with much of what we have been saying already. Two-thirds of an organization's financial performance is dependent on its employee strategies. If this were true then one would expect that most managers would spend a corresponding amount of time on employee strategies. I think you would agree with me that this is definitely not the case, and that the actual percentage of time spent on employee strategies is not even close to that number. In reality, employee strategies are devolved, or it would be fair to say they are outsourced, to HR.

Levin's studies conclusively demonstrate that in the best organizations, the management of human resources and strategic development are intrinsically linked, and that **change is best effected when personal goals are aligned with corporate goals.** As we have seen repeatedly, creativity is a state of mind, a state of attitude, and a state of being – it is a human and social phenomenon.

Rensis Likert, a psychologist who researched the impact of management styles on performance, did pioneering work in determining the characteristics of organizations that make the greatest use of human capacity. He concluded that such organizations consist of highly effective work groups linked together in overlapping patterns by other similarly effective groups. He further describes the type of management styles exhibited by organizations, including the one that best facilitates a supportive group system:

1. The Exploitative – authoritative system – instructive – subordinate – motivation only by rewards

2. The Benevolent – authoritative system – condescending – little communication and little teamwork – motivation mainly by rewards – staff feel no responsibility

3. The Consultative system – management has some but not complete trust in subordinates – some communication – moderate teamwork – motivation is by rewards and some other elements

4. Participative – group system – good teamwork – communication – confidence – rewards economic as well as other types – performance based – employees feel responsible for the organization's goals

Likert asserted that in order to achieve the Participative model, the following must be put into practice:

1. The motivation to work must be fostered by a total human approach to management

2. Employees must be seen as people with their own needs, desires and values and hence their self-worth must be maintained or enhanced

3. An organization of tightly-knit and highly effective work groups must be built up which are committed to achieving the objectives of the organization

4. Supportive relationships must be built up in each group – characterized not by actual support but by mutual respect

5. The background of the groups which form the nuclei of the Participative group system are characterized by the following features:

    • Members are skilled in leadership and membership roles for easy interaction

    • The group has existed long enough to have developed a well-established and relaxed working relationship

    • The members of the group are loyal to it and to each other since they have a high degree of mutual trust

    • The values and goals of the group are an expression of the values and needs of its members

    • The members perform a "linking-pin" function and try to keep the goals of the different groups to which they belong in harmony with each other

Levin then described the main motivational tools required by management for developing the right type of organization:

1. Approval, Praise, Recognition

2. Trust, Respect, High Expectations

3. Loyalty Given, That It May Be Received

4. Job Enrichment

5. Good Communications

6. Cash Incentives

The work of Maslow, McGregor, Levin, and Likert not only reinforce each other, they bear a remarkable resemblance to the principles adopted by Toyota. Remember how that company started out on its journey into Lean Production. For ease of reference, the steps taken are again included below:

1. A quarter of the workforce were fired
2. The remainder of the workforce were guaranteed lifetime employment
3. There was to be flexibility in work assignments
4. Steep pay progression by seniority (in terms of experience) rather than function, with bonuses tied to profitability
5. Employees active in initiating improvements rather than simply reporting problems
6. Employee granted full access to Toyota facilities (housing, recreation etc.)

We can also compare these to some of the principles utilized by Lockheed Martin's legendary 'Skunkworks', the source of some of the greatest advances in the history of military aviation. Amongst many others, the Skunkworks is credited with the development of the Blackbird SR 71 reconnaissance plane, the first to fly at speeds in excess of Mach 3, and the F 117, the world's first stealth fighter. The items summarized below were taken from a list provided by ASTECH Engineering, whose source is Kelly Johnson of the Skunk Works:

1. The Skunk Works manager must be delegated practically complete control of his program in all aspects. They should report to a division president or higher.
2. The contractor must be delegated and must assume more than normal responsibility to get good vendor bids for subcontracts on the project.
3. Push more basic inspection responsibility back to subcontractors and vendors. Don't duplicate so much inspection.
4. The contractor must be delegated the authority to test their final product in flight. They can and must test it in the initial stages.

5. The specifications applying to the hardware and software must be agreed to in advance of contracting. A specification section stating clearly which important military specifica-tion items will not knowingly be complied with and reasons is highly recommended.

6. There must be mutual trust between the military project organization and the contractor with very close cooperation and liaison on a day-to-day basis. This cuts down misunderstanding and correspondence to an absolute minimum.

7. Because only a few people will be used in engineering and most other areas, ways must be provided to reward good performance by pay not based on the number of personnel supervised.

It is reassuring to note that much of what we have explored so far is entirely consistent with the idea that organizations are a human and social construct and human assets are its greatest store of value. The principles are tried, they are true, and they are tested. What is more, they have been around for far longer than we think. The following is an extract from a paper entitled, *A Short History of Empowerment*, by Bob Webb.

1800s Railroad Construction

In 1864, the Central Pacific Railroad Company was pushing construction of the railroad from Sacramento California into the Sierra Mountains. Someone at the Central Pacific noticed the efficient work habits of Chinese. It was obvious that Chinese ingenuity could do the impossible, so the company decided to experiment with a Chinese construction crew. Company managers also did something unheard of by American managers; they adapted the worker responsibility style of the Chinese, giving full control of the project to front-line work teams. As a result, track laying increased until it reached a record ten miles in one day, a record that still stands today. The worker responsibility concept was so successful; most railroad construction companies adapted it. (This is not true for the operation of the railroads where the desire for power and control came roaring back. With high profit margins, control and abuse was affordable.)

There is the evidence. For more than 140 years now, the means by which employees could be organized in teams and empowered in a way that optimized productivity was already available. It is amazing that organizations have ignored this very useful piece of history – but then we have said that they are slow learners.

Bob Webb does provide some perspective on the psychology of managers, and why their actions defy rational expectations. This is also exactly where economic theories of profit maximization break down.

In the eastern industrial complex, the worker responsibility concept was foreign. It was socially unacceptable for an engineer to ask a front line worker for advice. (This attitude is still true today) The contrast between east and west leadership methods became visible during the construction of the Panama Canal, one of the manmade wonders of the world.

1904 - The Panama Canal
John Wallace was the first chief engineer of the Panama Canal. He developed his engineering and management techniques in the eastern railroads and was a member of many engineering societies. His leadership style was by control. In Panama, his eastern leadership methods worked against him. His attitude, "workers needs are of little concern to the company or the project. Workers are to be treated as machines."

In the eastern states there were ten men waiting to be hired for every job. Under abusive conditions, the work force could be maintained and workers could survive. Not in Panama! Because of abusive living and working conditions, workers died by the thousands and there was no one to take their place. In Panama, it became obvious Mr. Wallace knew nothing about leadership associated with motivation and efficiency. After one year, he threw in the towel. He blamed his failure on lack of money, not leadership.

John F. Stevens became the second chief engineer. His formal education was limited to grade school and he did not belong to impressive engineering societies. He came from western rail-

road construction camps where work teams were now the norm. In the western construction camps, worker turnover was lost productive time and finding replacements was extremely costly. Mr. Stevens learned how to motivate and maintain worker loyalty by treating workers as valuable asset.

The type of people who came to Panama were the same type that ventured west of the Mississippi River, highly independent, self-confident, stubborn, strong-willed, hard working. Stevens knew how to organize work environments that energized and motivated this type of worker. The Panama Canal was completed as scheduled and under budget.

If responsibility leadership is so efficient, why are not more companies using it? Answer: Most leaders do not want to give up control. Control is job security and/or a feeling of importance. The typical CEO will let a company go bankrupt before trusting others with responsibility he thinks should be his.

Bob was motivated to write the article and tell his story because of the management control philosophy and abusive working conditions he encountered in various parts of the world. He credits his experiences at the Panama Canal with transforming his life – he worked under John F Stevens and became one of his disciples. His contribution brings to the fore a fundamental issue that we are yet to look at in this book – the irrational behavior of managers. It provides at least a partial explanation for the failure of organizations to implement much of what we know to be correct, as well as the tendency to resort to fads.

Managers will defy good business logic because of their need to exercise control, and their insecurity, which arises from a need to be seen to be in charge and to be the one coming up with all the right ideas. This explains why managers make decisions that to everyone else are plainly stupid and sub-optimal.

It was for such reasons that Henry Ford refused to recognize and appoint managers within his business and almost destroyed the company he had created – he wanted to retain control.

Then there are the organizations where, because there is a desperate need to satisfy the markets with the right numbers, essential programs are cut prior to year-end, wasting money and progress. Once the year-end is passed and the markets are happy with the 'numbers', the programs are restarted. Organizations waste millions every year simply to keep analysts, investors, and the stock markets happy with numbers that are in some respects meaningless.

Ignorance may be bliss but there is no value in it.

The irrational behavior of managers invalidates every economic theory of the firm that ever existed – profit maximization is for the birds. Managers do not consistently make rational decisions in the interest of an organization – their decisions are often based on their own self-interest, and they include the need to satisfy their own insecurity.

It is for this very same reason that managers prefer to go with the flow and join the ranks of the faddists. Adopting the fad may not be the most rational decision, but if everyone else is doing so and you have already paid the consultants for telling you that is the way to go, then from a career perspective, it is a relatively safe decision.

In many instances, downsizing, rightsizing, and other such reorganizations are bonus and reward driven – not objective rationalization in the best interest of the business. When that is the case, and when after some time the organization eventually realizes that this was perhaps not the right decision, the manager who executed the reorganization has either been promoted or moved on to some other organization – with another 'notch' on the CV and more money in the pocket. It is then left to others to pick up the pieces. This particular point is brutally reinforced by Dr. Barbara Ehrenreich, the multi-award winning American journalist, author, and champion of the people. In her latest book, *Bait and Switch: The (Futile) Pursuit of the American Dream* Dr. Ehrenreich notes:

> *So, by eliminating other people's jobs, top management can raise its own income. The trend was clear in the midnineties: CEOs who laid off large numbers of employees were paid better*

than those who didn't. In the last few years, outsourcing has reaped the greatest rewards for CEOs: compared to other firms, compensation has increased five times faster at the fifty US firms that do the most outsourcing of service jobs.

Put in blunt biological terms, the corporation has become a site for internal predations, where one person can advance by eliminating another's job.

I often wonder precisely what managers and executives could be thinking when they engage in such folly given that the remaining employees cannot possibly be inspired to give of their best.

Such behavior is irrational.

The extreme form of management irrationality is greed and many executives have disgraced the annals of our time. The management of organizations like WorldCom, Tyco, Parmalat, and Enron recklessly gambled away their organization's value and ultimately its existence, in pursuit of personal wealth.

Former Enron CFO Andrew Fastow testified in court that his creative accounting antics, the very same antics that led to the demise of that company, were driven by reward and prestige.

We should also note that the share price of companies that lay off their workers often increases. This tends to be a reflex action to cost cuts, as in most instances stockbrokers and analysts have no way of assessing the value of people being made redundant.

In such instances, irrational management behavior is accompanied by irrational stock market behavior.

Understanding and influencing the irrational behavior of managers is a yet unexplored area of anthropology and we will not attempt to find all the answers in these pages. However, we should be grateful for the work of Andrea Gregory and Lisa Smale, founding partners of The Good Boss Company, www.goodboss.co.uk, which describes itself as:

...a campaigning consultancy group formed in 2005 as a centre of excellence in research into bosses' behavior. It offers leading-edge learning resources and materials, training and coaching, to improve bosses' capability in the UK.

The Good Boss Report 05-06 provides us with the following summary findings:

1. Nearly one in four of Britain's bosses are bad or dreadful, according to UK employees, and only 4% would rate their bosses 10 out of 10

2. Nearly half (48%) of employees with a bad boss think they are bad because they are in the wrong job

3. More than half (58%) have actually looked for another job because of their bad bosses.

4. Employees believe the main causes of their bad bosses' behavior are:

   • Poor training and development (44%)

   • Poor management by their own bosses (44%)

   • Overwork (34%), and

   • Under-staffing (28%)

What these unquestionably demonstrate is that **for best results, managers must be developed and their personal and professional objectives aligned with those of employees, the organization, and other stakeholders.**

This particular lesson is vitally essential and is one that should not be forgotten. It is a firm basis with which to unite the varying human and social elements that constitute an organization.

Managers must be allowed to live and breathe within the same human and social context as the people who work for them. The motivation of managers is as important as the motivation of employees.

The problem with many of today's organizations is that management rewards are based on the bottom line for a particular period, not overall long-term performance.

So as not to unduly depress you, I would like to end this chapter on a brighter note – showing just what enlightened management can achieve, even in the face of the kind of hostile competition that exists in the airline industry. This 1995 extract about Southwest Airlines, the low budget US carrier, highlights the success of one organization whose management has learned the lessons of history.

Southwest Airlines is an excellent example of social invention that helps people discover their true capabilities. The social environment combines humor with responsibility. Employees work in teams without outside supervision. At job interviews, the prospective employee must show a sense of humor along with other self-development attitudes. Only those that match the ridged personnel profile are hired. The result is a highly motivated, efficiency work environment that attracts customers. The facts speak for themselves. (As of 1995)

1. *Founded in 1971 as a low-cost regional air carrier*

2. *An early leader of worker responsibility*

3. *The company limits emphasis on the formal organizational structure. Decision-making is by worker/management committees. Leadership meetings are taped and shared with employees.*

4. *The company has been profitable every year since 1972, including 1991, when it was the only major airline in the black.*

5. *Has 176 planes and one of the most modern in the industry.*

6. *Flies more passengers per employee, 2,318 versus 848 for the industry*

7. *Has the fewest number of employees per aircraft, 79 versus 131 for the industry*

8. *Has the fewest number of customer complaints in the industry.*

9. *90% of its employees are union members.*

10. *Plane turn around time at the gate is 15 to 20 minutes compared to one hour for other major carriers.*

11. *Each plane flies 10 flights, per day, twice the industry average.*

12. *The company has never had a major accident.*

13. *Many of the company's employees are now millionaires.*

Southwest Airlines is growing and other airlines have noticed. They are trying to implement worker responsibility programs of their own. The choice is, move decision-making responsibility to the front-line or go out of business. The days of command-and-control leadership are over.

A more recent article in the online edition of the Chicago Tribune written in May 2005, attests to the continued success of Southwest Airlines.

Specializing in short hauls and leisure business, Southwest is considered the most efficient and financially conservative company in the airline industry. However, investors must first determine whether they feel comfortable about investing in this volatile industry at all.

Southwest features streamlined procedures at gates, uses a single type of aircraft to save on maintenance, finances its growth internally and has a loyal customer base. Thirty-two straight years of profitability are impressive.

We have historical, practical, and living emblems that individually and collectively inform us that business objectives are best achieved when we create social harmony and synergy in the workplace; when we cater to the entirety of human need.

Drucker's refrain is worth repeating, "You cannot hire a hand, the whole person comes with it."

Therefore, what we have to do now is revisit the person, the individual, and the aspects of their life and who they are that organizations will need to come to terms with.

THE HUMAN ASSET MANIFESTO

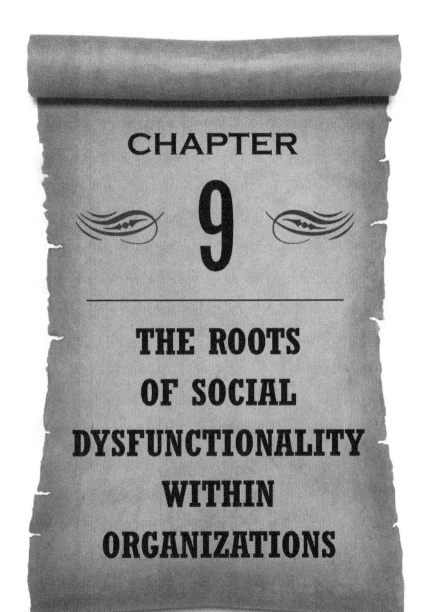

CHAPTER

9

THE ROOTS OF SOCIAL DYSFUNCTIONALITY WITHIN ORGANIZATIONS

THE HUMAN ASSET MANIFESTO

THE ROOTS OF SOCIAL DYSFUNCTIONALITY WITHIN ORGANIZATIONS

We have developed a comprehensive overview of the human and social context within which organizational development, productivity, innovation and competitiveness may be enhanced. We have taken on board the idea that human assets are the ultimate repositories of knowledge and value. We have also developed an appreciation of the conditions under which they are best motivated and engaged.

In this chapter, we will develop further insights into why organizations are socially dysfunctional by analyzing how they have evolved relative to the societies around them. We will see how the asymmetry in the development of these two has created tensions that are akin to a collision of giant tectonic plates, and further examine what this implies in regards to the development of human assets.

The Industrial Revolution will once again act as our point of departure.

Since their emergence some 300 years ago, corporations have retained the same basic structure of owners/investors, managers and employees. In stark contrast, it is impossible to overstate the social changes that have taken place since that time. Kings, popes, archbishops, and the landed gentry no longer control or dictate the pattern of life the way they used to.

At the outset of the Industrial Revolution, work was in many ways considered a duty and moral obligation. In certain parts of Europe, the idea of the Protestant work ethic conveniently coincided with the labor requirements of the new technologies. Later, as national identities became increasingly prominent, work became a matter of national pride.

In western societies, social change took a giant leap forward during the Industrial Revolution. By the time Henry Ford had hit his stride with the Model-T some 200 years later, the idea that ordinary people could have and enjoy the use of items only previously available to the privileged few was becoming the accepted norm. This very concept accelerated the transition from mass production to mass consumption – a switch from a production-focused society to a people-focused society.

These changes in affluence and standards of living have done much to change people's social outlook. We have modern-day examples of this change. The gradual reforms now taking place in China, and earlier democratic developments in South Korea and Taiwan, are prime examples of how material changes in living standards shape attitudes to political and social freedoms.

From a historical perspective and one that is even more relevant to our case, the rise in mass production coincided with the progress of democracy in both Europe and North America. The trend continues today – **the more people believe they have something to live for the more they value their lives, and the more they want be self-actualized.** When a society progresses towards mass consumption and consumerism, it also progresses towards a more liberal and open political system – individual freedom of expression becomes more important.

In the past twenty-five years, we have seen it happen in South Korea and we are witnessing it in China. Yet, these are in no way unique, the development of democracy in the US and the UK have followed a similar pattern.

Thus, in western countries, the journey from subsistence to mass consumption was accompanied by the transformation from social acceptance and accommodation to social liberation. Nothing reflects this more than the attitude to war.

At the Battle of Gettysburg in 1863, when ordered by General Lee to muster his division to repel a possible Union counterattack, General Picket replied, "General Lee, I have no division" – some 13,000 men had been wiped out in a suicidal charge against the Union lines.

Today such losses are deemed unacceptable. More US soldiers died in their civil war, almost 600,000, than all subsequent wars combined – that includes World War I, World War II, Korea, and Vietnam.

In Europe, men celebrated the outbreak of World War I. They threw their hats in the air and rushed off to enlist. The names Somme, Marne, and Gallipoli remind us they were treated as expendables. In the first day alone, the British Army suffered over 60,000 casualties at the Battle of the Somme. Their generals kept sending them 'over the top'.

By World War II, many accepted war as something that had to be endured, not celebrated as a test of loyalty to one's country. Churchill, the man who led his country to victory against all odds, lost his seat in the elections immediately following the war. The idea that one should be more to their country than mere cannon fodder was taking hold.

People were beginning to believe that their lives were more valuable than any king, priest, aristocrat, or government could suggest or imply. Ultimately, they recognized the economic disconnect between their own miserable existence and the prosperity of their rulers.

By the time Vietnam came around, the draft was unpopular and few now want to go to Iraq. Even when they do, there is absolutely no way that the kinds of casualties seen in previous wars could ever be deemed acceptable.

To appreciate further the social transformation of the past several decades, it is important to consider the changes in society in terms of specific goods and services. I once watched a documentary on 1940's UK life. It featured a middle-class family. They had no central heating, no television, no telephone, no car, no washing machine, and no dish-washer. In modern western societies, a family can have all of those, plus a VCR, stereo, and DVD player, and still be considered poor!

Social and political liberation has changed our individual expectations and perception of work.

Thirty years ago when people talked about professionals, they referred to a very narrow band of people – mainly lawyers,

doctors, teachers, and accountants. If you had a degree, you were certain to get a good job with great prospects for promotion. One's profession was a badge of honor and a personal differentiator. It was the era of keeping up with the Joneses and a growing and noticeable minority could distance themselves from the crowd by way of their chosen profession.

Today the word profession can be extended to almost any vocation, including gardeners – partly because people have made a very worthy occupation of providing these services to other people.

In contrast, the numbers of people with degrees or equivalent qualifications have proliferated. MBAs are being turned away and a PhD does not guarantee you a job. The US alone currently has 50 million students in tertiary education. An article in *The Sunday Times* article by Zoe Brennan asks, "Is it worth getting a degree?" The question is based on research that shows that the monetary value of a degree is falling away sharply. The research also shows that almost 40% of the 18-19-year-old population are participating in higher education.

For these reasons, **climbing the corporate ladder is no longer a feasible proposition – there are too many qualified people competing for too few positions at the top.**

In western industrialized societies, white-collar workers and professionals are the new masses, the new proletariat. Thirty years ago, it was the factory worker. What that means is that for most people, with a few notable exceptions, their work and their profession is no longer a significant differentiator. It should therefore be no surprise that the focus of people's lives and identification have shifted from what they do for a living, to what they live to do – consume.

The era of mass consumption has given way to the era of the mass consumer.

Mercedes and BMWs are now more affordable, with Mercedes in particular deliberately targeting the mass market. Whatever the make, small cars in general now exhibit luxury features and levels of reliability that would have been unthinkable only a few years ago – the clock in a Mercedes is no longer an extra – that was not the case ten years ago. Many luxury goods producers have gone downmarket – as celebrity trends and the need to follow and look like celebrities has taken hold.

It is no longer a question of keeping up with the Joneses – Angelina Jolie, Jennifer Lopez, David Beckham, and Brad Pitt have taken their place. This of course explains why, according to the official statistics, in 2004 cosmetic surgery grew by 65% in the UK and 44% in the US, where the industry is said to be worth more than US$12 billion. I should point out that all these estimates are believed to be grossly understated.

Now more than ever, individual taste, fashion, how we look, and what we consume, determines and defines who and what we are.

We want quantity, but with quality and loads of choice. Now more than ever, there is no distinction between employees and customers in terms of their individuality, uniqueness, desires, self-esteem, need for attention, and last but not least, a compulsion for self-fulfillment.

The young woman with breast implants, a pierced navel, Louis Vuitton bag, and Jimmy Choo shoes, whose Starbucks order is a white chocolate mocha latte with whipped cream, and who holidays in Ibiza, works for you.

The McGregor Consulting Group defines the consumer society in the following terms (for the purposes of this book, I have omitted many of the wider social and environmental issues they mentioned but they are all extremely valid):

1. People build identities largely out of things and as such the key issues for enjoying life is the consumption of goods and services

2. To consume is the surest perceived route to personal happiness and social status

3. Activities that previously belonged in the domestic sector are being integrated into the market sector – this is necessary because households have been transformed from workers to consumers

4. Everybody is a walking advertisement

5. Social space is reorganized around leisure and consumption as central social pursuits and as bases for social relationships

6. The consumer is placed at the centre of the good society as an individual who freely and autonomously chooses, pursue choices through rational means and creates a dynamic society through market-exercised power over economic institutions (consumer is king/queen - sovereign)

7. Central to the evolution of a consumer culture is the commercialization of leisure and the mechanization of the home (free up time and energy to shop and provide more things to buy)

8. Peoples consumer choices (taste and style) are seen to be indicators of who they are as a person and of their moves within the games of class, prestige, status, hierarchy, and fashionability

9. If a consumer society sees consumers as sovereign, then the people who waste, squander, and destroy are sitting on the throne!

10. Some say that, in a consumer society, consumption has replaced work as people's central life interest (ironically we have to work in order to spend)

In every sense, the consumption of goods and services, and in their lifestyles, people are consumers first and employees second.

If we go back to Maslow's Hierarchy of Needs, we should not be surprised that higher-level needs for self-fulfillment and self-actualization are now a dominant feature of industrialized societies. Consequently, people increasingly gain more pleasure and identity from their lifestyle and consumption, and less pleasure and identity from their profession or work.

This is a different experience from that of prior generations.

As McGregor asserts, people do have to work in order to spend. However, there can be no pretensions that they check their human and social needs and vanities in at the door when they get there.

The outcome of this clash between individualism and corporatism is as follows:

1. Corporate objectives and individual ambitions are diverging at an increasing rate

2. Corporate focus and emphasis on financial objectives is increasingly meaningless to staff

3. Automation and productivity is viewed by employees as a ruse to replace people with machines – resulting in a sub-optimal approach to strategic development

4. One's workplace or job is increasingly seen as somewhere one goes or something one does to pay the mortgage, rather than a valid vocation

5. It is difficult to motivate staff; training and development spending is less than optimal

6. Corporate communications become difficult as people don't really pay attention to what is being said – money wasted on offsites

7. There is a disconnect between management and staff; employees do not trust their managers to act in their best interest and are generally cynical of corporate objectives

8. Few people get excited about work – my wife once told me that my problems at work were because relative to those around me, I was too enthusiastic about what I was doing. Sadly, it turned out she was right.

9. People work until such time that they can find another job some where else – counterproductive given that settled organizations facilitate greater creativity

10. Long working hours act as a disincentive, even in highly-paid investment banking – also, studies show that employees lie under pressure and there is a cost to this

11. More and more people are seeking a greater work-life balance – not just flexible hours, but less hours overall – more part-time work favored

12. Managers adopt a let's-take-the-newest-fad approach to management; reorganizations, downsizing, change management,

MBOs, Knowledge Management, etc. etc. etc – increases all round frustration and further unsettles the work environment

13. Managers outsource their single most important task, the development of people as human assets, to HR – it is totally detrimental to strategic development

14. Staff tend not to go beyond the call of duty – stifling innovation and creativity

15. Teamwork, the essential ingredient of innovation and knowledge development, is difficult to promote and sustain

It is within the context of the above, and the fact that investors, and to some extent managers have retained their absolute primacy over employees and other stakeholders, that organizations have become socially dysfunctional.

Organizations and their human assets have different or mis-aligned objectives.

Organizations only capture a relatively small proportion of their employee capabilities – totally consistent with what we have seen in the research by Towers Perrin. Employees operate at levels well below their optimum and productivity is impaired. As the work-life dynamic continues to diverge from corporate objectives, corporations will become even more socially dysfunctional and productivity will continue to become even more impaired.

The big question is; what particular issues will organizations have to focus their attention on, in order to reduce this social dysfunctional-ity, and improve their performance? We should not be surprised that they relate to age, gender, race, religion, and all the base characteris-tics that define each of us as individuals.

We have seen that it took several generations before societies began to take full advantage of the innovations brought about by the Indus-trial Revolution. This was later repeated when electricity became available. We have seen two generations of Lean Production and still Detroit and other automakers are yet to grasp its lessons. Similarly, it has taken a whole generation for the IT revolution to usher in improvements in productivity. It is obvious that there are strong generational barriers to learning that need to be overcome.

One of the major challenges facing organizations will thus be the extent to which they can integrate and optimize the capabilities of the next generation of workers.

The other side of the above problem will be the challenge of retaining and optimizing mature workers, the over 40's, whose talents organizations have habitually proved themselves so adept at wasting or disregarding their talent.

Perhaps the greatest challenge will be for the traditionally male dominated business world to recognize both the intrinsic value of women as well as the purchasing power they have become. Not far behind that will be the ability with which organizations manage the mixture of race, religion, and ethnicity that is an ever-increasing feature of the modern workplace.

The consumer society, its accompanying social revolution and the dynamics of diversity will if not suitably managed, accelerate the divergence between individual and corporate objectives. This will further exacerbate the need for organizations to create and develop the right environment for nurturing human assets.

Organizations will rise and fall based on their ability to manage these challenges, and make the necessary adjustments in their business – it will not be easy. In the next few chapters, we will look at the specific nature of each, as well as the opportunities and pitfalls each of them presents.

We will however start with customers, external human assets.

THE HUMAN ASSET MANIFESTO

CHAPTER

10

MODERN LESSONS IN THE HUMAN AND SOCIAL EVOLUTION OF CUSTOMERS

THE HUMAN ASSET MANIFESTO

⟶≫⟨ 10 ⟩≪⟵

MODERN LESSONS IN THE HUMAN AND SOCIAL EVOLUTION OF CUSTOMERS

Earlier, we saw how Ford and GM have been suffering because of their inability to adapt their production methods to changes in the external environment – namely the price of oil, and the need for their customers to switch to fuel-efficient vehicles. It would be remiss of us not to set aside some time to focus specifically on the inability of other industries and organizations to understand the human and social changes that drive customer demand, and the consequences of their failure to adopt new and more relevant business models.

It should come as no surprise that some of the industries most susceptible to human and social changes are those most concerned with lifestyle, leisure, and entertainment.

For a long time, the music industry rested on its laurels, much like Edison did with his phonograph. It failed to take account of the changes that were being brought about by the Internet. For some reason, it had not occurred to them that with the onset of the digital age, many of their consumers would express a preference for digital distribution over the Internet, rather than having to go out and buy CDs.

So intent was the record industry in maintaining its grip on how people accessed their music that they were unable to counter the inevitable – someone else initiating and providing the service that they should have made a priority. Napster was to emerge the biggest and best known of these services, and by offering free digital download of songs, it threatened the very viability of the record companies.

Eventually, after a series of lawsuits, titans of the record industry, such as AOL Time Warner and EMI, were forced to sign an agreement with Napster, an upstart of the digital age, to legally distribute their music online. That was only the beginning. Apple with its iPod and iTunes music store is now the leading distributor of digital music and Microsoft and a host of others have joined the party. These new players are slowly but surely eating away at the sales of traditional CDs.

The new digital format has brought about other changes. Whereas before one had to purchase a whole album even if you were interested in only one or two of the songs, digital downloads allow consumers to cherry-pick their favorite songs and make their very own compilations.

The digitization of the distribution of music has resulted in a significant reduction in industry costs by cutting out the middlemen. It has disrupted the industry value chain and changed its economics. **The failure of the music industry to recognize the human and social needs of their customers has resulted in a massive loss of profits and erosion of their leadership.**

Had the industry embraced the new technologies and made a better attempt at understanding what it meant for consumers in terms of pricing and accessibility, things might have been different. Rather than being scared of the quality and ease of digital downloads, they should have invested in digital rights technology and intellectual property protection, which would have allowed them to become leaders rather than followers in the digital revolution.

Instead, **the music industry has been relegated to fighting legal battles with 12-year-olds for illegally copying its music.**

It is the failure to recognize the human and social needs, not the mere introduction of technology, which has undermined the titans of the music industry – and now their worst nightmares are about to come true.

Early in 2006, a group called the Arctic Monkeys reached the top of the UK charts without the aid of a record label. Their marketing strategy was based around giving away samples of their songs through the Internet, and performing at promotional gigs. By the time their album was released, they had already developed a large following. In their first week, the band's album had outsold the combined total of all the other albums in the top 20.

What is even more interesting is the fact that the Arctic Monkeys play a brand of music that is socially conscious and relevant – not exactly what records companies look for these days when they are signing artists.

Maybe this spells the end of some of those annoying boy and girl bands the record companies love to concoct and throw at us.

We just might get lucky!

Another industry more focused on navel gazing and its own profit, at the expense of the human and social needs of its customers, is the film industry. For decades, people have gravitated towards cinemas and movie theatres to watch the latest film release, and the industry cleverly segmented its market by timing those releases – cinemas, DVDs, Cable and Satellite TV, and terrestrial TV.

Originally, the studios had managed to segment the global film market by releasing films at different times, but video piracy caught up with them. For a time, the industry managed to continue its practice of segmentation with the global DVD market by way of regional encryption and different release dates, both of which allowed the industry to take advantage of price differentials. This particular ploy required the cooperation of hardware manufacturers. However, it was rendered useless by the fact that vendors and others could, with a simple procedure, alter DVD players, thereby allowing them to play films from any region.

There was an even bigger problem with regional encryption – most PCs would play DVDs irrespective of the format.

Thus, the industry relented somewhat, but sadly, it did not learn.

Not all movie fans want to be herded into cinemas, many of which are smelly and uncomfortable, despite recent upgrades. The proliferation of wide-screen and plasma TVs, plus hi-fi equipment with Dolby Digital 5.1 Surround Sound, has meant that consumers can to some extent now reproduce the cinema at home.

The pace of life has also changed dramatically. Rather than standing in line to get cinema tickets, or trying desperately to find a parking space, it is far easier to either rent or purchase a DVD on the way home, and enjoy it in the comfort of your living room, as and when you want to – not just when the cinema is open.

TiVo and other digital recording devices allow consumers to effectively create their own TV stations, and watch programs as and when they want to, in accordance with their own lifestyles. They want to do the same with films.

The convenience of viewing a film at home is desirable for many other reasons. Viewing at home means that urgent bathroom breaks don't result in missing part of the film, and eating is not limited to hot dogs, popcorn, and giant sodas. The prices of the average DVD is such that it now costs the same as a trip to the cinema for two – except that when you buy the DVD you can watch it over and over again, with all the cinematic extras, at no extra cost.

It is therefore no surprise that consumers don't necessarily want to wait for a new film to be released on DVD several weeks or months later, before watching it in the comfort of their home.

Despite all of the above: home equipment levels; convenience; pricing; and lifestyle, the film industry still insists on the time-honored sequence of launching films first in the cinema, followed by DVD, satellite and terrestrial TV.

They will now have to have a rethink.

On January 31, 2006, Steven Soderbergh's new film, "Bubble," was released simultaneously in cinemas, on DVD and on pay-per-view TV. The film industry is outraged, claiming that it will destroy their business and most of the big cinema chains are refusing to show the film.

In an article, entitled *'Bubble' hits theatres, TV, DVD on same day*, Gary Gentile, writing for the Associated Press, describes the full impact and future implications of this film:

> *The country's largest theatre chains are snubbing the film because they object to it being sold on DVD and shown on cable TV the same day it debuts in a handful of theatres owned by the same company that produced the movie.*
>
> *"Bubble" isn't the first film to be released this way. But the combination of a high-profile director and the backing of maverick billionaires Todd Wagner and Mark Cuban have studios and theatre owners paying close attention this time.*
>
> *"It's the biggest threat to the viability of the cinema industry today," John Fithian, president of the National Association of Theatre Owners, said of the so-called "day and date" release strategy.*
>
> *The move comes as new technology is giving consumers faster access to music, movies, TV shows and other content via multiple devices, including laptop computers, portable video screens, even cellphones. Theatre owners have faced challenges from technology before, most notably television and the VCR. But this is the first time major studios have contemplated releasing films in competing formats at the same time.*

Rather than complaining, the big film studios might be well advised to come up with ideas that better reflect consumers' tastes and lifestyles, rather than improbably trying to turn back the tide.

Thus far, we would not be surprised that those industries – cars, music, and film – which more than most have come to reflect consumer lifestyles and trends, are the ones most affected by changes in the human and social dynamics within society. However, there are others.

Take, for example, the US airline industry. There is scarcely a major US carrier that has not sought bankruptcy protection at some time in recent years. The following extract from *Money Week* sums up their predicament:

Since the deregulation of the airline industry in the 1970s, more than 20 airlines have filed for Chapter 11, but the situation is now so bad that around half of American air passengers are now flying with airlines that are technically bankrupt. Last week's Chapter 11 declarations from Delta, the third-biggest US carrier, and Northwestern, the number four, mean that four of America's six main carriers are under Chapter 11 protection. United (second-biggest) has been in bankruptcy since 2002 and US Airways (sixth) will shortly come out of bankruptcy protection by merging with America West.

Yet, in earlier chapters, we met Southwest, an airline that is both successful and profitable. Jet Blue (about which we shall talk more later) is an airline with a similar success story.

Why is there this dramatic difference in success and failure within the same industry?

Well, to begin with, Jet Blue and Southwest have managed their human assets a lot better. The older carriers are still fighting with their unions over pay and categories of workers. They should have followed Toyota's example. In principle, they have been unable to convince enough or sufficient numbers of their employees that they have a vision of the future in which all stakeholders have a vested and reasonable interest.

Secondly, the old airlines had structured themselves with costs, rather than customers, in mind. Their hub and spokes configuration meant that for the average passenger it was not always possible to travel directly between two cities – their voyage usually involved a stopover at a major hub, which acted as a connecting point for all a carrier's flights in a particular region.

Once the industry was deregulated, the new carriers like Jet Blue and Southwest came in, and guess what? They started a revolution by picking up passengers from one airport, and taking them directly to their final destination. Now who would have thought such a thing possible?

They also did something else; something that showed they truly accepted the wider human and social evolution of their times. They recognized that air travel was no longer a privileged activity. What mattered most was the need for ordinary people to travel either for leisure or in the course of their business. Air travel had become for many a practical necessity, in a way that the motor car had become a practical necessity several decades earlier.

As such, **the new airlines threw out the bad food and pretentious but discourteous stewardesses, and the era of cut-price and no-frills flying was born. Airplanes became nothing more than airborne buses.**

European airlines such as Easy Jet and Ryanair have followed a similar path to Jet Blue and Southwest and have had similar success.

Many blame the demise of the legacy carriers on the deregulation of the airline industry. Yet, **airline deregulation in the US occurred as far back as the late 1970s – almost 30 years ago. The failure of the legacy carriers cannot be blamed on deregulation. The legacy carriers have failed because of their inability to adapt to the evolution of the human and social needs of their customers.**

In this regard, the similarities with the US auto industry and the inability to learn and adapt are striking. In both cases, without genuine change, they will continue to be genuine failures.

The failure to adapt to the human and social changes of customers is present in many industries and arises in many ways.

Many years ago, if you were a frequent traveler and spent a lot of time in hotels, you would, at the end of your stay, be presented with a large telephone bill. Ripping off customers by way of excessive telephone charges was a favored pastime of hotels – that is, until mobile phones came along. Since then, the only reason to touch the phone in your hotel room is to either order room service or book your wake-up call.

THE HUMAN ASSET MANIFESTO

Peeved at losing this valuable source of revenue, and rather than accepting change with good grace, some hotels have been engaged in blocking mobile phone signals, in the hope that you will once again resort to using their phones.

It is just another example of the paucity of thinking, and the inadequacy of the human and social dimension, present in some businesses. Rather than trying to push back the tide of human progress, hotel executives would be much better off providing good interactive Internet broadband facilities (some already do, but alas not enough of them).

The soft drinks industry also has human and social problems that it has systematically failed to address. Much of the industry's success has come about through targeting teenagers, a strategy which has included the positioning of vending machines in schools. With obesity on the rise, and the sugar content in soft drinks seen as a major contributor to that problem, manufacturers are now being targeted by parents, consumer groups, and legislators. In an article, entitled the *Liquid Candy, How Soft Drinks Are Harming America's Health*, The Centre For Science in The Public Interest notes the following:

> *Soft drinks provide large amounts of sugars (mostly high-fructose corn syrup) to many individuals' diets. Soda pop provides the average 12- to 19-year-old boy with about 15 teaspoons of refined sugars a day and the average girl with about 10 teaspoons a day. Those amounts roughly equal the government's recommended limits for teens' sugar consumption from all foods.*

It is highly unlikely that the industry's problems will disappear overnight – look how the tobacco industry has been dogged by lawsuits and problems over the past two decades. One cannot help but think that they would be better off recognizing the social issue and leading the change, rather than having to fight a battle which will relentlessly continue to set public opinion against them.

In Europe, where the industry is worth some $US45 billion, soft drink producers are responding by voluntarily ceasing the advertising of their products to children, and are set to place less emphasis on selling their products in schools. They did not take this action lightly –

they are trying to forestall the imposition of far more draconian measures by the EU.

Overall, this is an industry that has chosen to be dragged kicking and screaming into recognizing the need for human and social change, rather than leading it.

We have come to understand that organizations are slow learners and, as such, the above examples should not come as a total surprise to us. We should however also recognize that some organizations have been nimble in recognizing and adapting to change, and some are leaders.

McDonald's has responded to the backlash of improper diets and obesity, and in particular, Morgan Spurlock's groundbreaking documentary, Supersize Me, by improving the nutritional balance of its meals.

Given its bewildering array of coffees and other beverages, Starbucks is the ultimate lifestyle consumer brand – it says we have something for every individual need. Its fair trade initiatives are also going down well with its customers.

Some retailers, like Wal-Mart in the US (although it may become undone by other human asset problems) and Tesco in the UK, are doing their best to bring branded goods to the masses. **The erosion of social barriers in the distribution of goods and services is one of the features of mass consumerism.**

An article published in The McKinsey Quarterly of January 10, 2005, entitled New Strategies for Consumer Goods, written by Peter D. Haden, Olivier Sibony, and Kevin D. Sneader, sums up the predicament of the purveyors of branded consumer goods.

> *The surge of discount retailing and the spread of private-label products are putting ever-greater pressure on the price of branded goods. Companies have extracted much of the financial benefit from restructuring their portfolios and concentrating on core brands. And though managers doggedly pursue further improvements in productivity, most of the obvious gains have already been achieved.*

Some branded product businesses are looking to leverage the human and social changes of their customers.

In association with Bono, lead singer of the Irish rock group U2, American Express, Gap, Converse, and Giorgio Armani have launched the Red Label line of branded goods. The intention is to attract customers with a social conscience by giving up a small percentage of sales to help AIDS victims in Africa. CORDIS, an EU body, (it stands for Community Research & Development Information Service) provides us with further insights into this developing trend, and just how important it has become.

> *About a quarter of Europeans, suggest that a business's social image is a "very important" factor in their choice of product or service supplier. Research in the UK showed that 17% of the population had boycotted a company for ethical reasons; 19% had positively used a company with a good ethical reputation; and a further 28% had done both.*

We should also take careful note of the cooperation between business and the entertainment industry, something that has now gone well beyond the use of popular music in adverts. It's a far cry from the 1950s when the establishment was concerned that music would corrupt our morals. Those were the days when Frank Sinatra described rock 'n roll as, "The most brutal, ugly, desperate, vicious form of expression it has been my misfortune to hear."

I guess things have moved on a little bit since then.

Just in case you are somehow persuaded that this is all about Corporate Social Responsibility, then allow me to disturb your tranquility and introduce you to the wider implications of human and social evolution on consumer trends.

The biggest shock to established names and brands in the west will come with the emergence of Indian and Chinese brands. These countries between them represent some 40% of the world's population. It is quite likely that as more of their populations move into the middle classes, they will take with them more of their traditional identities and national and regional sentiments. This will eventually propel emerging consumer brands into the premier league of global players, and that will have a profound impact on the existing global players.

The idea of the global village, and with it the global consumer, purchasing major western brands will be swamped by an overwhelming tide of human and social evolution in the world's most populous countries. If we look at the way in which Japanese brands have emerged in the past 20 years, then it might give us some idea as to what will happen in the future.

The reality is that in the not too distant future we will be moving to a more Asia-centric world. That suggests Asian culture, goods, services, and tastes will pose a significant challenge to the established order.

It will be some time before Brand China and Brand India emerge. In the interim, organizations will have other worries. In the next chapter, we will see how the changes in some of the industries mentioned above are being turbocharged by the younger generation.

However, before we move on to that younger generation, I would like to leave you with one final thought.

Now, I am definitely not one to advise anybody on just how close they need to get to their customers, but it is fair to say that the following observations are entirely consistent with Maslow's ideas, and specifically the importance of first satisfying the most basic of human needs. The following extract is thus self-explanatory. It is taken from an article in the *Washington Post* of January 21, 2006. The article was written by Mike Musgrove, a Washington Post Staff Writer, and its title is, *Technology's Seamier Side, Fates of Pornography and Internet Businesses Are Often Intertwined*. It reads as follows:

> *Online pornography, a $2.5 billion business and growing rapidly, pioneered such now-commonplace practices as streaming video, trading files and making online purchases. By comparison, sales of music downloads totaled $1.1 billion last year.*

THE HUMAN ASSET MANIFESTO

It's an old joke that every new technology is driven by porn: A big attraction for digital cameras, some hold, was the ability to take bedroom photos without having to take film to the snickering teenagers at the corner photo shop. And a force behind the rapid spread of VCR and, later, DVD sales was the ability to watch blue movies without being seen at a theatre.

More recently, when Apple announced an iPod with video playback capabilities, there was a stampede among adult entertainment companies to announce that they were making video programming available in the player's format. Mobile porn is already such a booming business that it has its own trade show, the Mobile Adult Content Congress, which will take place in Miami next week. Scheduled speakers include representatives from Virgin Mobile UK and Vodafone, as well as porn actor Ron Jeremy

"Of course pornography has played a key role in the Web," said Paul Saffo, an analyst with Silicon Valley think tank Institute for the Future. Explicit images have been key in the advent of many technologies, he said. "Porn is to new media formats what acne is to teenagers," he said. "It's just part of the process of growing up."

I will allow you to draw your own conclusions.

However, before you move on to the next section please read the Statement of Affirmation on the next page. It represents a summary of the principles established in this section. I hope that you will also be moved to act on the suggestion that follows.

The Human Asset Manifesto
Statement of Affirmation 2

- *I believe that people are the source of innovation*

- *I believe that people are the source of competitive advantage*

- *I believe that people are the source of productivity*

- *I believe that organizations should place people before technology*

- *I believe that customers and suppliers are vitally important human assets*

- *I believe that the more people are engaged and motivated the better their performance*

You can evidence your support for this statement and by doing so help to send a strong message by going to www.thamanifesto.com

THE HUMAN ASSET MANIFESTO

LIBERTY,
EQUALITY,
FRATERNITY

THE HUMAN ASSET MANIFESTO

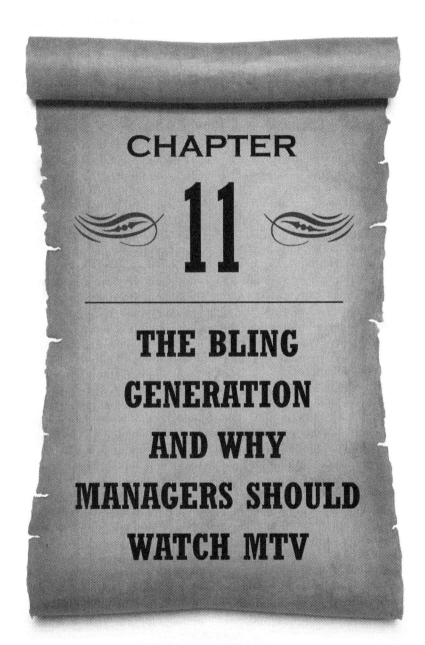

CHAPTER

11

THE BLING
GENERATION
AND WHY
MANAGERS SHOULD
WATCH MTV

THE HUMAN ASSET MANIFESTO

11

THE BLING GENERATION AND WHY MANAGERS SHOULD WATCH MTV

James Poniewozik at www.time.com describes MTV's hit show *Pimp My Ride*, as "My Wheels, My Self." An article in Motor Trend, www.motortrend.com, has at its subtitle, "How do you know MTV's *Pimp My Ride*, has hit the mainstream? Because corporate monolith General Motors has joined the tattoo party."

The article then goes on to describe how GM is using West Coast Customs, the same people featured on the show, to 'pimp' one of its premier offerings, a Chevrolet 2006 HHR sport wagon.

Sorry, I may have gone a little too fast for you. Most people reading this have no idea what I am talking about. The trouble is they should. **The customization of cars is becoming one of the biggest things in the car industry, and nothing has done more to boost this than MTV's Pimp My Ride.**

The program is the No. 1 MTV show in the US, Japan, Germany, the UK, and many other countries.

What do they do on that program?

Each week, they select one very lucky person with some decrepit old car and West Coast Customs transforms that car into an amazing new set of wheels, complete with an extensive range of personalized additions. It is a celebration of the individuality and consumerism, much of it conspicuous, which has become part of youth culture.

For a long time Detroit completely ignored the idea of 'blinging out' cars. That is until they realized that it was a multi-billion dollar industry with a huge built-in element of celebrity endorsement. Hence, the above reference to GM joining the tattoo party.

This is just one of the programs dedicated to the "bling generation". Bling generally refers to the current propensity to conspicuously exhibit one's jewelry. However, for me, it sums up the tendency of the young to customize everything or otherwise acquire the latest and greatest in cool gadgets – blinging out.

Funny! I typed the word bling into my computer and it came up as an incorrect spelling. That is another thing about the bling generation; they are changing our vocabulary faster than ever before.

The bling generation is into the cult of celebrity like no other generation before it. It has a different focus. A BBC News item reported that **kids nowadays know the cost of an iPod, but not the cost of a pint of milk.**

The bling generation is taking the era of the mass consumer and all its attendant worship of materiality to new excesses. Lois Curren, Executive Vice President, MTV says, "MTV research shows that viewers go out of their way to customize different areas of their lives, from downloading music to shopping, and we noticed they started doing this with their cars."

Have a look at some of the things that are in *Pimp My Ride's* customized cars and you will get an idea of what I am talking about:

• Recording studio
• Refrigerator
• 40-inch flat-screen TV
• Clothes dryer
• Smoothie machine
• Working sink with makeup vanity
• Voice-activated jukebox
• Fireplace in trunk
• Bowling-ball polisher
• Gaming centre with three Xbox consoles
• Underbody TV monitor (for viewing while working on car)

- Karaoke machine
- Ping-pong table
- Espresso machine
- D.J. station with twin turntables and mixer
- Lava lamp
- Digital drum set
- Chandelier
- Goldfish tank in back seat (with fish named Ike and Tina)

This is in addition to the regular gear such as hi-fi systems, ghetto-blaster speakers in the trunk, chrome rims, and amazing paint jobs. The website, www.thetruthaboutcars.com sums up the commercial realities:

> *Lest we forget, automakers from Chrysler (300C, Charger) to Mercedes (CLS500) to GM (HHR) are selling more and more cars with built-in bling. The wilder the design, the greater the degree of pre-existing product "individuality," the lesser the need for ANY modification, urban or otherwise.*

Another MTV program I would like to introduce you to is *Cribs*. In Cribs, the viewer is invited into the homes of celebrities to see just how they live; they see their bathrooms, inside their refrigerators, their gadgets, inside their wardrobes, their computers, and their games.

Armed with the information provided by *Pimp My Ride* and *Cribs*, and their own individual styles and love for creative anarchy, the bling generation is driving whole industries. If you watch the music videos, programs, and ads on MTV and the other music channels, the list is truly impressive.

1. Cars
2. Games and Game Consoles (Microsoft launched the Xbox 360 on MTV)
3. Computers
4. Fashion and clothing (they have usurped Vogue and Cosmopolitan)
5. Mobile phones – Internet, Music, Radios, Ringtones, Cameras, TV Programs, Gaming

6. MP3 & MP4 Players, iPods
7. Movies ('best kiss' is one of the categories at the MTV Movie Awards)
8. Jewelry – the very essence of bling
9. Food and drink – One rap song entitled "Pass The Courvoisier" by Busta Rhymes and P Diddy boosted sales of that product by over 30%
10. Cosmetics
11. Home accessories
12. Music (of course)

You have to watch MTV if you want to know the zeitgeist! Why? It is the zeitgeist. It is where the trendsetting young engage with the culture of celebrity and mass consumerism. The rest of us simply sit back and await the aftershocks.

Sometimes, that aftershock hits our wallets!

More importantly, if you are running a business, you might not want to be in a position where you are following up after the aftershocks. By then, it might be too late.

Even when you create products for one purpose, the bling generation will recreate it or alter its dynamics and effectively its economics.

Mobile phone companies did not think much of text messaging. Then one year when school exam results came out in the UK, they had the largest number of text messages ever in one day. Suddenly, mobile phone companies realized that they had a real winner on their hands. Pfizer created Viagra thinking it would mostly be used by older men. Wrong! Young men have been using it in droves. Apparently, it negates the undesirable effects of a night of binge boozing. I suppose you could say that it too enhances performance and increases productivity.

Crazy Frog has brought about an amazing change in the world of music and mobile phones. The Frog ringtone (another word my word processor fails to recognize) reached No. 1 in the charts during 2005.

The sound of the Crazy Frog character is that of a Swedish youngster imitating his friend's moped. Another Swede created the caricature. The combination was bought by Jamster, a German, company who delivered it as a ringtone. Later it was made into a No. 1 chart hit, much to the annoyance of Coldplay – it outsold the group's single by a margin of four to one.

What does that mean for CDs, mobile phones, record companies, and mobile phone companies? It means that they have had to completely rethink and redefine their approach to consumers. Even Apple with its marvelous invention the iPod is running scared.

The fate of major industries is being determined and influenced by youngsters and adolescents. Without watching where the zeitgeist is at, you just might be surprised at what is going to happen next to your business.

Microsoft's new Xbox 360 is said to be capable of making a 1,000 billion calculations per second. That is one trillion calculations per second or one teraflop. Sony's PlayStation 3 is rumored to be even more powerful. Ten years ago only supercomputers were capable of doing that, not to mention the fact that **NASA only used a fraction of that power to put a man on the moon.**

The Xbox and its Sony competitor are not merely targeting their energies at the bling generation. They know that eventually the rest of us will not be able to resist the total package. The Xbox 360 console does all of the following:

1. Internet connectivity
2. Music
3. Videos
4. View TV
5. Store digital media
6. Play Games

The bling generation is setting the trend but eventually we will all be looking at the integrated home entertainment center and deciding that is the way to go.

That is an important and highly relevant feature of the symbiotic relationship between the blingers and those who seek to innovate and ensure that their products will remain relevant for the foreseeable future (in these days that could mean just a couple of years). Therefore, while the global gaming industry is estimated at some US$35 billion, these games boxes are looking beyond to Internet commerce, the music industry, hi-fi and audiovisual equipment manufacturers, etc. etc. etc.

So maybe you are not ready to buy one of the new games consoles or maybe you don't want the car with the chandeliers. No problem. That's not the point.

The bling generation is having the same impact on culture, consumerism, and computers that Paris haute couture had on the world of fashion in its heyday. The difference is in the sheer size and scope of their influence. Haute couture was only for the select few – but the splash it made sent waves throughout the world of fashion. The bling generation is making a very large splash and it too is sending out waves. Except these are no ordinary waves, these are tsunami-like waves that will engulf us all one way or the other.

Car manufacturers will be offering increased levels of personalization. You will get more gadgets on your mobile phone than you ever dreamed of. You might buy that new style of dress or shirt – lifted straight from one of those red carpet events that have become a staple of the music channels. Moreover, you will continue to struggle with the new language spoken by your kids – a language with which you are unfamiliar.

The next time you replace a piece of video or audio equipment in your living room, and you think of the movies, programs, and podcasts available on the Internet, you just might think about an Xbox or a PlayStation 3. Traditional hi-fi and audio-visual equipment manufacturers had better be watching MTV because those items might be their biggest competition in the future.

For the skeptics out there – I have news for you. The following extract from a February 2006 Reuters article entitled, *IBM launches business computers based on game chip*, just might interest you.

*IBM, <IBM.N> the world's largest maker of business comput-
ers, on Wednesday introduced new computing systems that it
said extend the processing power of video-game microchips to
corporate data centers.*

*The systems will open up new capabilities for businesses in the
medical and military sectors, for example, as companies seek
ways to use increasingly demanding and graphics-intensive
computer applications, IBM said.*

*Driving the systems is the so-called Cell processor, developed
by IBM, Toshiba Corp. <6502.T> and Sony Corp. <6758.T>
for gaming consoles including Sony's PlayStation 3, scheduled
for release later this year. IBM is now installing the Cell in
its "BladeCenter" computer servers, a compact way of building
large data centers that run corporate networks.*

**The upshot of all this is that powerful microprocessors are going
into the game consoles used by the bling generation, before they
arrive in corporate data centers and military applications.**

Whether we like it or not, the bling generation eventually gets to
us all. Smart organizations are and will be using their trendsetting
capabilities to get to the rest of us. From a consumer perspective, the
blingers are determining our collective futures.

The bling generation not only significantly influences your choice of
products; some blingers are already working for you – the rest are on
the way. If you manage to exploit their unique capabilities you may
triumph. If you don't, things could become quite difficult. As such, it
is worth taking a closer look at the bling generation from a social and
work perspective.

What I call the bling generation is actually defined as two separate
groups by Dr. Rick and Kathy Hicks in their book, *Boomers, Xers
and Other Strangers, Understanding The Generational Differences
That Divide Us*. Xers by definition were born after the Baby Boomers, between 1965 and 1976, although for the purposes of our discussion we are really focusing on those born towards the latter end of

that period. The more significant group for our discussion is the Net (Internet) Generation, those born between 1977 and 1997.

First, a brief word on the Xers.

Xers are frustrated by the fact that a preponderance of Boomers in the work force has left them out of the best jobs – despite their qualifications. They are experiencing the impact of the white-collar proletariat. Since hierarchical progression is limited, they seek self-actualization in other ways. Therefore, they are keen to prove their capabilities and their competence by having greater responsibility, greater autonomy, and greater meaning in their jobs.

I hope that this is all sounding familiar.

At the same time, the research by the Hicks shows that unlike the Boomers before them, the Xers believe in having a much better work-life balance. Xers will not sacrifice all for work. Additionally, because of the relatively limited possibilities for hierarchical promotion as well as the rebellious nature of the Boomers who went before them (they say if you can remember the 60s then you weren't there), Xers do not have lot of respect for authority. In fact, to them competence is far more important than authority.

Of course, they were heavily influenced by MTV.

The Net Generation is even more influenced by MTV ("I Want My MTV" is their refrain) than the Xers. They care even less about authority and formality than the Xers.

The Net Gen is also the first generation to grow up with computers at home. It is amazing because I don't recall using my first calculator until I went to university in 1977, and I was reading Physics and Chemistry. **By the time Net Gens became adolescents, they were locking themselves into their rooms and surfing the Internet for endless hours.**

Consequently, their technology skills are far superior to those of previous generations. This should not be too difficult to understand. Competing with them is like trying to beat Tiger Woods at golf – he started playing when he was three years old. No amount of practice is going to help you.

According to the Hicks, Net Gens are born into technology and they assimilate it rather well. They are the world's first true multi-taskers – they can have their TV, games, Internet, email and instant messaging all going at the same time. This allows them to learn things in parallel rather than in traditional linear strands. Thus, they digest information rather readily, but it also means that they are easily bored.

I received positive proof of this from a very kind lady. Kind because she has the patience to proofread my manuscripts and although we have never met, she is based in Edinburgh while I am based in London, we have during the course of our professional engagement, managed to construct a very human relationship. On proofing the manuscripts for this book, she was moved to send me the following note on her daughter who happens to be a Net Gen.

Dear Jonathan…

I thought you might be interested in this snippet, which backs up your Net Gen reflections. My daughter is most definitely of the Net Generation (born 1989), and she can be found every evening in her room with the Internet accessed, iTunes playing, DVD on, e mail up, mobile phone on and instant messages appearing at regular frequent intervals. She is also taking her Highers this year (she has designs on reading Medicine at Oxford). At the start of this academic year, she told me she intended to take six Highers – English, Maths, Chemistry, Physics, Biology, and French. As she also plays for the school hockey team (for which she trains 3 times a week), is in choir, orchestra, jazz band, madrigal group and wind ensemble, and had just landed a lead role in the school musical, I gently suggested that she may want to take only 5 Highers, and pick up the sixth one next year. She thanked me for my suggestion, but told me she would keep to her plan, as she didn't want to be bored! Would she do well in a large organization? I suspect not.

I am sure you all join me in wishing Clare the best possible future. Maybe it is a good thing she is looking to do medicine.

The confidence that they have in the use of new technologies means that they come to work with attitude-plus – knowing that they are much better at manipulating and optimizing the use of new technologies than their elders are.

You may recall how many times we have said that from the Industrial Revolution to the IT Revolution, it takes at least one generation and sometimes several before the productivity potential of new technologies can be optimized. Net Gens provide today's organizations with the possibility to place this optimization on automatic pilot.

The Net Gens are the key to the acceleration of productivity in the digital age. Allow me to illustrate.

Another friend of mine shared with me the experience of lending her mobile phone to her nine-year-old daughter. Within minutes, her daughter was using functions on the phone that her mother never knew existed. This is not a case of the Generation Gap. In fact, this particular condition is known as the **Generation Lap – we have been surpassed and left behind in the slipstream by those whom we believed were our young Paduan Learners.**

It's a bit like Luke Skywalker being better and more powerful than Yoda. Amazing that is!

It is no small wonder that product innovators focus on this group – they set the trends for change. Never before have marketers had such direct access to such a young, experimental, and trendsetting market.

The gaming industry provides a prime example of what happens when a new generation takes over. Traditionally, Hollywood moviemakers refused to cooperate fully with game developers. Twenty years ago, if you bought a Star Wars game expecting to see real likenesses of Luke, Princess Leia, and Hans Solo, you were in for a big disappointment. It has taken a new generation of managers to link the gaming industry directly with movie titles and characters – they remembered the days of their own disappointments. This change is redefining the nature of both industries and providing a healthy lifeline to struggling studios.

It took a generation to learn lessons that should have been obvious if the movie studios had focused on the human and social aspects of their decisions.

In January 2006, Mike Potter of Ithaca College won the first annual CellFlix Festival for cellular short films –shot entirely on a cellular phone. His winning entry, a 30 second shoot, as required by the rules, was entitled Cheat – an amusing story about his grandparents. In the video, grandpa describes how on Sundays he would read out the newspaper headlines to grandma. Grandma is then asked whether the headline is true or not – if she is right, she gets a kiss. Then grandpa makes his great admission – sometimes he cheats!

The Ithaca college website describes the competition as follows:

The CellFlix Festival is an annual competition dedicated to the development of creative content for mobile delivery. It's all about imagination, fantasy, and story – created through and presented on the small screen.

If you're a filmmaker, a storyteller and a dreamer of big dreams – and you could use an extra US$5,000 to help make those dreams come true – pick up your cellphone/smartphone and get busy.

You must shoot the story on your cellphone/smartphone, but you can edit it any way you choose.

Produce the best 30-seconds of small-screen cinema, and walk away with the US$5,000 grand prize – and the satisfaction of knowing that you're helping to make the world a smaller and more beautiful place.

The wider implication is this; organizations can either kill or harness the proficiency and dexterity of the Net Gens and that will be wholly dependent on their ability to socially integrate the different generations. The Net Gens care even less about authority and bureaucracy than the Xers. They respect competence more than position and authority. Their confidence makes them highly individualistic and competitive and they need space to explore their creativity. Tradition means nothing to them. Developing them into team players will take some doing.

A recent study done on behalf of Vodafone in the UK entitled Working Nation confirms much of the above, but also highlights possible sources of conflicts between the age groups. Here are some of the relevant extracts:

The Confidence Of Youth - *The report finds that younger age groups have a very strong self-image and place a high value on their contribution to the workplace. For many employers, this perception is inflated. Almost seven in ten (67%) young people (16-25 year olds) see themselves as particularly innovative. However, only 38% of employers say that they feel young people are more innovative than older people.*

Diversity: A Prerequisite For Success? – *The ageing profile of the working population means that some employers increasingly recognize the need to work hard to integrate and inspire different age groups within their workforces. 69% of employers believe that companies will fail if they don't employ diverse workforces 75% of employers believe they should do more to help the young and old work better together 62% of employers agree that companies need to provide older workers with more flexible working, allowing them to retire later if they so desire. Employers recognize that there is a need for change, but identifying the issue is only the first step. Do employers need to promote diversity and flexibility through active policies? As yet, the majority of employees feel there is more talk than action.*

Positive Self-Image – *The research identified that the self-image of the young can make both employers and older people see the younger co-worker as arrogant and over-confident. This can be a source of conflict and limit genuine integration in the workplace. This strong self-belief and self-perception is clearly* *a source of confidence for the young. For example, young people see themselves as particularly innovative (67%); but this is a point of view not necessarily shared by others. Significantly, the Working Nation study shows that employers are less sure about the innovative mindset of the young, with only 38% agreeing that young people are more innovative than older people.*

Variety Is The Spice Of Life – *Future success for businesses may depend upon employers' abilities to attract, retain and create the right kind of working environment for both young and older employees. However, achieving this equilibrium demands that employers recognize that both young and mature employees bring different skills to the business and that both have very positive contributions to make. Although the majority of responses resonate with this concept, the Working Nation study indicates that there are also diverse perceptions. For example, 66% of employers (74% running SMEs) believe that customers don't like to deal with young, inexperienced workers. But, at the same time, 68% agree that you need young people to make for a more dynamic workforce. Flexible working is regarded highly by employees but many of those surveyed feel that it is not the reality of today's working life. Moreover, both employees and their employers surveyed were suspicious of any claims of flexible work practices.*

In Japan and much of Western Europe, the slowing and in some cases declining birth rate has meant there will not be enough younger workers to replace the older workers that many organizations are now so happily discarding. Everything that we know about corporate history suggests that they will wait until the problem has reached a crisis point before they begin a mad scramble to attract and retain the best workers.

If they are smart, or should I say if they manage to wake up, they will find their salvation in the largely untapped talent that represents 50% of all *Homo sapiens*.

Women are the subject of our next chapter.

THE HUMAN ASSET MANIFESTO

CHAPTER

12

AND ON THE SIXTH DAY GOD SAID "LET THERE BE WOMAN!"

THE HUMAN ASSET MANIFESTO

AND ON THE SIXTH DAY GOD SAID "LET THERE BE WOMAN!"

From so many different perspectives, identity, expression, consumption patterns, purchasing power, leadership styles, and workforce participation, women are proving beyond doubt the need to focus on business within a human and social context. **The female revolution is as important as any other social dynamic of the past 300 years.** Sadly, many organizations neither recognize this nor pay it the attention it deserves.

To understand the truly prodigious nature of this revolution, and what in particular has to change in the future, we have to start with what I consider a very interesting observation.

I often wondered why there are two distinctly different types of women at work. One set who seem well balanced, and the other, aggressive and unrelenting in their ambition – just like men many of you would say, but in truth even more so. I have only recently come to realize why this might be so. **In a traditionally alpha-male dominated environment, women who wanted to get the top were convinced, and perhaps rightly so, that the only way to get there was to be more aggressive, more ambitious, and perhaps even more deceptive than their male competitors were.**

This reminds me of an anecdote.

> The CIA had three recruits, two males, and one female. The three were separated for their final test. The test they were told was a matter of national security – it would require them to go into a room and shoot a defenseless man who was gagged and bound to a chair. The first man went in and came out

expressing his relief. The gun had fired blanks – he would not have the murder of a defenseless man on his conscience. Good said the CIA trainers. You have passed the test. The second man went in, and he too came out expressing relief that the shots were blanks and he too was passed by the trainers. Finally, the woman went in. After a long delay, she came out fuming. "Would you believe that bastard simply refused to die? When the shots had no effect I gun-butted him several times but he still would not die. In the end I had to break a chair leg and ram it through his heart!"

If you found it funny, it means that there is more than a hint of truth in it.

I am not for one minute suggesting that every woman who has ever made it to the top has adopted this approach. However, it has been patently obvious that many have. The inability of women to challenge or indeed change social stereotypes has meant that for many of them, success only came about when they were able to morph or change their identity. In other words, many of those who chose such a path probably took a deep breath before plunging in.

In many cases, they even discriminated against other women. It is another function of the extremely competitive mindset, borne out of a sincere belief that only a few women are ever going to make it to the top.

Quite apart from the resentment this breeds amongst both their male and female counterparts (or should we say competitors), it defeats the idea of value in diversity.

Others, the majority of women, are still struggling to have their potential fully realized. I recently spoke to a female business colleague of mine who lectures other women on how to become more assertive in terms of pushing their agenda in the working environment. A major executive recruitment agency is advertising seminars on gender communication strategies, ostensibly to help women improve their chances of success in a male-dominated world.

While these are worthwhile approaches, they are at best interim or stopgap measures. The real problem lies elsewhere – within the very nature of men.

Few men will admit, but most women will agree, that whether it is home or work, it seems that men are programmed by some illogical and supernatural force to ignore what women say. Indeed, a few men even boast of it. The issue therefore is that if we want more women executives and more women in prominent positions, there has to be a definitive change in how women are received and responded to by their male counterparts.

As such, while training women to be more assertive may be a good idea, we should also train men to be more receptive.

In reality, women will only gain true success if their accomplishments are made on their own terms and in their own way – not those dictated by men.

The "modern" organization has failed to keep pace with the social revolution and nowhere is this more apparent than in the hiring, promotion and retention of women. It reflects the broader attitudes within male-dominated society. .

At the time of the Industrial Revolution, women did not have the right to vote. When they married, they as well as their possessions became the property of their husbands. No surprise therefore that women of that era rarely featured in business or commercial activities.

By the early 20th century, most women in the western world were given the vote. However, real change only came about during and after World War II when the shortage of working men resulted in the wholesale recruitment of women into the workplace. As so much of history is written by men, it is no wonder that there is a failure to recognize that Allied successes in World War II were largely the result of the millions of women who made mass production of armaments and other materiel possible. Even more remarkable is the role played by women pilots in the Battle of Britain – they transported planes from one airfield to another, thus freeing up male pilots for combat duties.

Nevertheless, the real lesson here is that men only suddenly woke up to the value of working women during wartime when they had no alternative – so much for the idea that above all else, men are imbued with rational thinking.

The fact that women were allowed to work as of necessity seems to have governed their participation at work for several decades after the war. Women remained incidental to the workplace in terms of promotion, equal pay, and their knowledge capabilities. Most executives in the male-dominated society refused to accept the idea that women could play the role of mother and business executive – in truth, many still don't.

This began to change in the 1970s and 1980s. However, it was perhaps unsurprising that those organizations that did promote women generally chose those who conformed to the male ideal of whom or what a manager should be. Hence, the phenomenon I described at the beginning of this chapter – women who tried to be more man than their male counterparts.

Nothing signified the macho-powered women more than the female business suit with exaggerated padded shoulders and expansive collars, made popular by TV soaps such as Dallas and Dynasty. Alternatively, women would wear pinstriped business suits that were for so long the preserve of businessmen.

These were not just fashion statements. They represented female projection of power in a male-dominated world. To aspiring women they made a very bold statement to their male colleagues – we are one of you. For those women who wanted to get ahead, this form of "power dressing" remained dominant for some time.

It was not until the 1990s that the female social revolution really began to take shape. **As more young women took their place at work and assumed greater economic independence, they apparently adopted the Mae West view of marriage – "Marriage is a great institution, but I am not ready for an institution."**

The impact of this on demography, birth rate and the number of young people entering work is quite significant. So significant in fact, that hiring, recruiting, and promoting women will become an absolute necessity in the near future. Men still have not to come to terms with the consequences of this social change. Examining it further provides us with a framework for better understanding what it is – the dawn of a Female Age.

To begin with, it was inevitable that not all women were going to take the power-dressing route. Led by cultural and media icons from Madonna to the Spice Girls, and more latterly Beyonce and Destiny's Child, young women in particular have begun to assert their individuality as well as their femininity and indeed their sexuality, in all spheres of life. The office has not remained insulated from these trends.

Gradually, it was becoming OK to dress like a woman in the office, irrespective of profession or level within the organization.

If the power dressing way of the 1970s and 1980s characterized the need for women to ape their male counterparts of the period, the Wonderbra defined the nature of the social revolution in the early 1990s. With slogans such as "look into my eyes and tell me you love me" and "who cares if it's a bad hair day," the Wonderbra heralded a change in female assertiveness and female attitudes. A study by a group of students of the University Of Michigan Business School noted:

Towards the latter 1980's and into the 1990's, women were comfortable for the first time with not only their professional success, but their sexuality as well. This brought on changes in fashion.

In a further description of the phenomenon and the hype that was created around it, they noted:

The first Wonderbras were packaged with a yellow card reading "The One and Only Wonderbra" urging consumers to "accept no substitutes." The Wonderbras were delivered via a caravan of armored vehicles and limousines carrying models, bodyguards, and security guards.

Three New York City department stores, Macy's, A&S, and Lord and Taylor, carried the exclusive supply. In mid-August, the Wonderbra was introduced in ten other cities in similarly unique ways – cable cars in San Francisco, pink Cadillacs in Miami, and a motorcycle escort in St. Louis. The full national rollout occurred later in fall 1994.

Women have moved on from the Wonderbra era but then it had only signaled the beginning of the new age. They have gone much further. Not only did feminine intimate apparel suddenly mushroom into a multi-billion dollar industry, women's clothing, styles, and attitudes all experienced massive change.

Younger women are now at their most assertive and expressive. Nothing captures this more than the red carpet parades, seen at every movie premiere or major entertainment. They have become the stage on which young female icons of the day to send a message to their adoring fans.

Girl power is on the rise.

So important has this become that labels such as Versace and Burberry, once reserved for the well-heeled, have made their range affordable for the millions of those young women who aspire to be, or at least look like, their icons. Whole industries are now trying to capture the trend in social change, female assertiveness, and economic independence that have accompanied this.

It is very different from the day when feminists burned their bras as a symbol of their release from sexual stereotyping. Women have now embraced their sexuality in a way that defines them not for men, but for how they see themselves.

This is a very important distinction. **Women's sexuality has become an expression of their identity not their subjugation, and it would be foolhardy to think that this is merely a matter of** attire. **The impact of this change is both social and political, and it has influenced women of all ages.**

We should not be surprised that this is so.

For centuries, men of all nations, religions and ethnic groups have exercised control over women, principally by exercising control over their sexuality. Wherever women have taken control of their sexuality, including if, when, and how many children they have, they have also taken control of their lives.

This is one the truly great revolutions of recent history.

This change in female behavior is entirely consistent with the changes brought about by the consumer society that we initially dealt with in the chapter *Why Corporations Are Socially Dysfunctional*. It is entirely consistent with the consumer society proposition that people are defined by what they consume.

As such, any effort to constrain or place women within a male context when looking at promotions or hiring would be entirely inconsistent with the zeitgeist. Intuitively, it leads one to conclude that such an approach is entirely counterproductive.

There is another very significant lesson here, one that we first looked at in the chapter where we dealt with Maslow, *"You Cannot Hire A Hand, The Whole Person Comes With It"* – Drucker. Self-actualization is an aspiration cherished by most humans – to be whoever or whatever they want to be. It therefore follows that an organization can only maximize the talent of its employees, if those employees are allowed to express themselves in a way that is consistent with them as individuals.

It is within this context that **allowing women to be who they are and what they are, and indeed actively promoting that principle, is one of the most important tasks of the modern organization**. As women represent half of the available talent pool, it makes no sense to restrict the search for the best employees, the best executives and the best managers to the male half of the pool.

In western countries at least, the case is further strengthened by the fact that in terms of university graduates, there are more females than males.

As the purchasing power of women increases, and the demographics of purchasing power change along with it, it is hard to see how male-dominated organizations can properly reflect the tastes of female consumers. It is also unlikely that such organizations can now or in the future, properly market their products to women – especially when the changes in tastes, independence, and purchasing power have been so dramatic.

Data Monitor, the market analysts, examined the income and spending of women in eight leading markets: Britain, France, Germany, Italy, the Netherlands, Spain, Sweden, and the United States. Here is what they were able to determine:

1. More women than ever have gone into tertiary education, entered high-earning careers, delayed marriage and having children, or stayed single

2. Women are staying single for longer, with the result that for many women the 20s and early 30s have become the Freedom Years offering independence and self-sufficiency

3. While marketers have always acknowledged women to be a powerful consumer force, this has been mainly due to their role as purchaser for the entire household. In recent years, however, women have become independent and confident consumers

4. Consequently, the amount spent by women in Europe and the US is expected to rise to €2,000 billion by 2007, compared with €1,400 billion in 2002

Over a period of five years, the purchasing power of women in the western world will rise by 43% or some €600 billion!

The work of the management guru Tom Peters supports this trend and goes even further. In his book *Re-Imagine*, he states:

"American women constitute 43% of Americans with a net worth of US$500,000 or more; said women significantly influence 75% of financial decisions."

"As of the first quarter of 2000, more women than men were using the web; 6 out of every ten new web users were women."

The first point in particular should make investment banks change their attitudes towards women. Trading floors are still a male stronghold. The following extract from a New York Daily News article entitled, *Wall St. Women fight back* by Thomas Zambito tells us all we need to know.

The women of Wall Street are attacking the brotherhood of babes and booze that's lingered as an ugly backdrop to the world of high finance.

And they're going after the one thing their firms prize most: their cash.

Recent multimillion-dollar sex discrimination payouts involving Morgan Stanley and UBS AG, Europe's biggest bank, have encouraged more women to take on an all-boys network, according to sex discrimination attorneys...

This week, six women from the New York and London offices of the German investment bank Dresdner Kleinwort Wasserstein filed a US$1.4 billion lawsuit in Manhattan Federal Court claiming they were denied promotions and six-figure bonuses won by male counterparts.

This is a prime example of an industry that has lost touch with a large portion of its human assets – and is paying the price for it.

The upshot of all this is that the rise of the consumer society has been accompanied by an even greater phenomenon – the dramatic transformation in female purchasing power and where that power is being put to use. There is no question that its impact goes well beyond the fashion and retail industries. A study by Women to the Top (W2T), a

European group dedicated to bringing more women into senior management, gives us a clue. Their work indicates that in the US nearly half of all shareholders are women, women buy half of all computers, and women are responsible for 83% of all consumer purchases. The numbers for Western Europe are broadly similar.

American women are the world's largest economy, followed by American men in second, and all of Japan third! As traditional male blue-collar jobs end up in other parts of the globe, the power of the female economy in both Western Europe and the US will only grow.

Those who have not realized the extent of this transformation in spending power are missing out – big time.

One industry that has become acutely aware of their deficiencies in this regard is computer games. This multi-billion dollar business predominantly employs males and thus it is no surprise that most games are of the loot-and-shoot-them-up variety (*Grand Theft Auto*, the world's largest title is a prime example) primarily aimed at young men. There has been very little attempt to create the kind of games that women prefer. As Lisa Rabasca of Monitoring Psychology emphatically informs us:

> *In comparison, few Internet or computer games or software programs target girls, except Barbie Fashion Design, a program that allows girls to create outfits, jewelry, and hairstyles for Barbie.*

Gaming manufacturers have now made a startling revelation – women play games too! Fancy that! Now who would have thought such a thing!

They have also realized that more women would play games if they were created or developed with women in mind.

Realizing just how much money they have lost by not focusing on the female market, games developers are now scrambling to redress their myopia and are now employing more women. Currently in the UK, only about 11% of the industry's employees are women.

The industry's employment demographics have been a poor reflection of the social demographics of their potential consumers, resulting in billions in opportunity losses. You may recall from an earlier chapter how it took a change in generation for that industry to come of age in terms of its overall offering. Taken together, the failure to pay attention to issues of gender and age dramatically illustrates how diversity can influence the bottom line.

Part of the problem is that women and men view technology, as they do everything else, differently. Some of you may even be muttering under your breath the idea that men are from Mars and women are from Venus. Another extract from the article by Lisa Rabasca of Monitoring Psychology may help to reinforce that view:

> *When adolescent boys and girls are asked to design a machine, boys typically will draw a vehicle--something fast with twin valves and piston turbojets. Girls, on the other hand, will design something practical, like the "Feed-and-Chore Doer," a contraption created by one girl that converts into an umbrella, a shovel and a rake, depending on the weather and the owner's needs.*

Rabasca further maintains that men and women differ in their use of technology:

> *"Women talk about technology as a tool to do things with, men talk about it as a kind of weapon," said psychologist Cornelia Brunner, PhD, a researcher with the Education Development Centre's Centre for Children and Technology in New York City. "Women talk about using it to create, men talk about the power it gives them. Women ask technology for flexibility, men ask it for speed. Women talk about using it to share ideas, men talk about the autonomy it grants them."*

Those who develop IT applications of whatever sort or for whatever reason should take careful note.

If organizations want to take advantage of the growing economic power of women, then they need to ensure that the gender demographics of their organization more accurately reflect that of society or the potential target market. The more organizations reflect the gender demographics of their societies, the more likely they are to be responsive to changes in the tastes and needs of demographics, and the more likely they are to remain competitive.

W2T support this claim by citing two studies that indicate a strong relationship between women in executive management and long-term profitability. One is a study of Fortune 500 companies by Roy Adler of Pepperdine University in the US, which shows that firms with the best record of promoting women into executive positions significantly outperformed the median firms in their respective industries. Another study by Cranfield Business School in the UK, who publish a Female FTSE 250, shows what they describe as a "consistent and growing correlation" between share price and women in management. An extract from the Cranfield Report for 2004, written by Dr Val Singh and Professor Susan Vinnicombe of the Cranfield Centre for Developing Women Business Leaders reads as follows:

> *There were some significant differences between companies with and without women directors. In previous years, we have indicated that market capitalization was significantly higher in companies with women on the board and the same trend continues this year.*

These conclusions are supported by the Scottsdale National Gender Institute in the US.

In order to understand the nature of this particular phenomenon we need to examine further just why gender demographics are so important. For that, we can turn to a study by Babson College's Centre for Women's Leadership and the Commonwealth Institute in Boston. They found that female executives focus on and prioritize customers, employees, and corporate culture, in stark contrast to the traditional business drivers of success such as sales growth and market share, routinely preached by the male-dominated business establishment.

In Re-Imagine, Tom Peters spends a great deal of time exploring the working styles of women and why it is so consistent with bringing out the best in modern organizations. He based the following observations on work by Harvard psychologist Carol Gilligan, *In a Different Voice.*

- Men are rights-oriented. Women are responsibility-oriented
- Men have an individual perspective (The core unit is me) Women have a group perspective. (The core unit is we.)
- Men take pride in self-reliance. Women take pride in team accomplishment.
- Vision: Men, focused. Women, peripheral.

These traits and working styles are supported by a whole raft of studies, in my view most notably by Helen Peters of the Hagberg Consulting Group. The Group defined the leadership traits and qualities most required for the next millennia, which they called Leadership 2000, and summarized them as follows:

- Traditional hierarchical organizations are a thing of the past.
- People and processes are as important as tasks and results.
- Employees will demand, and the fewer layers of management will require, empowerment at all levels of the organization.
- Teamwork leads to success and the team must come before the star.
- Workforce diversity and the globalization of business will require far more acceptance of individual differences and flexibility in management approach and style than ever before.
- Managers will spend more and more of their time in situations where they do not have to command authority; they will not necessarily be the technical expert but rather the synthesizer of cross-functional activities encompassing different fields of knowledge.

Their research showed that women managers more closely match the criteria for Leadership 2000 than their male counterparts do – the main reason being their greater team orientation.

Yet, there is no question that these criteria can only be fully realized if organizations allow women to be women, and not constrain them within male dominated power-structures.

You might also note the reference to the human and social changes that are part of Hagberg's considerations, as well as the fact that these values reflect those we met when we looked at Toyota and its Lean Production methods.

It appears that without question, female executives are more cognizant of the need to nurture and develop human assets than their male counterparts – exactly what is required for the 21st century human organization. Given what we have learned so far, it is not surprising that their presence in executive management makes both a qualitative and quantitative difference in performance.

Organizations should take careful note.

Women are either conspicuously avoiding or delaying any entanglement with the institution of marriage. If they do eventually get married, it is highly unlikely that they will have as many children as their mothers. These are primarily the result of women's social evolution, and the control they now exercise over their sexuality, which we noted earlier in this chapter.

All these factors are resulting in a decreasing birth rate, ageing populations, and ultimately a decrease in the number of people available for work. Europe and Japan are particularly affected. In the latter case, it is estimated that one in four women over 30 are single and record numbers are foregoing marriage and childbearing altogether.

In the coming years, talent will be at a premium. As such, the most successful organizations will be those that can attract, retain, and promote women. In Japan, a country where women are rarely promoted to senior positions, they are now waking up to the fact that their previously undervalued and ritually despised female colleagues have now become invaluable.

While western countries are somewhat more enlightened than their Japanese counterparts, they are not exactly paragons of virtue in this matter. Dutch and German companies are reputedly very poor at promoting women into senior positions. The UK is better with the US another step ahead.

Economic necessity, maintaining competitive advantage and shortages in the available talent pool will ultimately dictate the changes all organizations will have to make.

In September 2004, the UK Equal Opportunities Commission or EOC reported that chronic skill shortages are damaging Britain's productivity. It also noted that in many of the sectors that were experiencing skill shortages, there was an inexcusable lack of women workers and applicants – a shameful waste of the nation's available resources. It cited the building industry whose workforce was less than 1% female.

This position is both absurd and illogical when one considers the huge increase in the number of single homes and flats in the UK, many of them belonging to financially independent women. Pierre Williams of the House Builders' Federation best sums up the extent of the change in this market:

> *"There has been a colossal shift in the make-up of new housing to reflect the fact that more people are living alone…There has been massive growth in building of flats."*

In a report, entitled *The State of the Nation's Housing*, The Joint Centre for Housing Studies at Harvard University reports:

> *Meanwhile social and economic trends have given women a more powerful presence in housing markets. Between 1980 and 2000, the number of households headed by unmarried women increased by almost 10 million. Over the same period, the median contribution of wives' earnings to dual-earner households rose from 30 percent to 37 percent. As a result, unmarried women now head a larger share of households and married women make larger contributions to household income than ever before.*

There are similar trends in Japan and practically any country where women are delaying marriage and increasing their financial independence.

Remember what we said about corporations being slow learners. It appears that we are back to World War II when changes in attitudes to women only came about because men had no other choice. As such, it is no surprise that organizations are now fast asleep at a time when they should have their eyes open, scouting for the best available talent regardless of gender.

Nevertheless, when the financial cost of this comatose slumber finally dawns on them, they will be compelled to act, as they will have no choice. When they do, it will place women in a strong position. Organizations will have to make a determined effort if they are to avail themselves of the best women have to offer. The best women will be seeking out the best employers. They will rank those prospective employers using some of the following criteria:

1. Overall policies in respect of the recruitment, retention and promotion of women

2. The relative number of women in management

3. Overall employment flexibility and work-life balance

4. Employment flexibility relating to maternity leave and return from maternity leave

5. Gender equality in terms of reward structures

6. Overall corporate culture as it relates to women

Indeed, there is already one organization, Aurora, which assists women in achieving these aims. According to their website:

> *Aurora provides a FREE service for women to research and compare companies. This service provides evidence about how companies attract, retain, and advance women and this is know as their 'gender capital'.*

Organizations that want to develop their human assets, improve productivity and maintain their competitive advantage will ignore these changes at their peril. More importantly, those who want to get ahead and stay ahead will recognize that they need to act post-haste.

Failure to respond to these gender realities will ensure that organizations suffer increasing dysfunctionality – and a diminution in their human assets.

Fortunately, this is the age of the Internet, and it does provide organizations with a partial solution to some challenges. The transformational changes in ICT that have occurred in the last 15 years facilitate greater flexibility in working practices. Telecommuting is a very practical way to bring more women into work while enabling them to enjoy a greater work-life balance.

Jet Blue Airlines, one of the few success stories of the US domestic airline industry, employs hundreds of people who work from home, doing tasks such as customer reservations. Telecommuting makes it possible to save on building and office costs, and improves the flexibility of employee working conditions for those who need it – many of them women with families.

There is no question that employees like this arrangement. Jet Blue has a staff turnover rate of 3.4% and attracts high caliber staff. In contrast, the turnover rate at conventional call centers is 39%. One survey indicates that 70% of US managers believe that working from home makes people more productive.

"Homesourcing" is superior to outsourcing by a factor of 12. It is no wonder that Jet Blue wants as many people working from home as possible.

The critical difference between Jet Blue and the myriads of call centers is that Jet Blue uses technology to accommodate people, whereas call centers use people to accommodate technology. Everything we have learnt so far tells us that the former is far superior.

Yet, this is only one solution. Gender dynamics will require organizations to make comprehensive adjustments in their tactics and operations. First, it is most important that women be allowed to be women;

in order to truly capture the diversity of thought and action businesses require. Then to make the most of that talent pool, they should be treated with equanimity and actively promoted, in order to reflect better the demographics of potential markets.

A failure to adapt accordingly will result in organizations experiencing increased social dysfunctionality, with consequences for their productivity, profitability, and even longer-term sustainability.

In closing, it is perhaps most appropriate to recall the words of Betty Bender. "When people go to work, they shouldn't have to leave their hearts at home."

I am positive that most women would agree with that sentiment.

CHAPTER

13

PEOPLE DON'T GET LESS CREATIVE AT FORTY – THEY SIMPLY TIRE OF KNOCKING THEIR HEADS AGAINST BRICK WALLS

THE HUMAN ASSET MANIFESTO

13

PEOPLE DON'T GET LESS CREATIVE AT FORTY – THEY SIMPLY TIRE OF KNOCKING THEIR HEADS AGAINST BRICK WALLS

In late 2005, I attended a reunion of the Cass Business School MBA graduating class of 1992. How things had changed. After 13 years, most of us were now somewhere in or near our 40s, for which we bore the proud hallmarks of a commensurate increase in girth.

A lot had changed. The Internet, mobile phones, and emails were not in common use in 1992. I also remembered that it was around that time that everyone was rushing to learn Japanese language and culture. It was the commonly-held belief that Japanese business practices were going to take over the world. The idea of a single nation having a single business culture has since proved to be the fallacy it always was. You will note for example that not all Japanese automakers followed Toyota's model. Indeed, one of them, Nissan, had to be rescued by Carlos Ghosn, a Brazilian born to Lebanese parents, who is the CEO of Renault, the French automaker.

What culture is and what it actually represents in business is one of the most misunderstood issues of our time.

However, what was even more interesting about the particular group of people at this reunion was that a good 80% of us were now either working for ourselves or for a small business in which we had an interest. Compared to 13 years ago, this was a complete reversal. At that time, most of us were working for large institutions.

THE HUMAN ASSET MANIFESTO

As I surveyed the group, I thought to myself that large organizations have missed out on a great talent pool, and wondered for just how long they would be able to discard such talent in the way they are obviously doing now.

Those who had left larger organizations were adamant that they were far happier in their current circumstances. Those who had remained in the employment of large organizations were more than forthcoming in stating their gripes.

Twenty or so years ago, many of these people would have been welcomed into organizations with open arms and would have been promised long and rewarding careers. In return, they would have believed that they were joining organizations that would provide them with avenues to make the most of their chosen vocation and skill sets.

The question is what happened in the intervening 20 years that turned bright and enthusiastic people into a group that for all intents and purposes would not touch a large organization with a barge pole.

The reason why is simple enough. Contrary to popular belief, people do not get less creative at 40 – they simply get tired of hitting their heads against a brick wall. They become so battered that invariably they realize that the world of big business no longer holds their interest, no longer enables them to fulfill their personal or professional ambitions, and utilizes very little of their skills.

Finally, out of sheer frustration, anger, mutual consent, or having been pushed when they became "difficult" – they leave. Leaving with them are the years of knowledge and expertise, which in truth their former organizations should have done their best to hold onto.

From an organizational perspective what is truly sad about this is that in most cases, their former managers would not even be able to appreciate what they were losing. The obsession of the modern organization with downsizing, rightsizing and reorganizing has only served to make a bad problem even worse, as highlighted in this extract from Accenture by David W. De Long and Thomas O. Mann.

Companies typically are not aware of the risk of lost knowledge until the damage is done. For example, no one expected anything but cost savings when a 1995 workforce reduction at Delta Air Lines sent many experienced mechanics out the door. But problems arose when the less experienced crews that succeeded them took longer to troubleshoot and repair aircraft, causing flight delays, cancellations, angry customers and a serious jump in Delta's cost-of-seat-per-mile. "It was a very expensive lesson," says Jim Smith, director of performance and learning for Delta's Technical Operations Division. So was the experience of a major credit-card company: A new analyst, unfamiliar with how the company ranked prospects, mailed solicitations to people least likely to respond rather than most likely.

Frank Lekanne Deprez, director of ZeroSpace Advies and senior lecturer, Nyenrode University, the Netherlands, shows us just how dangerous this callous disregard for the knowledge of serious workers can get by citing another airline example:

One major airline, for example, recently lost more than 1,200 veteran maintenance technicians to early retirement. That's more than 25,000 years of specialized experience fixing some of the world's most sophisticated airplanes.

Deprez further elaborates by indicating what older and more experienced workers actually represent in human and social terms.

Research by Hamilton Beazley identified that just 30% of expertise is explicit, whereas 70% resides in people's minds (and personal hard disks!). Preserving that kind of knowledge takes more than "brain drain" strategies and putting information and knowledge into company databases.

Indeed, the fact that as much as 70% of an employee's knowledge and expertise is intrinsic to them as individuals is solid proof that humans are assets, and that they are best recognized, nurtured and developed in human and social terms.

The failure to retain mature and experienced staff can almost be viewed as criminal negligence when we consider that an organization is a living interactive network of people. It therefore means that constantly replacing or getting rid of them represents a rupturing of the informal networks and communications that are the very lifeblood of the organization.

I was once told a very instructive tale about an organization that did an evaluation of salespersons' productivity. While most of the salespersons were average, by far the most productive was an older man who had been around for a long time. He did not always use the latest sales tools but he knew his way around the organization exceptionally well. More surprising was the salesperson that came second. This youngster was relatively new to the organization. Although not quite the same standard as the number one, he too was some distance ahead of the pack. On further investigation, it turned out that the youngster actually sat beside the old man and worked closely with him.

Proof, if any ever was needed, of the importance of human contact and interaction in improving performance.

It is one thing to have and then ultimately lose experienced employees; it is quite another thing to make the most of their skills while they continue to work within an organization.

Have you ever wondered how it is that a person who, having worked in an organization for years, who seemingly drifts along as part of the corporate deadwood, suddenly becomes a successful entrepreneur once they leave?

The truth is they didn't suddenly become an entrepreneur – they always were an entrepreneur. The problem was their organization was either unwilling or unable to tap into their skills.

Large organizations are extremely poor at engaging and utilizing the skills of their people. In other words even if they manage to retain mature employees, they fail to recognize their value.

As employees gain experience, it places them in a position to offer far more to an organization than they were originally contracted to do. Yet, they find themselves constrained and bogged down by the bureaucracy and office politics that passes for much of modern management. After a few years of knocking their heads against the brick wall, they simply tire of it. Finally, when they resort to doing only what is necessary, or take the line of least resistance, the organization responds by saying they are no longer enthusiastic or creative.

Wrong, wrong, wrong. Their organization killed them.

The modern organization is like a machine that slowly grinds away and strips individuals of their greatest human quality – the freedom to be the very best they can be.

I am sure many of you over 40s reading this book will be able to identify with what I am saying and I have certainly had my own experiences. What is more, many of you, irrespective of age, have already experienced the great frustrations of working for organizations that simply do not engage you in a way that makes you able to give of your best.

I once asked a head of HR in one organization I had spent many years working for, what it would take for me to get promoted. He was very blunt. He told me that I was highly creative and that I had done many things that were obviously of great benefit to the organization. However, he advised me that in order to get promoted, I had to make a personal choice. My creativity meant that I too often challenged the established order – promotion would require greater efforts at conformity on my part. **He stressed that my career was entirely in my own hands; stay creative, add value and remain in my position, or conform and improve my chances of promotion.**

Initially I was taken aback by this advice – in business logic terms, it made absolutely no sense. However, I realized that my adviser was being perfectly honest and, for that, I am eternally grateful to him. He was very accurately reflecting the nature of the organization for which we both worked. The only thing bad about his counsel was that it was true. **I was working for an organization that did not value its people in a way that it should.**

THE HUMAN ASSET MANIFESTO

I must raise another issue. **There is no question that as we grow older we get less tolerant of the BS and the politics that increasingly dominate corporate life. Additionally, the desire to be self-actualized and free from artificial barriers of rules and hierarchies increases.** What is more, the higher up you go, the more changes you try to effect, and the more you try to engage constructively, the more that BS stinks.

It can be no surprise that those with a more mature outlook on life, or those who are genuinely concerned about effecting positive change, are the ones most frustrated by such rubbish. Alternatively, the politicians and the faddists, those who are preoccupied with playing or who merely wish to hang on to their own jobs, are promoted, much to the detriment of all the other stakeholders.

When it comes to dealing with mature people, organizations are immensely immature.

There is another aspect to this. With academic achievement now widespread, it is impossible to provide employees of any generation with a defined path to the top. There are far too many people trying to squeeze through the same narrow door. It is thus imperative that rather than hierarchical promotions, employee progression is based on greater responsibilities, challenges, and sophistication in the tasks they are given.

Unfortunately, it appears that the older one gets, the more mundane work becomes.

I must finish my little story. Sometime later, when I complained about the lack of performance on the part of a number of people in the organization, and the fact that it negatively affected my work, I was told by someone in HR that I was too performance-oriented!

Well at least the organization was consistent!

I am sure that you would not be surprised when I say that I did not last much longer in that particular organization. As it turned out, I made my choice – I was definitely not promotion material. If I had been, perhaps I would not have been writing this book – I must have made the right choice. I am also sure that in one way or the other, my personal experience has been replicated many times over in many different organizations all over the world.

Organizations like to recruit youngsters, sincerely believing that untainted youth will bring fresh ideas and new impetus to their business. When younger workers are recruited, they are expected to provide a new dynamic, new ways of thinking, new ideas, and new enthusiasm.

Then organizations spend their time finding ways to kill or suppress that enthusiasm as the youngsters too come across brick walls. It seems that organizations forget that every older worker experienced youth at some stage of their life, and in a sense got 'older' because the organization got busy knocking the enthusiasm out of them.

It brings to mind Drucker's deadwood anecdote. **What employees become is largely due to the environment managers create for them.**

Organizations have turned the wasting of talent into a fine art.

The same principle applies when moving from one organization to another. How many times have people of all ages left their old organizations behind with the expectation of a fresh start. After throwing themselves into their new organization with all the enthusiasm they can muster, it usually does not take long for them to realize that they are going to face the same old problems as they did in their old company – same meat, different gravy.

After a while, their enthusiasm is dulled, and they settle into their old routine, with the same old habits, the only difference being if they were smart, they are getting a higher salary for the same pain.

Google, the Internet Technology company that is all the rage these days, has an interesting take on all this. Quite apart from the vast number of PhDs they employ, they also have a policy of not hiring people who are more than a year or two out of university. Google believes that any period of experience in the normal world of business world adversely affects the mindset and attitudes with which prospective employees would approach their work.

It is a sad reflection on the corporate world but frankly, I don't blame Google.

As with women and the younger generation, the long-term demographic changes now taking place within society, particularly Japan, Western Europe, and the US, will ultimately force organizations to treat their mature employees with much greater care.

IBM for one is making note of these changes. In a press release announcing its strategies to deal with the issue, it cites the following statistics:

> *Among countries in the European Union, the number of older workers (50-64 years) will grow 25%, while younger workers (20-29 years) will decrease by 20% over the next two decades. And in the US, by 2010, the number of workers between ages 45-54 will grow by 21 percent, the number of 55-64 year-olds will expand by 52 percent, and the number of 35-44 year olds will decline by 10 percent. As these workers become eligible for retirement, organizations risk losing major skill sets and their competitive advantage in the global economy. Exacerbating this issue, many organizations do not have a clear view of which skills they may be about to lose to retirement.*

Whether most organizations are listening or not is entirely another matter. Nevertheless, whether they like it or not, their listening skills and their efforts in relation to the retention and utilization of older employees will be of great significance to their future success.

CHAPTER
14

RELIGION, RACE & ETHNICITY

THE HUMAN ASSET MANIFESTO

CHAPTER

14

RELIGION, RACE & ETHNICITY

We have already examined why diversity in terms of age (young and old) and gender are so important. Before we leave this topic, there are a number of other diversity issues that also require attention. As with the previous issues, they are concerned with having a demographic balance that reflects that of the wider society and using that to improve the quality and value of human assets. However, they are also concerned with issues of decision-making and reputation.

Foremost amongst these are those relating to religion, race, and ethnicity.

Religion

During the Christmas of 2005, many western companies were afraid of putting up Christmas decorations for fear it would offend people of other religions (meaning Muslims). It was a gross misunderstanding of the nature of Islam and how it relates to Christmas.

The truth is that Christ is also revered as a prophet of Islam – something that most Christians seem to be unaware of. I might also add that I have visited a Muslim country at Christmas time and while the celebrations are not exactly the same as in the west, the tradition is certainly recognized and upheld, especially in hotels with western visitors. Then of course, there are places like Dubai that fully intend to capture Christmas commerce and actually promote seasonal shopping.

It seems that the only thing these organizations accomplished through their ignorance was to upset those of their Christian staff, and perhaps even some of their customers, who may not have liked their decision.

I wonder if they had actually asked their Muslim staff what they felt about Christmas – I am almost sure they did not. Most Muslims I know happily celebrate Christmas with the rest of us.

More fundamentally, this represents a woeful lack of understanding and a failure to have an appropriate dialogue with people of other religions. I am 100% sure that if these organizations were to do a poll of their non-Christian staff, those staff would have told them that they enjoyed Christmas celebrations just like everybody else.

The decision by those organizations is symptomatic of what passes for political correctness – ideas created by well-intentioned do-good-ers who often do not understand the interests of those they claim to be protecting. **Political correctness for the sake of being politically correct often means that there is an absence of a frank and open discussion about the real issues.** In the absence of such frank discussions, political correctness is a way of being "suitably nice" – but often it cannot hide the fact that it stems from ignorance.

There should be an end to largely meaningless and quasi-symbolic attempts at political correctness. Focus instead on genuine education and understanding. With the ever-increasing religious diversity within societies, organizations need to improve their efforts at understanding the real issues.

Not understanding religious issues can be costly.

In that regard, I will never forget an anecdote that was told to me several years ago. There was a project in a relatively remote part of Malaysia (or it could have been Indonesia) where having ensured that they had provided excellent living quarters, the project managers could not understand why they were having difficulty in recruiting workers. Finally, someone told them they had forgotten to build a mosque. Only once the mosque was completed was the project able to move forward.

Race & Ethnicity

Perceived racism at work is a highly significant issue and I have come to realize that in many respects it is not dissimilar to the issue of women at work. **Rarely have I come across a person of color on either side of the Atlantic, and I include myself, who does not believe that they have to work twice as hard to make progress within an organization.**

It is important to note that, irrespective of what anyone else thinks, it is merely sufficient that such a perception exists. Whether they are true or not, the fact is that people's perceptions are their reality. As such, these perceptions have to be addressed, and they can only be properly resolved by having frank discussions on either side.

Further, there is absolutely no question that the record strongly indicates that firms have been poor at promoting ethnic minority staff. There is no question that cultural biases do exist. All peoples of all nations and all races are subject to such biases. They are part of who we are. **Unfortunately, inherent biases allow all of us to remain within our comfort zones. Worse, they blind us to the obvious.**

A former Danish work colleague turned to me one day and asked if I could believe that there was a Rastafarian sect that ridiculously depicted Christ as a black man with dreadlocks. Interesting, I responded, while pointing out that this was no more ridiculous than the common western depiction of Christ with blonde hair and blue eyes, even though he was a man of Middle Eastern descent.

Such is the source of cultural biases and what we believe others whom we don't consider of our ilk to be capable of. Biases limit our thinking; that means that we don't place ourselves in position to make the best use of every single person around us. We can only optimize all our human assets when we move beyond our inherent biases, outside our comfort zones, and learn to appreciate all sources of knowledge.

My own view and experience is that **most people are not racist, what they lack is an enlightened alternative perspective** – whatever their background, black, white etc. They also lack a perspective of what alternative cultures have to offer, and how that fits into their perspective and what they want to achieve.

THE HUMAN ASSET MANIFESTO

Recent events in France and New Orleans indicate that much of the world has a long way to go on this issue. In France, it appears that if your name is Ahmed, you are 15 times less likely to be recruited than someone named Antoine.

Some 20 years ago when I arrived in London, already a Chartered Accountant with several years' experience, I wanted to work in the City. **Thus, it was that in 1986 I was told directly by a number of recruitment agencies that the City did not employ black people. I was stunned.** When I eventually did get in, I recognized that they were not lying – there were very few black professionals working in the City of London.

Things have changed considerably since then. The UK has made considerable progress and it is now a different country. The UK still has some way to go, but it is nowhere near as bad as continental Europe.

Ultimately, the answer to, and at least a partial resolution of these problems may again be found in the actual demographic changes themselves. In Europe, the majority white population is ageing while that of the ethnic minorities is on the rise. France's ethnic minorities are already 10% of the population.

There will come a time when many white westerners will have to depend on the work and labor of young ethnic minorities to receive their pensions – if they did the maths, they would start loving and educating them right now.

Generally, for organizations to remain competitive, it will be imperative for them to better reflect the demographics of their societies.

Professions

Someone once described to me their experience of working in a German industrial firm where almost all the senior managers and executives were lawyers. The result he said was gridlock –decision-making was slow and ponderous.

Similarly, too many accountants could lead to an overemphasis on finance and financial control, as against developing new markets.

This particular philosophy is best captured by the following well-known anecdote:

> An accountant was sent off to far away land to see if there was any market for the company's product – shoes. The accountant returned saying that no one in that country wore shoes so there was no market. Although saddened by this news, the management was not disheartened – they decided to try again. This time they sent their marketing manager. The marketing manager came back in a state of sheer ecstasy. He proclaimed to all and sundry that he had discovered a wonderful opportunity – a land where no one wore shoes, thus presenting the biggest market opportunity the organization ever had.

Any management team that has a preponderance of any one view will be less than balanced in its decision-making process and ability. That goes for lawyers, accountants, and marketers.

Social Class & Other Connections

A similar case can be made in respect of people of the same social circles, or people who attended the same school or university. This is unless of course the business is exclusively focused on the relevant niche sector of the market where that might be the appropriate strategy.

Where the executive management of a business consists almost exclusively of people who share a very similar and very narrow set of perspectives, it risks inward thinking and a decoupling of management from the rest of the organization. I know of at least one organization that operates likes this.

Outsourcing

It might seem strange that I have placed it here but given the global nature of business and the increased level of outsourcing it is very important. Many western companies have been seduced by the idea that when you outsource to some poor country with lower levels of labor and working standards, the welfare of the workers is no longer your problem.

THE HUMAN ASSET MANIFESTO

Obviously, this is no truer than it was for BA and Gate Gourmet. There have been a number of high profile cases like Nike, whose cost savings began to erode its reputation when the exploitation of the workers manufacturing their shoes became an issue. Nike did address the problem, and many organizations are now making these considerations a part of their Corporate Social Responsibility or CSR.

Organizations must take suitable responsibility for all those people who make a reasonable contribution to their goods and services or risk damage to their reputation. Quite apart from that, it also sends a message to employees and customers; we don't only do good when we have to, it is a part of our ethos irrespective of the circumstances.

However, before you move on to the next section please read the Statement of Affirmation on the next page. It represents a summary of the principles established in this section. I hope that you will also be moved to act on the suggestion that follows.

The Human Asset Manifesto
Statement of Affirmation 3

- *I believe that every individual has a unique capability*

- *I believe that every individual can make a unique contri-bution*

- *I believe that the greatest value is created when individuals are most valued*

- *I believe that where there is unity of purpose there is great value in diversity*

- *I believe that an understanding of human and social evolution is fundamental to an organization's success*

You can evidence your support for this statement and by doing so help to send a strong message by going to www.thamanifesto.com

THE HUMAN ASSET MANIFESTO

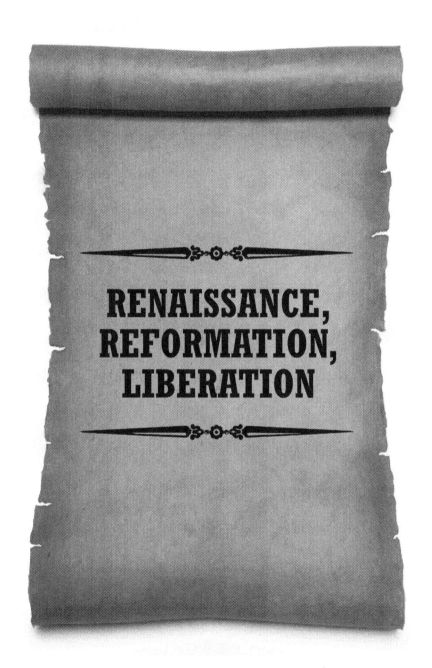

RENAISSANCE, REFORMATION, LIBERATION

THE HUMAN ASSET MANIFESTO

CHAPTER

15

LIES, DAMN LIES, AND MANAGEMENT SPEAK

THE HUMAN ASSET MANIFESTO

15

LIES, DAMN LIES, AND MANAGEMENT SPEAK

We are almost at the point where we can make recommendations in respect of the changes organizations must effect in order to optimize their human assets. Almost but not quite – there are a few more things that I believe are really worth highlighting. They are important because so many managers talk the talk, but do not walk the walk.

Making a complete break with the thinking of the past requires that you acknowledge and recognize the inadequacies in your immediate environment.

Business is littered with words that profess good ideas and intentions, but in reality have come to mean something entirely different. Managers use and abuse these words in order to suggest they are doing the right things, when the reality could not be further from the truth.

Managers might say all the right things, but invariably there is a huge gap between their rhetoric and their actions. Don't believe the hype. Don't be fooled by management rhetoric and warm words.

In order to aid your break with the past, I have put together a choice list of words in common usage, together with what I believe to be their real definitions. The extent to which these definitions apply to an organization provides an indication of its focus on human assets and the development of its people.

THE HUMAN ASSET MANIFESTO

I have incorporated these words and definitions into a questionnaire that allows you to perform a quick and dirty evaluation of your organization. I have named the questionnaire The Human Asset Test© or THATest©

To complete THATest© simply copy the questionnaire on the next page, indicate the appropriate mark to your department or organization (as you wish) and divide the score by the number of responses you have given. I have devised a scale of 1 to 5 for this exercise and you must assign the marks as follows:

5   This very accurately reflects my department/organization
4   This is a good refection of my department/organization
3   This moderately reflects my department/organization
2   This only slightly reflects my department/organization
1   This is not a reflection of my department/organization

A high score means that your organization does not focus on its human assets and is poor at developing its people. A low score means that your organization focuses on its human assets and is good at developing its people.

You can visit The Human Asset Manifesto website at www.thamanifesto.com where you can complete THATest©, very importantly, register your support for our mission to change the way organizations think and behave. Having completed this exercise, the brave new world we are about to describe will be even more meaningful to you.

Support our mission for changing they way organizations think and behave by recording your scores on www.thamanifesto.com

Management Speak	What They Really Mean	1	2	3	4	5
Listening Skills	Something that is required of employees, but for some strange reason is not required of managers					
Employee	Someone who is neither allowed to or supposed to think					
Colleague or Co-worker	Someone with whom you work, but have little idea as to what they actually do					
Reorganization/ Restructuring 1	A ritual management performs every year to trick people into believing they are doing something					
Reorganization/ Restructuring 2	What managers do when in doubt or refuse to face reality					
Outsourcing	A fad where organizations transfer or rid themselves of employees, only to see things get worse afterwards					
Salary	The minimum amount paid to employees in order to ensure they turn up the next morning					
Culture	The best and most flexible excuse as to why things don't get done within an organization					
Manager	Someone who has a position of authority but who tends to adopt a cover-my-ass approach to business decisions					
Management	The most politically savvy people within the organization					
Team	Any arbitrary collection of employees that management desig-nates is a "team"					
Teamplayer	The extent to which an employee, whether a team member or not, keeps their mouth shut, and toes the corporate line					
Consultant(s)	Any individual or group that repackages the latest business fad into something management can cover their ass with					
Leadership	Something managers talk about a lot, but have little clue as to how it should be exercised					
People	The single word that is paid the greatest amount of lip service by management					
Strategy	Something so dear to the heart of management that they keep it to themselves					
Human Resources 1	A good philosophy made bad by a bureaucratic department.					
Human Resources 2	Two words that are paid the 2nd greatest amount of lip service by management					
Productivity	Something managers ask employees to improve without any idea of the challenges or how to do it themselves					
IT	Something that management spends a lot of money on with very little to show for it					

THE HUMAN ASSET MANIFESTO

CHAPTER

16

NEW PARADIGM,
NEW APPROACH,
NEW ORGANIZATION

THE HUMAN ASSET MANIFESTO

CHAPTER

NEW PARADIGM, NEW APPROACH, NEW ORGANIZATION

"High performance organizations give control to the people who do the work – they are in control, not being controlled," John Seddon, In Pursuit of Quality.

This single quote expresses so much of what we have covered so far.

The Human Asset Manifesto statement in the very first chapter of this book embraces and strongly supports the idea that people are at their very best when they have the freedom to act and perform. The Industrial Revolution, Toyota's Lean Production, Maslow's self-actualization, and a host of other examples covered so far, prove this beyond doubt and so does the failure of modern management methods to engage and motivate the vast majority of their employees.

Having developed such a progressive and eminently rational philosophy of business and organizations, it enables us to reject a world based on Scientific Management principles, an obsession with fads, and a rigid adherence to standards.

Liberating and developing human capabilities is the key to optimizing human assets.

This liberation and development of human assets is the basis of a new paradigm, a new approach to business, and a new type of organization – The Human Asset Organization©. It establishes the development and optimization of human assets as the primary and legitimate foundation for organizational success.

THE HUMAN ASSET MANIFESTO

It is within this framework of liberating and developing human assets in order to optimize them that we can make the recommendations necessary for the reformation of organizations, and by so doing extricate them from feudalism. The recommendations are the flesh and bones of the new paradigm.

1. Redefine The Organization From A Human And Social Perspective

The best way for organizations to recognize fully the primacy of human assets is by defining their activities within a human and social context. This is a necessary first step. Without a recognition and acceptance that much of the current approach is wrong, and that the people-based approach is the most appropriate, it is impossible to effect honest change.

The best business visions are human and social in context. Ken Olsen, Chairman and founder of Digital Equipment Corporation, famously said; "There is no reason for any individual to have a computer in their home." It was about the same time that Bill Gates developed his vision of the computer as something that should be available to everyone – history records the rest of the story.

A business is best defined by customer needs – the people it serves. Who they are, where they are, what they buy, when they buy, where they buy, and how they buy. How they can be reached. The success of business is dependent on the extent to which an organization identifies with its customers' experiences as well as current and future needs.

Increasingly, it is also concerned with their human and social needs of society and the environment.

Innovation is a human and social activity. More than ever, it is dependent on the free exchange and adaptation of knowledge within the organization, as well as from customers, suppliers and other purveyors of knowledge – irrespective of their demographics.

Innovation is about finding new human and social applications for new technologies. It is also about finding new ways of improving distribution and ease of customer access to new products. The failure of AT&T to capitalize on prize inventions such as transistors and wireless telephony was due to their inability to articulate a social vision for their products – and reliance on what a consultant told them.

Sales and distribution are human and social activities. The delivery of products and services is a personal experience for the customer. We also know that satisfying the customer experience is best understood when a business places itself in its customers' shoes.

Marketing is a human and social activity. It is the responsibility of every person within an organization. Every contact, every discussion, every exchange of ideas, every inquiry, is part of the client experience.

Purchasing is a human and social activity, as the ongoing exchange of knowledge between the business and its suppliers is critical to product development and evolution.

Client relationship management is a human and social activity. The ability of an organization to sustain competitive advantage and improve productivity is increasingly dependent on the level and quality of dialogue, feedback, and knowledge exchange with customers.

Management is a human and social activity. The complexity of modern organizations is such that no single organizational structure and no amount of restructuring will adequately reflect business and customer needs. The ability to deliver knowledge-driven customer products and services requires open lines of communication and exchange of knowledge on a continuous basis throughout the organization, as well as between the organization and its customers.

The entire organization is a social network of suppliers, customers, employees, managers, and other external stakeholders. The success of these relationships will determine the success of the organization. Recognizing this is the first and most important step in the change process.

It is within this framework that we may redefine the organization in its human and social terms as consisting of the following interactions.

- Employees with themselves as individuals (i.e. the degree of self-actualization)
- Employees to Employees
- Employees to Suppliers
- Employees to Clients
- Employees to Managers
- Employees to External Knowledge Sources
- Employees to Technology & Systems
- Organization to Other Stakeholders
- Clients to Employees
- Client to Technology, Systems & Processes
- Suppliers to Employees
- Suppliers to Technology, Systems & Processes

2. Assiduously Promote Interactions Between All Human Assets

This is a direct consequence of redefining the organization in its human and social terms. Once that process is complete, then management must continuously work to develop the relationships between an organization's assets, in order to optimize the value of their relationships. This will greatly facilitate the next stage, the development of knowledge and the fostering of innovation.

3. Make The Development Of Knowledge A Priority

We have proved that knowledge is human and social in its evolution, development, and application. We have also just defined the sets of interactions that in turn define an organization. It therefore follows that in order to improve productivity and develop competitive advantage, organizations must promote and facilitate continuous, efficient, and effective exchange of knowledge in each of these interactions.

That means knowledge from suppliers and clients must be embedded in products and services. Employees must exchange knowledge in order to improve the quality of products and services. Systems, processes, and technology must facilitate rather than inhibit the flow of knowledge, and external knowledge sources should always be exploited.

4. Harmonize Corporate Objectives & Individual Goals

At the outset of this book, we clearly illustrated that the vast majority of people are uninspired and demotivated by their work. Under such circumstances, it is impossible to optimize human assets and in particular get people to collaborate and exchange knowledge. It follows that ways must be found to motivate and engage employees in a manner that is consistent with their best interests, as well as, those of their organization.

As such, organizations must articulate and express corporate goals and objectives in a language that employees can identify with, and develop a personal affinity. The best way to do this is to ensure that business strategies are translated, expressed, and communicated within the context of individual and personal goals and objectives.

Organizations must always put themselves in the shoes of the employee and ask the question: "What's in it for me?"

Organizations can visibly demonstrate that personal and corporate goals are consistent by reducing the emphasis on profits, and improving the focus on personal, team and group performance targets.

5. Ensure Employee Rewards And Recognition Reflect The Organization's Success

Employees must believe they have a vested stake in the organization, which is related to and based on their performance, the performance of their team, and ultimately the performance of the organization.

Without this, it will be impossible to maintain the alignment between corporate and individual objectives.

6. Ensure Individual Manager's Goals & Objectives Are Consistent With Employee Goals & Corporate Objectives

The objectives of all managers must be consistent with those of their employees and thus by definition, the organization – including their reward structures. Failure to ensure this will result in inconsistent performance.

7. Assiduously Promote Collaboration, And Align Organizational, Personal & Team Rewards

This is absolutely critical. Without such an alignment, it is impossible to develop value networks – teams working in harmony to create value-added products, solutions, or services.

Organizations must assiduously cultivate teamwork and collaboration at all levels in order to enhance innovation and product quality, as well as improve the integrated delivery of products and services.

8. "Put Your People First & Watch Them Kick Butt" - Rosenbluth

Employees are at the core of the social organization. They are management's first clients. Managing is therefore a marketing activity – an exchange between human and social equals. In marketing, one never asks the question, "What do we want?" The marketing question is "What do you want?"

One of the best examples of this approach is Rosenbluth Travel – a company transformed from a small business to a global industry leader with gross revenues in excess of US$6 billion. It is the third-largest travel management company in the world.

Rosenbluth's ethos is to put employees first. It recognizes that only fully motivated staff can deliver the very best in customer service – employees can enrich or depress the customer experience, and that can be entirely dependent on their personal experience within an organization. You can never train for excellent customer service; the very best customer service comes from within and that is highly dependent on staff engagement and motivation.

When an individual first enters the Rosenbluth, depending on where they are located, they are taken to either the US or European head-quarters to meet people and understand just how the organization works. They are taken out lunch to celebrate their arrival. They then meet the executives of the organization who welcome them and serve them tea.

Rosenbluth provides people with the room to be outstanding and cre-ative – it places trust in employees to be the very best they can. It engages in perpetual learning, which it makes as fun-filled and enjoy-able as possible.

Employee focus, development, leadership, perpetual learning, and partnership are all at the heart of the Rosenbluth ethos.

Organizations that expect to achieve excellent customer service with-out excellent treatment of their employees can forget it.

9. Unleash Creativity By Creating An Open And Flexible Working Environment

Human Capital is at its best when people are self-actualized, when they can express themselves with freedom and spontaneity, in a sup-portive environment. Steps required to achieve this include:

- Profiling and matching people to positions to optimize their particular skill sets
- Customizing work and conditions to suit employee needs
- Cultivating and perpetuating a culture of openness and flexibility
- Expanding roles and responsibilities to match employee growth and experience

- Constantly encouraging new ideas
- Reviewing rewards and incentives to reinforce desired behaviors and engender a meritocracy
- Continuous learning – both formal and informal
- Organizing people into entrepreneurial units
- Cultivating entrepreneurs by linking organizational and employee results
- Not unduly punishing genuine business mistakes

One of the best models of worker flexibility is that currently employed by DARPA. DARPA is a small bureau within the US Department of Defense. DARPA stands for the Defense Advanced Research Projects Agency. For several years and at a cost of tens of millions of dollars, DARPA had been conducting research into autonomous ground vehicles. Not making the progress it expected, DARPA tried a new tack. They launched the DARPA Grand Challenge.

In 2005, a prize of US$2 million was offered to any group whose vehicle could travel a specified route through the Nevada desert without a human being at the wheel. The entire course was 131 miles, or approximately 208 kilometers, in length.

Over 20 teams entered the Grand Challenge – mostly small start-ups with dedicated people who happily contributed countless hours a week to developing their entrant for the challenge.

One such company was Sciautonics, made up of Rockwell employees who worked on the project in their spare time. Rockwell donated equipment, facilities, and half of the capital to the start-up, and will benefit, financially and intellectually, if their employees' project wins a contract, or simply develops new technologies because of their involvement in the challenge. The Rockwell teams did not win the challenge, but both they and their company gained invaluable knowledge.

The actual winner of the DARPA Challenge was a team from Stanford University, with teams from Carnegie-Mellon University in the runner-up position.

Of course, the biggest winner of all is DARPA. By encouraging entrepreneurs from whatever source, they were able to spend a relatively
tiny sum, especially compared to the tens of millions they had spent
in the past, while gaining the technical expertise they required.

10. Seek Out And Promote Innovation In Every Area Of The Organization

This is entirely consistent with everything we have said about how
knowledge and innovation emerge – there should be no boundaries to
sourcing new ideas.

11. Develop Strategies From The Bottom Up, As Well As From The Top Down

Where employees are properly empowered and are a major source of
innovation, strategic development cannot solely be a top-down exercise – strategy must also flow from the bottom-up.

This approach has been a driving force behind many Silicon Valley
companies whose major challenge is to maintain their creativity as
they grow and become a lot bigger. At Google, software engineers are
allowed to spend 20% of their time on projects of their own choosing
– the idea being to create a portfolio of projects, which then compete
for investment.

12. Make Technology A Slave To People, Not People A Slave To Technology

People are more important than technology. The example set by
Toyota shows us that, given the necessary intellectual and operating
freedom, people will devise new technologies, improve existing technologies, and find new ways of using technology.

Homesourcing, which adapts technology to the needs of people, is proving far better and far more productive than outsourcing to call centers.

13. Focus On The Human And Social Application of Knowledge

As the example of AT&T with its development of wireless technology and transistors, clearly shows the human and social applications of innovation can be more important than innovation itself.

14. Empower Employees

Many organizations talk about empowerment but very few seem to know what it means. Here is a list of items that should be included under this heading:

- Make work challenging
- Enlarge the scope and complexity of job functions
- Reduce the number of job categories and specialists
- Cross-train
- Continuously promote formal as well as experiential and group learning
- Facilitate and promote self-development
- Include employees in strategic decision-making and restructuring plans
- Devolve responsibilities to the lowest levels
- Adopt Participative Management principles
- Promote and facilitate change and innovation
- Promote and facilitate constant feedback at all levels, functions and reporting lines
- Provide incentives and reward desired behaviors

Tata Tea is an exceptional example of what devolving responsibilities to the lowest levels can achieve. The South Indian tea grower had for so many years run its plantations like, well...er, plantations, of the colonial era that is. Managers managed, workers worked, and over the years profitability steadily declined. Then management got wise. They started a participatory management scheme that devolved power to the workers, and gave those workers a significant stake in its equity. Speaking to Hindu Business Line, Mr. V. Venkiteswaran, Executive Director of Tata Tea, stated:

> *"We are planning to hand over the company to the workers, staff, and managers who know the business of running the plantations best. By this move, we will be shaving off a part of the large overhead expenses that the plantation business has been bearing until recently."*

The changes were effected in February 2005. By the company's December year-end, productivity had improved by 34% and the company reported its first profits in 5 years.

15. Flatten And Simplify The Organization Structure

The new way of working and doing business within a human and social ethos is only accomplished if people are not buried under layers of hierarchy and matrix management structures. Simplify and flatten organizational structures, and place greater reliance on communications, informal networks, teamwork, and collaboration to improve the flow of knowledge and coordinate business activities.

An organization is a living entity – let it breathe!

16. Allow Genuine Business Mistakes

Without experimentation, organizational learning is difficult.

17. Abolish Any Overreliance On A Rigid Adherence To Standards

Ticking all the boxes requires little skill. It is boring, demotivating, and may only produce one-off, short-term benefits.

While minimum standards must sometimes be imposed and considered, they should remain just that – minimum standards. The surest way for an organization to stand still is by establishing rigid standards that must be adhered to – especially when those standards have been devised by some governments or international bureaucracy. The best standards are those that emanate from within, and which everyone knows and sees as part of an evolutionary process that they identify with.

Both DARPA and Toyota clearly demonstrate the value of setting performance targets rather than rigid standards. This allows human and social innovation to move the business forward. It also facilitates the acquisition and development of knowledge from all possible sources.

Having everyone focused on genuine business objectives is much better than policing – if you cannot trust your employees then you have a much bigger problem

18. Create A Dynamic Working Environment

Rather than giving my own suggestions, I have included several extracts from Forbes on Wegmans Supermarkets – No 1 on Forbes List of "Best Employers to Work For" in 2004. I tried as best as possible to reduce the length of the extracts but there were so many nuggets of excellence I had to share them with you. I was so impressed by what I read that I will make it a point of duty to visit one of their stores the next time I am in the US. I hope you feel the same way.

Wegmans proves, just like Rosenbluth, that putting your employees first brings results. It also demonstrates how understanding and catering to employees on a deeper more emotional level creates the kind of dynamic working environment that customers will adore. The extract reads as follows:

> *The unusual motto of this privately held grocery chain is "Employees first, customers second." The Wegman family's rationale: When employees are happy, customers will be too.*
>
> *The 89-year-old Rochester-based chain is that rare breed: a grocer beloved by its employees—and one that is also trouncing its competitors in a very tough industry. Here's how the company does it.*

Walter's brilliant and pugnacious son Robert, who became president in 1950, added a slew of employee-friendly benefits such as profit-sharing and fully funded medical coverage. When asked recently why he did this, 86-year-old Robert leans forward and replies bluntly, "I was no different from them".

In an annual survey of manufacturers conducted by consultancy Cannondale Associates, Wegmans bests all other retailers—even Wal-Mart and Target—in merchandising savvy. "Nobody does a better job," says Jeff Metzger, publisher of Food Trade News.

But the biggest reason Wegmans is a shopping experience like no other is that it is an employer like no other. "You cannot separate their strategy as a retailer from their strategy as an employer," says Darrell Rigby, head of consultancy Bain & Co.'s global retail practice. Wegmans' hourly wages and annual salaries are at the high end of the market (the better to fend off unions)...

But salaries aren't the whole story. The company has shelled out US$54 million for college scholarships to more than 17,500 full- and part-time employees over the past 20 years. It thinks nothing of sending, say, cheese manager Terri Zodarecky on a ten-day sojourn to cheesemakers in London, Paris, and Italy...

The proof is in the stores every day. The smiles you receive from Wegmans employees are not the vacuous, rehearsed grins you get at big-box retailers. They are educated smiles, with vast stores of knowledge behind them, cultivated perhaps through company-sponsored trips to Napa Valley's Trinchero winery. After all, what good is it to offer 500 types of specialty cheeses if you can't explain the origin of each, what type of cracker to serve them on, even what wines they should be paired with? "If we don't show our customers what to do with our products, they won't buy them," says Danny Wegman. "It's our knowledge that can help the customer. So the first pump we have to prime is our own people." ...

Simply put, no customer is allowed to leave unhappy. To ensure that, employees are encouraged to do just about anything, on the spot, without consulting a higher-up. One day it could mean sending a chef to a customer's home to clear up a botched food order. It could also mean cooking a family's Thanksgiving turkey, right in the store, because the one Mom bought was too big for her oven. Is that expensive? Sure. Is it worth it? You bet. A Gallup survey found that over a one-month period, shoppers who were emotionally connected to a supermarket spent 46% more than shoppers who were satisfied but lacked an emotional bond with the store...

Wegmans can save some serious coin by encouraging employees to step up to the plate. When the company opened a new, US$100 million distribution centre in Pennsylvania last June to serve its newer Mid-Atlantic stores, it needed truck drivers. Rather than hire experienced (and expensive) pros, Wegmans allowed current store employees to apply for the job. Twenty-one weeks later Wegmans had two dozen drivers with commercial licenses; they had previously been cashiers and produce clerks.

19. Ensure Your Human And Social Values Reflect Those Of Your Customers And The Wider Community

This goes beyond the quality of service to encompass their concerns for the environment, being a good corporate citizen and generally reflecting those ideals that they believe represent a positive contribution to the community. This approach ensures that an organization encapsulates the human and social values of their external assets.

A survey by the Centre for The New American Dream, www.newdream.org, showed that "91% of college students and 88% parents say they would be likely to purchase environmentally friendly products if they were available at stores they shopped at."

Nothing makes employees more proud than the fact that their employer stands for something within the wider community – that is in addition to the positive benefits it brings to society. This is where CSR can play an effective role. Having employees actively participate in any such initiative or venture also greatly enhances its impact.

Concern and respect for the environment must be an integral part of this strategy. In a connected and more informed world, it is highly unlikely that a parent will be motivated to work for an organization if they are unhappy with its environmental policies and the legacy those policies might bestow on their children.

In the longer term, the only way for organizations to optimize customer human assets is to ensure that that they are in the forefront of social change.

20. Adopt A Consultative Selling Approach

Consultative selling is the specific mechanism by which organizations seek to improve the relationship with their customers, to better understand their needs, to better embed those needs into products and services, and ultimately to better satisfy those needs.

It is based on the concept that customers will only share knowledge of their business with those with whom they have developed a strong relationship. The stronger the relationship, the greater the knowledge transfer and thus the greater the opportunity to match client needs.

The methodology is supported by research that indicates that the top three providers get 75% of a customer's business.

21. Focus On Performance Criteria, Not Just On Financial Results

One of the best management lessons I ever received was from a friend whose business focus was helping organizations develop their consultative selling capabilities. Her name is Nikki Owen, Director of Trainique Limited, and her advice was, "You cannot do a result, you can only do a performance." Profits are merely the outcome of external conditions on an organization's performance in respect of marketing, innovation, and productivity. Performance is therefore a human and social construct.

This interpretation of profits directly facilitates a better linkage between corporate financial objectives and the human and social activities that underpin them. Illuminating the connection between people and profits provides the basis on which organizations can translate their financial objectives into human and social activities, as well as into personal goals and performance standards.

There are other very good reasons for focusing less on financial targets and more on performance targets. These include:

- Accounting systems inadequately reflect the true value of an organization's assets

- Accounting systems are certainly inadequate in terms of people assets – by most estimates these represent up to 80% of an organization's value

- Generally speaking, accounting systems are hopeless at expressing the value of knowledge assets

- We have devised systems that account for what happens when we lose a machine part from inventory, but not what happens when experienced employees leave an organization

- Profits are often one of the smallest numbers in the entire financial statements – so much of an organization's financial resources are consumed elsewhere

- Many organizations have become slaves to the markets, manufacturing their quarterly results to meet analysts' expectations, rendering them relatively meaningless

Reducing the emphasis on profits and accounting measures facilitates a more holistic and practical view of the organization and its objectives for both managers and employees.

22. HR – Keep The People But Abolish The Department

HR departments spend their time coming up with esoteric ideas to convince management of their worth, or even to simply gain their attention. Then, of course, there is a lot of associated documentation and form filling to go along with these ideas – proof that they have actually done something. When times get tough, or at the end of financial year when budgeted targets are under strain, HR projects are the first to get the chop.

Don't blame the people. Like everyone else, HR employees need to be liberated from an environment that stifles their creativity and sense of purpose, and placed in an environment where they are made to feel that they are making a valid contribution – without desperately trying to prove it.

Organizations should therefore disband their HR departments and redistribute the staff, making them an integral and important part of the organization – not as HR advisors, but as decision-makers with business responsibilities. This will assist in ensuring that business strategic plans have the appropriate human and social dimension.

There is one caveat. I do not subscribe to all HR ideas – as often the focus is more on methods than on people. However, there is a substantial level of strategic knowledge within the discipline.

Changing the remit may transform people from sedate Methodists to stirring Evangelicals!

23. Make Human Asset Development The No. 1 Priority Of All Managers

If people are an organization's greatest asset, then every single manager should focus on their development. This means that management rewards and incentives must be based on their ability to develop people in a manner that is consistent with unified corporate and individual objectives – including the development of client and supplier relationships.

The redistribution of HR as described above should assist this process, but it also means that managers must be inculcated with the appropriate values.

24. Cultivate A People Centered Focus Within the Organization

People strategies should play a leading role in every aspect of the business:

- Recruitment
- Retention
- Job Roles, Tasks, Responsibilities
- Training and Development
- Rewards and Incentives
- Strategic Decision-Making
- Customers
- Suppliers

25. Recruit People, Not Qualifications

Many organizations still believe in recruiting people with the best grades from the best universities – this is very myopic. They would have missed out on Einstein, who failed the entrance exams to the Swiss Federal Institute of Technology. He claimed that because he was a slow learner it made him better at pondering the mysteries of the universe. Earlier, we noted how the Industrial Revolution came about because of ordinary men, many of them uneducated.

The idea that only people with the best grades from the best universities should be selected is just another aspect of cover-your-ass management – we did things right, but not necessarily right things. As Paul Good once observed; "Few great men could pass Personnel."

Bill Gates and Steve Jobs, both university dropouts, would not have stood a chance.

26. Understand Your Employees' Challenges In Order To Improve Productivity

It is amazing how those who want to see improvements in productivity often have no idea of the challenges their employees face in delivering them. These could include difficulties in trying to sell a new product, coming to grips with a new system, or competing for business where the competition has better knowledge, systems, and tools.

In some instances, the challenges are provided by managers themselves, particularly where the decision-making and approval processes are slow.

Another and perhaps even more critical aspect is the time it takes to find information on products, organizational capabilities, client transactions, market conditions etc. In a world where knowledge is vitally important to the execution of transactions, the time taken to access knowledge can be a major success factor. In these instances, the efficiency and effectiveness of an organization's knowledge delivery process can either significantly enhance or significantly inhibit productivity.

Managers who want to improve productivity must first place themselves in their employees' position in order to come to terms with the specific issues involved.

27. Abolish Functional, Hierarchical, and Generational Barriers

The best ideas may come from the youngest person, the oldest person or those tasked to execute tasks at the lowest levels of the organization. Specific steps should include the following:

- Ensure both young and old are included in the decision-making process
- Create teams that are cross-functional, cross-generational, and cross-departmental
- Actively deploy and exploit the technology skills of the young

28. Actively Promote The Role And Career of Women

This goes far beyond any form of political correctness. From an internal perspective, women naturally possess those characteristics that are conducive to the development of people within a human and social context, and are consistent with optimizing human assets.

From an external perspective, the purchasing power of women, and the huge market changes for which they are responsible, are making it increasingly imperative that organizations ensure that they improve the representation of women in all areas of business. Otherwise, there is a considerable risk that they will not have the ability to adapt their products and services to reflect those changes.

Finally, women represent 50% of the available talent pool. Disregarding or not making the most of that potential is outright folly as well as an injustice.

29. Focus On Retaining Experienced Workers

Experience cannot be taught – you may never fully comprehend the extent of the value that experienced workers add to your business – that is, until they are gone.

30. Leverage The Capabilities Of Young People

The bling generation is far more attuned to technology, its uses, and how best to leverage it than their older counterparts are. They are also major trendsetters and thus bring fresh perspectives into an organization.

31. In General Terms, Actively Promote Diversity

Remember, the more your organization reflects the demographics of your target markets, the more likely it is that you will be able to adapt to changes. However, diversity is also important because it provides an opportunity to look at issues from several different perspectives. Thus diversity actively supports and facilitates innovation and new ideas.

32. Invest In And Assiduously Promote Socialized Learning

Make socialization an integral part of the learning process in order to develop and enhance:

- Teamwork
- Learning & development
- Competencies
- Sharing of innovation and standards
- Analysis of clients' needs
- Approach to client solutions
- Delivery of products and services
- Recognition of organizational dependencies
- Improve cross-functional integration

33. Train Your Clients And Include Them in Your Business

As products and services become more complex, training and developing clients assists their understanding of an organization's abilities. Where appropriate, organizations should also include clients in their in-house training. The levels of trust that can develop from such relationships greatly facilitate knowledge exchange, increase the understanding of their requirements, and improve the ability to incorporate their knowledge and ideas into products and services.

34. Incorporate Your Major Suppliers Into Your Business, And Have Them Train You

What is true of clients is also true of suppliers. Rather than trying to provide suppliers with detailed specifications of what you want, allow them to enlighten you in respect of their capabilities. Establish performance standards and let them fill in the details.

Where appropriate, you should also train your suppliers in respect of the aims and objectives of your business, particularly in terms of what you want to achieve with your clients. It will make them more cognizant of how they need to support your business.

Not making use of your suppliers' capabilities can be costly irrespective of whether it is a manufacturing or service entity.

I remember working for one investment banking institution that bought a new trading and sales system for financial products from one if its suppliers. For some time after the purchase of that system everyone was unhappy with its performance – for some reason it did not match the original presentation.

One day, after much discussion, the supplier sent in their own IT people to find out what was wrong. They spent a few minutes, made a few minor changes and suddenly things were much improved. It turned out that the bank's IT staff had not worked with the vendors as effectively as they should have, and had insisted in maintaining complete control over all aspects of the implementation themselves.

This failure to make adequate use of the vendor's knowledge and capabilities resulted in sub-optimal system usage, an inability to provide clients with the best service, missed transactions, and lost revenues.

35. Cultivate Ethical Investors

An increasing number of investors adopt an ethical approach to their investments. An organization that is centered on human and social values rather than simply meeting quarterly revenue targets should seek out investors who understand the longer terms benefits of such a strategy, and so further assist the alignment of organizational objectives with human and social values.

The demand by Exxon shareholders that they pay far greater attention to global warming (dealt with more extensively in a later chapter) is a prime example of a shift in investor sentiment that can be harnessed to effect change.

The existence of an organization such as the Investor Network On Climate Risk – www.incr.com – is evidence enough that this proposition is both desirable and possible.

36. Focus On Integrity And Build Trust

Promote integrity at all levels within the organization and ensure that there is a transparent and consistent standard to which all employees must adhere. The trust that it will engender will be critical to the development of a meritocracy that employees can believe in.

37. Stay In Touch With The Zeitgeist – Watch MTV

You never know where the next business idea is coming from. What we do know is that youngsters are setting the trends.

Nuff said!

38. Avoid Fads And Put An End To Constant Reorganizations

Nothing promotes more instability and cynicism, and is more counter-productive, than constant reorganization. Organizations must determine their customer service model, restructure along those lines, and then stick to it. Then the focus must shift to building informal connections, affiliations, strong relationships and linkages throughout the organization.

Training and socialization within training can play vital roles in this area, but so too must mechanisms that are more informal.

39. Communicate, Communicate, Communicate

This is critically important. It facilitates transparency, develops trust, and ensures that everyone completely understands organizational and individual objectives. Without this most other initiatives will flounder.

40. Provide Employees With The Right Technology And Tools

While knowledge is a human and social activity, there is no question that technology has facilitated our ability to analyze, synthesize and apply knowledge at a rate unheard of even 15 years ago. Organizations should ensure that their staff have the right technology and tools to compete effectively.

41. Punish Petty Politics And Bad Behavior

If consistent good behaviors are to be recognized and rewarded, then consistent bad behaviors, be they those of managers or employees, should be punished.

42. Evaluate And Assess Human Assets On Regular Basis

Having determined that people and people-related activities are your primary assets you should evaluate, manage, and assess them as you would any other asset.

Having established the basis of the reformation and the establishment of The Human Asset Organization©, how do we assess the status and/or progress of our efforts? What methodology should we be using?

The Human Asset Evaluator© or THAEvaluator© – it does exactly as its name suggests, is the subject of the next chapter.

CHAPTER

17

OH YES,
WE CAN MEASURE
HUMAN ASSETS
- INTRODUCING -
THAEVALUATOR©

THE HUMAN ASSET MANIFESTO

17

OH YES, WE CAN MEASURE HUMAN ASSETS – INTRODUCING THAEVALUATOR©

THAEvaluator© measures the extent to which an organization's assets have been liberated, developed, and optimized, as well as provide an assessment of its progress towards becoming The Human Asset Organization©.

If we are to manage human assets effectively, it follows that we must have an ability to evaluate and assess them on an ongoing basis. The problem with many traditional HR tools is that they don't always provide a direct linkage between people, organizational development, and strategic objectives. This is important if managers are to understand how their investment in human assets is directly related to organizational performance and strategy.

THAEvaluator©, www.thaevaluator.com, also directly links people and their performance with organizational strategy and objectives.

THAEvaluator© implicitly recognizes that, for example, training a sales team will not produce the desired performance if the organization's sales systems, client relationship management processes, or the levels of communication amongst salespersons are inadequate. Moreover, it also recognizes that if the sales team is not motivated and engaged it is unlikely that training will be of any value.

THAEvaluator©'s holistic approach is entirely consistent with Drucker's maxim; "You cannot hire a hand, the whole person comes with it." It examines the whole environment and rejects the piecemeal approaches that so often frustrate managers and wastes resources.

The approach is entirely rational. **It is highly unlikely that one can arrive at the best possible solution to a problem if one has not performed the best possible diagnosis. THAEvaluator© is the business equivalent of an MRI scan.**

THAEvaluator© recognizes the primacy of human and social interactions within organizations. It recognizes that such interactions convey knowledge, improve productivity, and assist in the development of sustainable competitive advantage. It provides an objective basis for optimizing the deployment of people and organizational resources in a manner that is consistent with both corporate and individual goals. In so doing, it also provides a framework for strategic development that is consistent with the human asset capabilities of the organization. This is particularly essential in the case of medium-sized firms with limited resources.

THAEvaluator© is based on the new paradigm introduced in the previous chapter where we redefined the organization in terms of its human and social interactions:

- Employees as Individuals
- Employees to Employees
- Employees to Suppliers
- Employees to Clients
- Employees to Technology & Systems
- Employees to Managers
- Employees to External Knowledge
- Employees to External Environment

For convenience, we have omitted those sections of the evaluation that require suppliers and clients to provide feedback on their experience, and concentrate on the internal elements.

Having thus redefined the organization, the next stage involves translating these relationships into business and business related activities and factors as indicated in Table 1 below.

TABLE 1
REDEFINING BUSINESS ACTIVITIES
IN HUMAN ASSET TERMS

Human Asset Interactions	Business Related Activities
Employees as Individuals	Self-Actualization, Performance
Employees to Employees	Teamwork, Collaboration
Employees to Suppliers	Buying
Employees to Clients	Selling, Marketing, CRM
Employees to Technology & Systems	Processes and Procedures
Employees to Managers	Culture, Management
Employees to External Knowledge	Innovation and Responsiveness
Employees to External Environment	Legal and Reputation Risks

Having redefined the business then the next step is to determine the relevant factors that determine the success of each of these relationships. Therefore, for example, an employee's self-actualization will be dependent on the level of motivation, engagement, knowledge, and skills – in short, their degree of liberalization and development.

Similarly, selling and marketing will be dependent on those specific skill sets, as well as knowledge of products, services, and client solutions. Systems and Procedures can be assessed based on their efficiency of use from an employee perspective. This might include how well they provide access to knowledge and/or information.

The development of THAEvaluator©, the nature of the questionnaire and reports, and the analysis it provides, are explained in the Illustrations below.

Illustration 1 – Developing THAEvaluator© is a pictorial representation of how the THAEvaluator© is developed by applying a range of assessment factors to business activities to produce THAEvaluator© questionnaire and relevant reports. The questionnaire is thus based on the specific experience of employees within each targeted organization or department.

THAEvaluator© assessment factors have been derived based on their ability to liberalize or otherwise motivate the level of interactions, as well as develop the knowledge, skills and other capabilities necessary to improve their quality.

Illustration 2 – Index of THAEvaluator© Questionnaire is an index of all the sections and subsections included in the questionnaire. The main sections are consistent with the list of Human Asset Interactions as defined in Table 1. The subsections are consistent with the Business Related Activities also as defined in Table 1. In this instance, the assumption is that the organization has four hierarchical levels and THAEvaluator© assesses the quality of employee relationships and collaboration at each level.

Illustration 3 - Demographic Data shows the additional questions such as age, function experience, gender etc, asked of each person completing the questionnaire. This is entirely consistent with what we explored in the previous section of the book, LIBERTY, EQUALITY, FRATERNITY – an evaluation of diversity is absolutely essential for the total evaluation of human assets.

All THAEvaluator© scores can be further interpreted and analyzed in terms of their demographic/diversity constituents.

THAEvaluator© adopts a holistic approach to assessing and developing human assets because partial solutions are not rational.

Illustration 4 – Extract From THAEvaluator© Questionnaire provides a specific example of the first section of the questionnaire; I.1, **The Employee As An Individual, Self-Actualization**. It demonstrates how the specific assessment factors are applied in developing this particular section of THAEvaluator© questionnaire. The scoring and compilation of results is performed using the following scale:

1 = Poor, 2 = Below Average, 3 = Satisfactory, 4 = Good, 5 = Excellent

Illustration 5 – THAEvaluator© DETAILED ANALYSIS REPORT, OVERALL SUMMARY provides an assessment of the value of human assets within an organization. It is arrived at by a compilation of all the scores in each section and subsection of the questionnaire. The recommendations are based on those included in the previous chapter.

THAEvaluator© Overall Summary score assesses the progress towards becoming The Human Asset Organization©.

Illustration 6 - EXTRACT FROM THAEvaluator© DETAILED ANALYSIS & RECOMMENDATIONS REPORT provides a comprehensive interpretation and analysis of the section on Self-Actualization. It specifically links the strategic context, performance capabilities, possible human asset development solutions, and provides an indication of what future improvements might bring.

A similar report is produced for every section and subsection in the Questionnaire (see Index). They provide a detailed analysis of the Overall Summary and human asset score.

The Detailed Analysis & Recommendations report is an assessment of the human asset performance capabilities of each strategic area of an organization.

Illustration 7 - EXTRACT FROM THAEvaluator© SIGNIFICANT FINDINGS REPORT is similarly prepared for each section in the index. This report is based on the idea that most of an organization's problems can be solved internally. Thus, each section shows which departments or units scored well and which scored poorly in terms of their human assets, relative to the particular strategic or business objective in question.

By providing a comparative analysis of the human asset capabilities of the different units within an organization, the Significant Findings Report assists in the identification of internal solutions.

A demographic analysis for the relevant section is also included, in order to assist the organization in determining the specific nature of the issues involved.

Illustration 8 - EXTRACT FROM THAEvaluator© RISK PRO-FILE & ANALYSIS REPORT is a reinterpretation of the Detailed Analysis & Recommendations Report. It is an extremely valuable tool. If human assets represent at least 80% of an organization's value, then it follows that they are not only the greatest source of value, but also its greatest source of risk.

In the event that an organization or unit gets a below satisfactory mark on any aspect of its human asset performance, the Risk Profile & Analysis Report examines and draws attention to the associated risks, enabling management to focus their attention accordingly.

Illustration 9 – THAEvaluator© Organization Value Proposition demonstrates how by combining the relevant section and/or subsections of THAEvaluator© Report, we can derive an assessment of some of the most significant strategic issues facing the modern business. These include:

- Selling more products to the same clients
- Quality and productivity
- Innovation and productivity
- Risk management

The number of reports and analysis available are limited only by the imagination. Part of THAEvaluator© output is a download of all scores, which facilitates ad hoc detailed analysis of any aspect of human asset performance within an organization.

Illustration 1 – Developing THAEvaluator©

THAEvaluator© Questionnaire and Reports are developed by **Redefining the Organization** in people relationship terms, translating those into **Business Activities**, and applying the appropriate **Assessment Factors** to each relationship

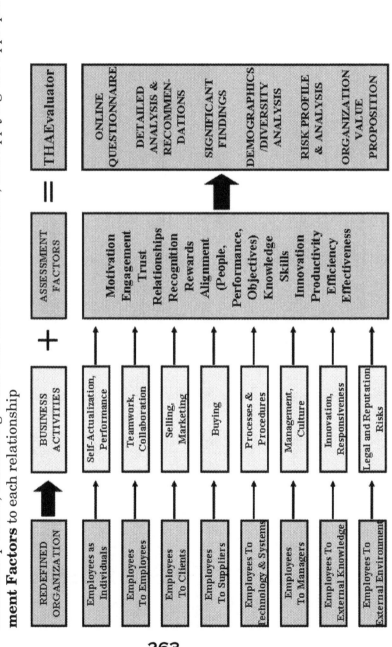

Illustration 2 – Index of THAEvaluator© Questionnaire

	THAEvaluator© QUESTIONNAIRE INDEX	PAGE
I	**THE EMPLOYEE AS AN INDIVIDUAL**	**X**
I.1	Self Actualization	X
I.2	Product & Technical Knowledge	X
I.3	Client Solutions Knowledge	X
I.4	Legal & Regulatory Knowledge	X
II	**EMPLOYEE TO EMPLOYEE – THE VALUE NETWORK**	**X**
II.1	Individual Unit Value Network	X
II.2	Level IV Value Network	X
II.3	Level III Value Network	X
II.4	Level II Value Network	X
II.5	Level I Value Network	X
III	**EMPLOYEES TO SYSTEMS, PROCESSES & TECHNOLOGY**	**X**
III.1	Knowledge, Learning & Development	X
III.2	Systems & Technology	X
III.3	Organizational Efficiency	X
IV	**EMPLOYEES TO MANAGEMENT**	**X**
V	**EMPLOYEES TO EXTERNAL KNOWLEDGE SOURCES**	**X**
VI	**EMPLOYEES TO CLIENTS**	**X**
VI.1	Client Knowledge & Consultative Selling Skills	X
VI.2	Client Relationships & Marketing	X
V1.3	Organizational Qualities & Competencies	X
VII	**EMPLOYEES TO SUPPLIERS OR MAJOR CONTRACTORS**	**X**
VIII	**EMPLOYEES TO OTHER STAKEHOLDERS**	**X**
VIII.1	The Community	X
VIII.2	The Environment	X

Illustration 3 - Demographic Data

Age
Under 26, 26-35, 36-45, 46-55, Over 55

Gender
Male, Female

Functions
Sales, Account Management, Professional, IT and/or Technical, Administrative and/or Clerical, Production or Maintenance, Other

Management Level
Senior Executive, Middle Manager, Supervisor, Staff,

Location
Country

Number of years in organization
1, 2, 3, 4-5, 6-10, 10+

Academic Qualifications
High School or Equivalent, Bachelors or Equivalent, Masters, Doctorate

Ethnic Background Or Origin
White / European, Hispanic, Arab, African, Japanese, Chinese, South Asian (India, Pakistan, Bangladesh, Sri Lanka), Other Asian, Other

Professional Qualifications
Lawyer, Doctor, Psychologist, Engineer, Accountant, Scientist, Economist, Mathematician, Other or None

Illustration 4 – Extract From THAEvaluator© Questionnaire

I   The Employee As An Individual
I.1 Self Actualization

QUESTION	SCORE				
1 = Poor, 2 = Below Average, 3 = Satisfactory, 4 = Good, 5 = Excellent	1	2	3	4	5
What is your assessment of your work in terms of the extent to which it is:					
Consistent with your personal goals?					
Consistent with your professional goals?					
Personally developing?					
Personally motivating?					
Challenging?					
Making the most of your skill sets?					
Fulfilling?					
Recognized?					
Respected?					
Rewarded?					
What is your assessment of your work in terms of the flexibility with which it allows you to self-manage:					
Your own initiative and ideas?					
The quantity of your output?					
The quality of your output?					
Your professional development?					
Your personal development?					
Your work-life balance?					
What is your assessment of your work in terms of the scope it provides for trying new ideas?					
What is your assessment of the extent to which your organization is liked and respected by:					
Employees?					
Clients?					
Suppliers?					

Illustration 5 – THAEvaluator© OVERALL SUMMARY

Strategic Framework	Score	Analysis of Score	Possible Solutions
Knowledge, innovation, and productivity are of the people, for the people and by the people. Improving productivity and developing a sustainable competitive advantage is highly dependent on an organization's ability to optimize the growth, management and deployment of its human assets. Implicitly, this requires a recognition, an understanding and a determination to prioritize human assets in all aspects of the organization's business Finally, human assets are at their most innovative and creative when provided with the right flexibility and environment.	1.00 Poor	The organization has failed to recognize the value and importance of human assets. Its ability to optimize productivity, innovate, and develop a competitive advantage is significantly impaired.	1. Articulate mission, values and strategic objectives in human and social terms
	2.00 Below Average	The organization has not placed sufficient emphasis on prioritizing human assets. This impairs its capability to improve productivity, innovate, and develop a sustainable competitive advantage.	2. Determine whether or not you have the right people profile and match people to jobs 3. Prioritize people development; make it an integral aspect of reporting 4. Focus on employee value
	3.00 Satisfactory	To some extent, the organization does recognize the value of human assets and reasonable efforts have been made to develop them. However, further improvements would improve capabilities to innovate and enhance productivity and competitive advantage.	5. De-emphasize quarterly financial reports 6. Educate managers, analysts and investors in the importance of human assets
	4.00 Good	The organization recognizes the importance of human assets and has worked to maximize them. This provides it with a capability to innovate, improve productivity, respond to its environment, and sustain competitive advantage.	7. Make developing human assets the primary responsibility of managers 8. Promote team-players and developers of human assets 9. Aside from core functions, abolish HR; place the staff in strategic positions within the organization
	5.00 Excellent	The organization fully recognizes the primacy of human assets and has worked to maximize them. This provides it with excellent capabilities to innovate, improve productivity, respond to its environment, and sustain competitive advantage.	10. Provide incentives for learning, entrepreneurship and experimentation
ORGANISATION'S THAEvaluator© SCORE = X			

Illustration 6 - EXTRACT FROM THAEvaluator© DETAILED ANALYSIS & RECOMMENDATIONS REPORT

I   The Employee As An Individual
I.1 Self Actualization

Strategic Framework	Score	Analysis of Score	Possible Solutions
One of Drucker's more famous dictums is; "You can't hire a hand, the whole person comes with it."	1.00 Poor	The organization and its employees have conflicting goals and objectives. They do not find their jobs either fulfilling or motivating and are in no position to make the most of their capabilities.	1. Recruit and retain people that best match a profile for strategic success
In order to even begin the process of optimizing human assets, individual and corporate objectives must be in alignment.	2.00 Below Average	The organization and its employees are only partially aligned in terms of their goals and objectives. They find their jobs only marginally fulfilling and they are not in a position to make best use of their capabilities.	2. Prioritize people and their development 3. Profile and match people to the positions that make the best use of their capabilities
It also means that organizations must provide an environment where the individual is freely able to express and take full advantage of their capabilities.	3.00 Satisfactory	The organization and its employees are reasonably aligned in terms of their goals and objectives. They find their jobs fairly motivating and fulfilling and are in general terms making use of their capabilities.	4. Set strategic objectives in non-financial terms 5. Articulate and express mission, core values and strategic objectives in employee/human terms 6. Expand job roles and responsibilities
Part of this motivation is the extent to which they take pride in not only their work, but also that of their organization.	4.00 Good	The organization and its employees are very well aligned in terms of their goals and objectives. They find their jobs motivating and fulfilling and are suitably positioned to optimize their capabilities to be creative, productive, and innovative.	7. Provide opportunities for self-help and development 8. Set broad performance objectives and criteria and reduce direct supervision
	5.00 Excellent	The organization and its employees are very well aligned in terms of their goals and objectives. They find their jobs highly motivating and fulfilling and are very well positioned to optimize their capabilities to be creative, productive, and innovative.	9. Align recognition and rewards with performance objectives

ORGANISATION'S THAEvaluator© SCORE = X

Illustration 7 - EXTRACT FROM THAEvaluator© SIGNIFICANT FINDINGS REPORT

I The Employee As An Individual
I.1 Self Actualization

Areas Of Excellence	Score	Areas Of Concern	Score
Employees within these areas of the organization have been provided with an environment that enables them to make best use of their capability to innovate, improve productivity, and develop competitive advantage.		Employees within these areas of the organization have *not been* provided with an environment that enables them to make best use of their capabilities. Their ability to innovate, improve productivity, and develop competitive advantage is significantly impaired.	
Division, Business Unit, Department, Unit 1	x	Division, Business Unit, Department, Unit 8	x
Division, Business Unit, Department, Unit 2	x	Division, Business Unit, Department, Unit 9	x
Division, Business Unit, Department, Unit 3	x	Division, Business Unit, Department, Unit 10	x
Division, Business Unit, Department, Unit 4	x	Division, Business Unit, Department, Unit 11	x

The above analysis may be used as a basis to compare and contrast the environments that give rise to both sets of THAEvaluator© Scores, and thus assist in the generation of internal solutions.

The following demographic indicators provide insights into some of the factors that may have influenced the scores in this section.

Age	Score	Function	Score	Hierarchy	Score	Years in Organization	Score	Ethnic Background	Score
Under 26	x	Sales	x	Senior Executive	x	1	x	White/European	x
26-35	x	Account Management	x	Middle Management	x	2	x	Hispanic	x
36-45	x	Professional	x	Supervisory	x	3	x	Arab	x
46-55	x	Administrative/Clerical	x	Staff	x	4-5	x	African	x
Over 55	x	IT & Technical	x	Average	X	6-10	X	Japanese	x
Average	X	Production/Maintenance	x	Gender	Score	10+	x	Chinese	x
		Other	x	Male	x	Average	X	South Asian	X
		Average	X	Female	x			Other Asian	x
				Average	X			Other	x
								Average	X

Illustration 8 - EXTRACT FROM THAEvaluator© RISK PROFILE & ANALYSIS REPORT

I The Employee As An Individual
I.1 Self Actualization

Strategic Framework	Score	Analysis of Score	Risk Implications
One of Drucker's more famous dictums is; "You can't hire a hand, the whole person comes with it." / In order to even begin the process of optimizing human assets, individual and corporate objectives must be in alignment.	**1.00 Poor**	The organization and its employees have conflicting goals and objectives. They do not find their jobs either fulfilling or motivating and are in no position to make the most of their capabilities.	Employees are generally very disgruntled with their roles and tasks. There is a risk that work is being improperly executed. This could be particularly damaging for product quality and customer care. / Work stoppages are a possibility and staff retention problematic.
It also means that organizations must provide an environment where the individual is freely able to express and take full advantage of their capabilities.	**2.00 Below Average**	The organization and its employees are only partially aligned in terms of their goals and objectives. They find their jobs only marginally fulfilling and they are not in a position to make best use of their capabilities.	There is a more than reasonable level of employee disgruntlement which if let unattended, could deteriorate further. The consequences of this could be damaging. Staff retention could be problematic.
Part of this motivation is the extent to which they take pride in not only their work, but also that of their organization.	**3.00 Satisfactory**	The organization and its employees are reasonably aligned in terms of their goals and objectives. They find their jobs fairly motivating and fulfilling and are in general terms making use of their capabilities.	Employees are reasonably content with their employment. There are some risks, however, if improvements in their work environment could greatly improve the extent to which they are engaged.

ORGANISATION'S THAEvaluator© SCORE = X

Illustration 9 – THAEvaluator© Organization Value Proposition

Strategic Objectives	THAEvaluator© Business Activity	THAEvaluator© Strategic Assessment
Selling More Products To The Same Clients	Product & Technical Knowledge Client Solutions Knowledge Client Knowledge & Consultative Selling Skills Client Relationships & Marketing The Value Network	The ability to integrate the delivery of an organization's full range of products and services to clients
Quality & Productivity	Management Self-Actualization Systems & Technology Organizational Efficiency The Value Network Supplier Skills	The efficiency and effectiveness with which products and services are integrated / developed within an organization
Innovation & Productivity	Self-Actualization Client Knowledge & Consultative Selling Skills Supplier Skills The Value Network Knowledge, Learning & Development Solutions Knowledge External Knowledge	The ability to capture and maximize internal and external knowledge
Risk Management	Management Legal & Regulatory Knowledge Organizational Systems, Processes & Technology The Community The Environment	The management of human, operational, legal, and reputation risks

THE HUMAN ASSET MANIFESTO

THAEvaluator©'s MRI scanning provides a quantitative and qualitative assessment of:

1. The extent to which employees are self-actualized, empowered, and motivated to work
2. The extent to which there are gaps or deficiencies in the knowl edge and skill sets required to complete certain tasks or to attain specified strategic objectives
3. Organizational relationships and knowledge flows between departments or divisions as an assessment of the integration and team work involved in developing products and services, and delivering them to clients.
4. The overall team, communication, collaborative dynamics through out the organization
5. The extent to which there is a consultative sales process that facilitates the optimum knowledge extraction and integration of client knowledge into products and services
6. The extent to which there are client relationship management processes and procedures that facilitate the integrated delivery of products and services
7. The ability to develop specific solutions that match client needs, whether for internal or external clients
8. The efficiency and effectiveness with which key knowledge systems and processes relating to the production of goods and services organization can be accessed and utilized
9. The extent to which productivity is impacted or proscribed by the inefficiencies in systems, processes, and procedures
10. The extent to which organizational culture influences knowledge creation, development and application
11. Management's role in creating an optimum environment for knowledge development and application
12. The specific factors that inhibit or enhance productivity (a part of the questionnaire specifically asks how they spend their working day)
13. The extent to which personal, professional, and corporate objectives are aligned (a key indicator of employee engagement)
14. Ensures that the application and utilization of knowledge is focused on improving productivity and developing competitive advantage

THAEvaluator© provides organizations with a total strategic development framework. It can be used as a comprehensive assessment tool in any of the following circumstances:

1. Acquisition of a Company, Division, Department or Unit
   a. Go beyond the numbers in terms of analyzing and assessing capabilities
2. Organizational & People Development, Training Programs
   a. Determine needs and factors that enhance or diminish your investment
3. Business & Strategic Planning
   a. Align strategic assets with strategic objectives
   b. Ensure resources are commensurate with ambitions
4. Improving Productivity & Maintaining Competitive Advantage
   a. Determine and then address the specific areas or factors that enhance or diminish productivity and innovation
5. Reducing Operational & Strategic Risks
   a. Identify areas where lack of motivation, poor management control or poor procedures give rise to significant financial and operating risks
6. Drive Performance
   a. Align employee objectives with corporate business objectives
   b. Provide an objective and comprehensive framework within which organizations can report human asset performance in relation to financial results

The first item is particularly relevant. THAEvaluator© provides a basis with which we may move beyond the inadequacies of evaluating organizations based solely on their financial results, by providing a qualitative and quantitative assessment of its human assets and their strategic performance capabilities.

Analysts, private equity firms, accountants, and investment and commercial banks wanting to develop a more comprehensive evaluation of target organizations should take note.

For consultancies, THAEvaluator© can be used as a pre-assignment diagnostic tool that facilitates identification of the core issues and a more constructive engagement. This represents a radical departure from the practice of consultants arriving at a client's offices, and offering whatever fad or particular skill set they have in their possession.

Once THAEvaluator© is brought into the equation, then both client and consultant have a basis for a more objective assessment of the issues, and thus a more rational approach to providing services.

For HR and/or Training Companies, THAEvaluator© provides the type of analysis that directly identifies the overall training and skill levels within an organization, and where specifically their services should be targeted. It ensures that training and organizational development requirements are suitably aligned with strategic objectives.

Consistent with our theme of adopting a holistic approach, THAEvaluator© facilitates ensuring that training and development initiatives actually complement and support each other – something that is not possible when a piecemeal approach is adopted.

Table 2 – THAEvaluator© HR & Consulting Framework, specifically demonstrates how THAEvaluator© creates a framework within which consultancies can offer their full range of products and services to clients, as well as supporting a comprehensive training program in conjunction with an organizational strategy.

TABLE 2
THAEVALUATOR©
HR & CONSULTING FRAMEWORK

THAEvaluator© Business Activities	Organizational Assessments & Surveys	Training & People Development
Employee Self-Actualization	Personal & Career Profiling Employee Satisfaction Recruitment, Retention	Career Interpersonal Skills
Collaboration, Teamwork and Value Networks	Employee Engagement Socialization & Cooperation	Team Building Communications
Product, Service and Technical Knowledge	Skills Profiling & Competencies	Product & Technical
Client and Consultative Selling Skills	Salesperson Profiles Salesperson Competencies	Selling Skills Negotiating Skills
Client Relationship Management & Marketing	Customer Service & Care Personal Profiling	Presentation Skills Client Management
Supplier Skills	Knowledge	Knowledge Management
Leadership & Management	Leadership & Management	Coaching, Leadership, Management
Systems, Processes & Procedures	Operational Performance Operational Risks	Corporate Procedures
Knowledge Development and Application	Culture Skills	Learning & Development Knowledge Management
Compliance & External Stakeholders	Culture, Integrity Corporate Responsibility	Compliance Corporate Responsibility

THE HUMAN ASSET MANIFESTO

CHAPTER

18

WHY ORGANIZATIONS MUST LEAD SOCIAL CHANGE IN ORDER TO SURVIVE

THE HUMAN ASSET MANIFESTO

18

WHY ORGANIZATIONS MUST LEAD SOCIAL CHANGE IN ORDER TO SURVIVE

The Human Asset Organization© is an idea that goes beyond the narrow confines of traditional business themes. This should not be surprising. Everything we have explored so far tells us that such an organization must be focused on the totality of the human experience, and not the mechanistic assumptions of the prevailing management ethos.

As such, in order that we might assist organizations in the liberation and reformation of their human assets, so that they become The Human Asset Organization©, it is imperative that we move beyond an analysis and list of recommendations, and articulate a wider philosophy.

The history of humanity is the history of ideas. Ideas change the world. History tells us that for good or evil, better or worse, the power of ideas is far greater than that of any logistics or form of technology.

The 20th century was a battle between the ideas of Karl Marx on the one hand, and the likes of Nelson Rockefeller on the other. This battle shaped and spurred spectacular changes in people, nations, civilizations, global financial systems, and scientific development.

Ideas tend to precede new processes, new technology, and new ways of doing things. In those instances where a discovery precedes an idea, the only way to test the quality or relevance of that discovery is by finding the idea that makes it valuable.

What is true for war and civilizations is also true for business.

IBM possesses thousands of scientific patents many of which are unused – on average the company licenses 3,000 patents a year. When Lou Gerstner took over in the early 1990s, the company started selling many of those patents and was making an estimated US$1.5 billion a year from these sales.

Then IBM had a rethink. It is now giving away many patents in order to encourage greater use of the open-source software that it champions.

IBM's big idea is this: if other organizations can make better use of their software, then allowing them to have it means that they can increase the market for open-source software to IBM's benefit. By creating an open-source software technical and economic sphere of development, IBM hopes to ultimately challenge the dominance of Microsoft.

IBM's big idea is to join forces with the open-source software movement and exploit human assets beyond its normal scope of activities. In effect, it is redefining the boundary, magnitude, and quality of its human assets and with them the organization's capabilities. The big idea is human in its context and greater than technology – it is pushing the boundaries of the human and social revolution that has characterized the IT industry to the next phase.

In this book, we have paid considerable attention to IBM and Microsoft. The competition between them has defined our era. What some may view as a battle of technology giants has actually been a battle to establish the most competitive idea for a human and social business model.

The battle between Microsoft and IBM is an ongoing battle of ideas that has implications for technology where each idea is followed by a change in the approach to technology. IBM's current support for open-source software is merely the latest riposte in that battle.

The ICT revolution would not have occurred without college dropouts working out of basements and garages. Silicon Valley was a social revolution, which eventually had huge implications for technology. It is the Industrial Revolution of the

modern age, made possible by new ways of working and more equitable ownership and reward structures – both of which are an anathema to the establishment.

Despite the fact that many dotcom companies crashed, their different approach to work, their creativity, and their propensity to share rewards more generously with employees/partners, has had a lasting impact on the world of work. Many traditional organizations lost their best talents to them. For similar reasons, investment banks lost much of their best staff to Hedge Funds and Private Equity firms.

How did traditional organizations respond to the challenge of these new entities and their new and more open way of working – dress-down Fridays!

That was it! Oh, we are losing our best talent so we should allow our staff to take their ties off once a week. They eventually decided on a bolder response in order to stem the flow of talented individuals. They changed dress-down Fridays into dressing-down every day of the week! Wow! I guess that really scared the competition!

In an attempt to retain 'talent', some organizations paid a select few inordinate amounts of money and share options. Sadly, this further skewed the distribution of rewards in favor of the senior ranks. It was thus the complete opposite of what the new organizations were doing.

While you may find this funny, the tragic reality is that most organizations will refuse to change their behaviors and attitudes even when it is obvious that a change is required. Until, that is, the day when they face dire circumstances when their very existence is threatened.

Organizations are slow learners – even when the way forward is staring them right in the face. Jet Blue Airlines, Pixar, and Toyota, have focused on their human assets, and are absolutely thriving at a time when their competitors are either in trouble, or on the verge of bankruptcy, as is the case with many US airlines. Yet those competitors are still failing to heed the message.

THE HUMAN ASSET MANIFESTO

It is for this reason that we need to articulate a philosophy and idea of The Human Asset Organization© that goes beyond our list of recommendations and provide an operating framework within which organizations can improve.

The answer to our quest is grounded in the evolution of both organization and society.

The basic structure of organizations and in particular the primacy of the investor-focused profit model has remained largely unchanged over the past 300 or so years. The structure prioritizes the interests of owners / investors followed by that of managers, with employees a very, very distant third.

Alternatively, the changes in society during that period have been phenomenal. We have gone from a situation where someone like me could have been bought by European slave traders for a few pounds, to a situation where we at least in theory strive for equality for all irrespective of race, religion, gender, etc. Mass consumerism is further extending the boundaries of this evolution.

This chronic disparity between the social evolution of the organization and the social evolution of society means that today's organizations are inherently socially dysfunctional. They are incapable of optimizing their human assets.

The first challenge of The Human Asset Organization© is to address the challenges arising from social dysfunctionality.

As noted above, while we have strived for social equality, organizations and society have fallen far short of perfection. Foremost amongst the internal challenges faced by organizations are those relating to age, gender, the environment, and wider human aspirations. In a composite example, Betsy Taylor of the "New American Dream" is quoted in the Organic Consumers Association stating:

> *"College students are bringing their values into the marketplace. Companies need to wake up and provide more environ-*

mental and fair trade products if they want to win lifelong loyalty from young consumers..."

"...people are starting to realize that simple consumer choices can help resolve complex problems such."

The article goes on to say that as many as 88% of students want their campus store to offer more environmental and fair-trade products. That item alone is four challenges all rolled into one; the bling generation, the environment, fair trade and global poverty.

The change in the social status of women, their role in society, their purchasing power, the need to make greater use of the available pool of talent, as well as the diversity that talent represents, are yet further significant challenges faced by organizations. Indications are that most organizations are yet to fully comprehend, much less address, them.

An ageing population and the need to retain experienced talent is another. The demographics of declining birth rates and an ageing workforce will make this a particularly difficult challenge, if mature workers continue to be cast aside or disregarded the way they are now.

There is more than ample evidence that advanced economies are still failing to optimize and leverage the value of ethnic diversity within their societies.

The Human Asset Organization© will incorporate and leverage diversity in order to assist in the eradication of social dysfunctionality, and improve their ability to optimize human assets.

There is another equally compelling perspective that directly links both the internal and external challenges being faced by today's organizations.

The idea that people must go to work to give up their freedoms and their ability to be creative, and accept a subordinate role to those who have invested money, is completely contrary to our social evolution and the very nature of humanity.

THE HUMAN ASSET MANIFESTO

The Human Asset Organization© recognizes that the greater the amount of freedom and control devolved to employees, the more successful the organization.

Most organizations have a long way to go to achieve this.

It must be one of the great anomalies of our time that people who live in liberal democracies go to work each day and surrender their liberty and freedom of expression.

In what is considered the seminal work on Knowledge Management, *Intellectual Capital, The New Wealth of Organizations,* Tom Stewart describes how management must change to optimize the value of intellectual capital. Stewart suggests that the job of management used to be to plan, organize, execute, and manage – POEM, while the way forward requires managers to Define, Nurture, and Allocate – DNA. The latter proposition meaning that managers must broadly define the nature and type of business, nurture its human capital, and allocate resources necessary for the task.

In one sense, there is no rational alternative to the DNA model given that it allows employees to determine how to make best use of their own knowledge and capabilities. Moreover, **the complexities of modern business are such that, except in their particular area of expertise, managers cannot possibly have more knowledge than the people that work for them.**

Implicit in DNA, the latter structure, is the idea that organizations must rely on the ability of knowledge workers to engage, actively participate, and freely give of their best in order to meet organizational objectives. From all we have seen so far, that also requires those workers to be fully engaged, motivated and rewarded.

This is entirely consistent with the notion that an organization is a living and breathing entity and that it must be considered within a human and social context. It also provides a model for organizations transitioning from a mechanical and scientific approach to the human asset approach to the organization, and into what Stewart describes as a Network Organization.

Based on the ideas we explored in the chapter on Maslow, for such an organization to be successful, the individuals within it must be self-actualized if they are to give of their best. It also implies a considerable degree of trust, commitment, and responsibility between them.

Leadership within The Human Asset Organization© is primarily concerned with providing a framework within which employees, both individually and collectively, can make the best of their abilities.

Then there is the question of equality of prosperity.

The Human Asset Organization© is one where all stakeholders are equally recognized. It is concerned with sharing its gains and rewards with employees on a more equitable basis. While doing so, it will also strive to make a positive impact on society.

This implicitly recognizes that while people spend a considerable proportion of their daily life at work, their ambitions and concerns cannot be divorced from those of the wider society. It also recognizes the significant role played by large organizations on issues such as free trade, the environment, and the quality of life.

From a philosophical perspective, divorcing the world of work from the idea of sustainable living and development is no longer possible.

Millions participated or got involved in Live 8. It is unlikely that they forget about that involvement when they walk into work the next morning. They would be less proud of their organizations if they believed that they operated in a manner that did not support free trade or debt relief for the world's poorest nations.

An increasing number of people are involved with NGOs and voluntary organizations. Images of the Asian Tsunami brought into our living rooms by the news media prompted individuals to donate more money for relief than their governments.

While we are far from solving the problem of global poverty, AIDS, Bird Flu, and SARS have finally made everyone realize that we do live in a connected world and that we are our brother's keeper.

People will be far prouder of their organizations if they believe they stand for something within the community. Conversely, they will be less than enamored of their organizations if they are not seen to be making a positive contribution. Remaining neutral will not be an option.

We might be reminded, however, that while many organizations do contribute to society, the overall public view is decidedly negative, as evidenced by this extract from New York Times of January 9, 2005, which we met earlier.

> *"More than ever, Americans do not trust business or the people who run it," reports Claudia H. Deutsch. "Pollsters, researchers, even many corporate chiefs themselves say that business is under attack by a majority of the public, which believes that executives are bent on destroying the environment, cooking the books and lining their own pockets." Deutsch cites polls from Roper and Harris, in which 72 percent of respondents feel that wrongdoing is widespread in industry, only 2 percent regard the executives of large companies as "very trustworthy," and 90 percent say big companies have too much influence on government.*

This affects all organizations both internally and externally – after all the public works for them. At the same time, it clearly defines the ultimate role and responsibility of The Human Asset Organization©.

Given the human and social challenges faced by organizations, the only rational conclusion that one could arrive at is that only those that are prepared to lead social change, rather than being shaped by it, will remain competitive. Those that ignore or resist social change will lose competitiveness, or reach a point where their very survival is threatened.

So for example, vehicle manufacturers that rely or wait on government legislation to set mileage and emission standards will lose out to competitors who have focused on these issues from a human and social perspective. So too will those food and beverage companies who fail to ensure that they provide more wholesome and nutritious products for public consumption.

The Human Asset Organization© will not await the pressure of government legislation, consumer associations, or environmental pressure groups before doing the right thing.

The Human Asset Organization© will work both independently as well as alongside these groups to lead social change, and not be dragged kicking and screaming into making them. This will greatly enhance its ability to achieve social harmony, and optimize its human assets.

The Human Asset Organization© is consistent with the noblest ideals of freedom and liberal democracy.

Recently, the most profound example of the need for organizations to lead social change was evidenced not by calls from consumers or legislators, but by the demands of a group of investors. **In what has to be considered one of the most extraordinary and instructive declarations of the liberal economic era, major shareholders at Exxon, the world's largest oil company, have berated its management for not paying attention to global warming.**

The point is well proven and rather than add any more to what I have already stated, I have simply reproduced below a copy of the letter the shareholders sent to Exxon. It says it all – especially the list of signatories at the end. I implore you to read very carefully every single word.

THE HUMAN ASSET MANIFESTO

Investor Network On Climate Risk
www.incr.com

May 15, 2006

Michael J. Boskin
c/o Mr. Henry H. Hubble
Secretary
Exxon Mobil Corporation
5959 Las Colinas Boulevard
Irving, TX 75039-2298

Dear Mr. Boskin:

We, as pension fund trustees and shareholders representing $525 billion in assets, are writing to request a meeting with you and other independent board members on the Exxon Mobil policy committee to discuss our concerns about what we view as our company's lack of strategic vision on climate change and its strategic implications for preservation of shareholder value.

We are following up an exchange of letters you have had with Connecticut State Treasurer Denise L. Nappier, who has been seeking such a meeting. You offered to have staff meet with investors to discuss climate change – and we are in discussions with your corporate secretary's office regarding such a meeting, which they are offering to hold in July.

The meeting we are requesting, however, is very different. We are major institutional investors in Exxon Mobil. We are interested in discussing with board members on the Public Policy Committee your plans to manage the transformation of Exxon-Mobil from a 20th Century oil company to a company that will meet the world's energy demands within carbon constraints in the a 21st Century.

In your February 24 letter to Treasurer Nappier you wrote that the Tomorrow's Energy report, released in February 2006, represents the board's position on climate change. If so, this is

288

troubling, as the Tomorrow's Energy report paints a picture of a company that fails to acknowledge the potential for climate change to have a profound impact on global energy markets, and which lags far behind its competitors in developing a strategy to plan for and manage these impacts.

The new report is built around what appears to us to be two serious contradictions. First, while the report states that "advances in technology are critical to successfully meeting future energy supply and demand challenges", our company appears not to be making any significant investment in new energy producing technologies. Second, while recognizing that the world is responding to climate change by putting limits on CO_2 emissions from burning of fossil fuel, there appears to be no strategic analysis of how these limits could impact the market for selling Exxon Mobil's major product – oil.

Outside analysts are also concerned. Goldman Sachs recently ranked oil companies on their environmental and social performance, which it concludes are important drivers of future performance and valuation. On climate change, the company scored 12th in its industry, far behind competitors like BP, Shell, and Total. For long-term investors, such underperformance is troubling. According to Goldman Sachs, "the companies that have the potential for creating significant value are those that have the most strategic options available to embrace a low-carbon world." For ExxonMobil investors, this is not encouraging.

A new report by IRRC, Corporate Governance and Climate Change: Making the Connection, rates 100 companies, including 20 companies in the oil sector, against a 14-point best-practice checklist. ExxonMobil received only 35 points out of a possible 100 in this analysis, again falling well behind its competitors.

Our company is in effect making a massive bet—with shareholders' money—that the world will remain addicted to oil for decades, even as its competitors are taking steps to hedge their bets and invest in renewables. As investors we are concerned that ExxonMobil is not preparing for Tomorrow's Energy and will lag significantly behind its competitors.

As shareholders, we ask to meet with you and other members of the policy committee to discuss these concerns, and to learn how the board plans to safeguard long-term shareholder value in light of the serious challenges presented by climate change.

Sincerely,

Phil Angelides, Treasurer, State of California
California Public Employees' Retirement System
Robert P. Casey, Jr., Treasurer, State of Pennsylvania
Evangelical Lutheran Church in America
General Board of Pension and Health Benefits of the United Methodist Church
General Secretary-Treasurer, International Brotherhood of Teamsters
Alan Hevesi, Comptroller, State of New York
Nancy Kopp, Treasurer, State of Maryland
David Lemoine, Treasurer, State of Maine
The Nathan Cummings Foundation
Sheet Metal Workers Pension Fund
Jeb Spaulding, Treasurer, State of Vermont
William C. Thompson, Jr., Comptroller, City of New York
Tri-State Coalition for Responsible Investment
Walden Asset Management
Steve Westly, Controller, State of California

The Human Asset Organization© will cultivate and attract those investors that support its human and social approach to business.

CHAPTER

19

DEFINING THE SOUL OF THE HUMAN ASSET ORGANIZATION©

THE HUMAN ASSET MANIFESTO

19

DEFINING THE SOUL OF THE HUMAN ASSET ORGANIZATION©

Having determined the principles that define The Human Asset Organization©, what it should do to optimize its human assets, and what it must represent, we need to define its soul – the power within that motivates individuals to come together to make such an organization possible. Implicit in this is the need to define the context within which self-actualized individuals will commit to work together to achieve organizational goals.

Let us first examine this issue from the individual perspective, and in doing so define what would really motivate you or any other individual to want to work for an organization.

Nowadays, there is much talk about a work-life balance. From a philosophical perspective, I have been wrestling with this issue myself, partly because I have been unsure as to exactly what it means. It is obvious that for too long some organizations have erroneously believed that working excessive hours improves productivity. There are many studies that suggest otherwise, so we won't even attempt to counter that point – the contrary position is a given.

There is ample evidence that people are moving away from high intensity and high salaried jobs in order to do more with their lives than simply slave away in front of their computer screens. With the help of my good friend and business colleague, Howard Bentley, I have now concluded that for those who want to be what they want to be, the idea of a work-life balance can be dispensed with.

Confused? Here is why and how Howard helped to convince me of this notion.

Howard facilitates organizational improvement and new ways of working. In his corporate engagements, he uses a number of audio-visual aids to communicate key messages to his audience. He works from home where he has a studio with all the equipment he needs.

Howard's basic philosophy is that work-life balance is not something he considers – by being who and what he wants to be, there is no great distinction on what we might casually refer to as his work, and his social activities. In other words, he has a natural life balance, dictated by how he has chosen to live and engage his passions. This includes helping to promote the 2007 Worldwide Scouts Jamboree in England, where they expect over 40,000 scouts from almost every country in the world.

Howard is not alone in adopting this philosophy. I received another fine example of living and working according to one's preferred lifestyle from Anne Palmer, Principal at BookMarketingSuccess.com. In an email to me, Anne explains the "natural order" within which she operates, including how she interacts with her clients, business partner Debra Dinnocenzo, as well as her own family.

> Since we have clients in many different times zones, I have several laptops set up around my home on standing-height work stations (Debra and I work from our home offices, meeting "virtually" most of the time), and as I walk around the house doing my "domestic thing," I'm able to see or hear mail arrive (except between midnight and 5 a.m.), and even negotiate with publishers while doing the laundry (but they never know that!).

> I believe that people aren't meant to live and work in "segmentation." People are integrated beings (like Drucker says, you cannot hire just a hand...the entire person comes with it!). We have achieved an enviable lifestyle of integrating work, play, family, friendships, etc., and we flow through all of these on a daily (and minute-by-minute) basis. The kids are now off to school, and my husband (who has the same work style) and I are going out for breakfast!

Both Howard and Anne are very successful people in the traditional sense, with the added advantage of thoroughly enjoying what they do.

How is this rationalized for the millions of people working within organizations?

By definition, The Human Asset Organization© is one where both personal and professional ambitions are linked to rewards and corporate objectives. What this means therefore is that in such an organization, employees must be free to operate within a framework that best suits and best facilitates who they are, who they want to be, what they want to achieve, and where they want to go. This is what facilitates individual self-actualization within an organization.

In this self-actualized state, individual objectives will move beyond the simplistic idea of a work-life balance – and what we are left with is a total life balance. It means that those who want to work from home will be allowed to, those who want to work fewer or unusual hours will be allowed to, those who want mix career and family life will be allowed to. The pursuit of higher education and taking a sabbatical to pursue other goals would be very consistent with this notion.

What is important here is whether, like Howard, you work for yourself or alternatively you work within an organization, **you first have to determine your "BE" – your reason for being, the higher purpose beyond a mere existence.** This is a truly important concept and one for which I am grateful to another friend and business colleague, Malcolm Lewis of Strategic Value Consulting, for taking the time out to discuss this topic with me. Malcolm's work is focused on assisting managers, executives and organizations to determine their BE.

Once an individual has determined their BE, the next stage is to find that organization or vocation that most suits their ambitions. This is critical at both the individual and the organizational level because this is where the two strands connect, or possibly disconnect, as the case may be. An organization that consists of individuals with common or shared values is far less likely to be socially dysfunctional, and far more likely to be both innovative and productive.

The Human Asset Organization© works with individuals to determine their goals, integrate those goals with the objec-

tives of the organization, and by so doing harness their entrepreneurial capabilities.

We met an example of this when we reviewed the DARPA Challenge (*Point 9, Unleash Creativity By Creating An Open And Flexible Working Environment*, in the chapter *New Paradigm, New Approach, New Organization*). In this instance, Rockwell provided their workers with seed capital to enter the DARPA challenge and shared the rewards of their efforts.

There is an abundance of entrepreneurial talent within organizations just waiting to be unleashed. **Yet, unbelievably, many organizations insist on exercising total control over their employees' intellectual capital. As such, if an employee does have a great idea, and many do, invariably it is never in their interest to share it with their organization.** It will remain locked away until such time that the employee can either share it with someone else or exploit it on their own – just like all those people who instantly become creative once they leave an organization.

The Human Asset Organization© will recruit and develop individuals and teams that have an idea and a BE which is consistent with the organization's objectives, unleash their creativity, and share with them the rewards of that development.

This is why organizations should stop recruiting people on the sole basis of their degrees and qualifications. They should also focus on the type of people they want to work with and their ambitions – they should determine their BE. This is not a prescription for acquiring a set of workaholic robots – diversity in backgrounds and values will always be important and a person can contribute to an organization's vision whether they work five or ten hours a day. What is important is that they share the vision.

For individuals living in more advanced economies who are less concerned with immediate survival, focusing on a BE will become an increasingly important aspect of life. In the earlier example of the 1940s middle-class family we had noted that in today's advanced economies, someone could possess all that family had and more, but still be considered poor. It follows that we can either engage in endlessly acquiring a plethora of new gadgets as quickly as they are thrown at us, or we can engage in developing how we contribute to society.

It is an accepted fact that while people in the developed world have increased wealth, they don't have increased happiness.

In *Bait and Switch: The (Futile) Pursuit of the American Dream*, the author Dr Ehrenreich appears to have some sympathy with our previously developed idea that white-collar workers are the new proletariat. She describes them as having done all the right things – got a good education, got a good job, and worked hard, even to the point of burning themselves out. Tragically, all they have to show for it is frustration, career turmoil, insecurity, burn out and a host of other less desirable traits. What is more, many have lost their jobs and encounter great difficulty in stepping back onto the corporate ladder.

From another perspective, people have become so 'bored' with regular life that much of what is now considered fun and leisure is the consumption of copious quantities of alcohol and drugs.

Having a BE provides a higher purpose to our existence.

We may arrive at a similar conclusion for organizations. If we once again reflect on the differences in the mission statements of Ford and Toyota we encountered in the chapter *Why The Car In Front Is A Toyota* you might recall Ford focuses on shareholder returns, while Toyota focuses on customer value. Toyota's BE goes beyond the acquisition of profits.

In addition to autos, we have examined a variety of other industries, such as airlines, music, computers, and consumer electronics, where those organizations that focus on human and social values are routinely more successful than their competitors are.

More organizations will need to make the transition from their current mechanistic model, replete with its Scientific Management approach, to a value-based system, that is focused on a BE. It is within this framework, where individual and organizational BEs are in harmony, that human assets are optimized, and with it innovation, productivity, and competitive advantage.

Throughout this book, we have proved that innovation, productivity, and competitive advantage have human and social roots, and reflect the human and social evolution of society.

It is therefore entirely logical and consistent that an organization's soul, its BE, and the reason for its existence, should be expressed in human and social terms and values – they should provide the framework from within which it conducts its business. This will have profound implications for its business model and the marketing of its products and services.

This is perhaps best understood by analyzing the basis on which organizations have evolved, the social factors that influenced that evolution and the competencies and qualities that were necessary for their survival at each stage. As usual, we will begin with our established reference point – the Industrial Revolution.

At the time of the Industrial Revolution and into the early stages of industrialization, the most important organizational competencies were centered on technology and technical competence. These included the ability to develop or make best use of emerging knowledge, and to translate that knowledge into products and services.

In social terms, it was an age when very basic goods, e.g. soap, that were previously only available to kings and aristocrats were being made available to ordinary people. Individual ambitions and expectations, save for the merchants and innovators of the time, were largely restricted to one's social class.

The organizational orientation, competencies and skill sets necessary for operating within that period are summarized in the table below.

Stage of Social Evolution	Organization Orientation	Organization Competencies
Industrial Revolution & Early Industrialization	Technical Production	Technology Execution and delivery

This early industrial phase eventually gave way to the era of mass production in the early 1900s. Although products and services remained functional, their proliferation and the transfer of knowledge meant that simply knowing how to make something was no longer sufficient. As such, organizations had to improve their structural capabilities – thus enabling them to produce large volumes of products and services at an affordable price.

Towards the end of the era, research and development assumed greater importance as organizations strove to outdo each other with respect to quality and efficiency. In social terms, the period saw a rapid expansion in the availability of basic goods and services.

The organizational orientation, competencies, and skill sets necessary for operating within that period, which ended with the outbreak of World War II, are summarized in the table below.

Stage of Social Evolution	Organization Orientation	Organization Competencies
Mass Production	Structural Capabilities Demand Price	Efficient systems and processes Distribution Competitiveness Industry expertise Industry leadership Reliability Cost Efficiency Research & Development

In the post-war period, people wanted more. The idea abounded that the average person's life was worth far more than the ability to sacrifice it for one's country. Individual expectations of life and the quality of life increased significantly.

To reflect the social trend, competition moved from mere productive capacity to focus on the need of the individual customer. Product variety, branding, marketing, and advertising all came to the fore and the new medium of television played a highly significant role. The organizational orientation, competencies, and skill sets necessary for operating within this period of mass consumption are summarized in the table below.

Stage of Social Evolution	Organization Orientation	Organization Competencies
Mass Production	Customer Product Price Location	Product and service quality Branding and Marketing Understanding of client's needs Innovation Client relationships Integrated delivery of products and services Customer care Client commitment Ingenious client solutions

By the 1980s, organizations had become multinational as well as multi-dimensional. Their greatest challenge arose from a need to operate in scale, while maintaining their customer focus in each market. This was especially difficult in the era of mass consumerism that was emerging around that time. In the era of mass consumerism, the demand for goods and services moved way beyond needs to an ever-increasing propensity to satisfy whims.

Many believed that the answers to the problems of the era lay in the organization structure. It started with matrix management but has since grown to encompass rightsizing, downsizing, outsourcing, and such machinations. That legacy is still with us.

During the period, the service sector of advanced economies experienced dramatic growth, further increasing the need to focus on people assets. Knowledge Management initially brought with it an emphasis on people but eventually it was subsumed by computers and systems.

It was an era when organizations should have placed their greatest focus on people and those that did reaped considerable success. The communications and IT industries came into their own as Silicon Valley brought with it new ways of managing, deploying and rewarding people skills.

However, by hanging on to the principles of Scientific Management, and by organizing people around computers rather than vice versa, the efforts of many organizations were considerably diluted. The organizational qualities and competences most suited to the period are summarized in the table below.

Stage of Social Evolution	Organization Orientation	Organization Competencies
Mass Production	Employees Clients Suppliers	Employee policies People quality Niceness of employees The sales or service experience Responsiveness Innovation

Mass consumerism will continue for some time. However, in a few years there will be 50 different functions on your mobile phone, of which you probably master fewer than five – if you are lucky. There will be 25 ways to access the Internet, and a further 13.5 ways to view a movie or an episode of your favorite soap. I exaggerate, but only slightly. The bewildering array of choice in our lives is already confusing and the indications are that this will get worse – consumers will continue to be slaves to their whims.

It is no small wonder therefore that a group of scientists in Holland have found that "Complexity causes 50% of product returns." Reuters reported as follows:

Half of all malfunctioning products returned to stores by consumers are in full working order, but customers can't figure out how to operate the devices, a scientist said on Monday.

Product complaints and returns are often caused by poor design, but companies frequently dismiss them as "nuisance calls," Elke den Ouden found in her thesis at the Technical University of Eindhoven in the south of the Netherlands.

A wave of versatile electronics gadgets has flooded the market in recent years, ranging from MP3 players and home cinema sets to media centers and wireless audio systems, but consumers still find it hard to install and use them, she found.

The average consumer in the United States will struggle for 20 minutes to get a device working, before giving up, the study found.

It has become a nightmare for traditional marketers. **Customer loyalty lasts only as long as the next best thing to catch their eye – tastes have become extremely fickle.** Merely pushing things at us is no longer a valid proposition and will become less valid as time goes by. What is needed therefore is a value proposition that pulls us towards their products – something that has an appeal beyond our whims.

At the same time, amidst the consumer binge that is taking place in more advanced economies, there is degradation of the environment, inequalities, and global poverty, hunger, famine and disease. As these issues increasingly dominate the political and economic discourse of our time, it is inevitable that today's organizations will be as subject to the human and social evolution they will provoke, as their earlier predecessors.

The Human Asset Organization© will embrace a value proposition that is consistent with the development of all human assets, internal and external. In this final stage of development, the organization can express itself and its ambitions in terms of the marketing of social values that are also entirely consistent and representative of its business objectives. The organizational qualities and competences most suited to the future are summarized in the table below.

Stage of Social Evolution	Organization Orientation	Organization Competencies
Human Asset or Social	Value (not profit) Driven Human & Social Marketing	Environmental policies Integrity and trust Organizational mission and values Organizational culture Commitment to the community

Social Value Marketing, the promotion of the organization's social values and its contribution to society (as well as the value of individual lifestyles) will be the way of the future, not because it is the nice thing to do, but because it will be consistent with an organization's value system and how it creates prosperity.

Expressing the utility of products and services in social value terms will be the most credible method of retaining customers and enhancing relationships. It will require organizations to define the social basis of their being and how they contribute to society.

The Human Asset Organization© will utilize Social Value Marketing to pull customers who share its values, as against endlessly engaging in the highly unpredictable rat race of pushing products and services at them.

It is because of this need to pull customers that L'Oreal, who marketed its cosmetics with the purely aesthetic slogan "because you deserve it", is trying to change its image by purchasing the Body Shop, a cosmetics company with ethical standards at the core of its activities.

The totality of the human asset approach takes us beyond CSR, while providing a framework within which the latter is wholly consistent with value in every sense. By defining its specific social value proposition, operationally, strategically, internally and externally, and linking that to values, missions, behaviors and actions within this framework, an organization can determine its BE, and define its soul. Their future success will depend on it.

It is for this reason that THAEvaluator© also includes an assessment of the Organization Competencies included in the tables above. The necessity for making this assessment is apparent when we study Diagram 1. Each set of organizational competencies effectively reinforces those of the period before.

What this tells us is that the most important competencies the modern organization can possess are its values. These values will ultimately determine the quality of everything else, and is entirely consistent with our view that human and social values are the roots of innovation, productivity, and competitive advantage.

Diagram 1

Stage of Social Evolution	Organisational Competencies
Industrial Revolution & Early Industrialization	Technology Execution and delivery
Mass Production Pre 1945	Efficient systems and processes Distribution Competitiveness Industry expertise Industry leadership Reliability Cost Efficiency Research & Development
Mass Consumption 1945 to 1980s	Product and service quality Brand & Marketing Understanding of client's needs Innovation Client relationships Integrated delivery of products and services Customer care Client commitment Ingenious client solutions
Mass Consumerism 1980s to Current	Employee policies People quality Niceness of employees The sales or service experience Responsiveness Innovation
Human Asset or Social Near Future	Environmental policies Integrity and trust Organisational mission and values Organisational culture Commitment to the community

Improved productive capacity improves technical proficiency and execution

Improved customer focus facilitates greater efficiency and competitiveness

Improved focus on employees improves their ability to innovate and satisfy customer demand

Improved focus on values provides a framework for improving human assets, people quality and customer orientation

Many organizations have adopted some form of CSR program, as indicated by the following article entitled SMEs with a Social Conscience, taken from the website of CORDIS, an organization devoted to European research and development (R&D), and innovation activities.

> *Businesses do not have to be big to act on social and environmental concerns. More than half of SMEs are involved in socially responsible causes. They are motivated by ethics, but find they gain business benefits.*
>
> *The 'triple bottom line' - financial, social, and environmental performance - features strongly on the agenda of prominent multinationals. It is also more of a priority than has been realized for Europe's SMEs, although it is much more informal and unreported.*

Many others are going a stage further and engaging in fair trade activities – paying a fair price and decent living wage for goods sourced from developing countries. This is a highly important development in globalization, especially when given the failure of our political leaders to address some of these issues.

Although I am positive that this is all well intended, for a variety of reasons I remain somewhat skeptical of the extent to which these activities are sustainable. They include:

1. Employees are unlikely to be impressed by their organization's philanthropic endeavors if they are not convinced that the organization acts in their own best interest
2. CSR will fail if consumers see it as a sales gimmick – the current level of trust is palpably low
3. CSR will pass or become diluted as every other fad, unless it is steeped in every aspect and fabric of the organization's business
4. In the longer term, the quality of an organization's efforts will ultimately depend on its employees. If the organizations professed culture and ethos fails to embrace those employees, then its efforts will fail

THE HUMAN ASSET MANIFESTO

In his book *Liberating the Corporate Soul, Building a Visionary Organization*, **Richard Barrett maintains that if organizations are to transform themselves from machines into living entities, then they must develop a value-driven strategic framework that encompasses every aspect of their business.** That is precisely what we are proposing. I particularly like the fact that Barrett's book is prefaced thus: *For those who have the courage to bring their whole selves to work.*

Barrett further goes on to say that the implications of this are such that the framework must encompass employees, the community and the society, and that it must be concerned with survivability, sustainability, and social inequality.

In these pages, we have also shown how such a framework supports the internal need for social harmony as a basis on which organizations must develop their capabilities to achieve their goals.

It is a sign of the times that the likes of Google, Microsoft, and Yahoo have all come under criticism for conforming to the dictates of the Chinese government by amending their software so that it restricts access to websites the authorities deem inappropriate. In the case of Yahoo, it has been alleged that cooperation with the Chinese government has even led to the arrest of individuals. Google, the darling of the stock market, saw its share price drop when the allegations, which it has not denied but rather tried to explain, first became known.

We also have the case of the major oil companies who made what many considered super-profits, and gained public disfavor as a result. Proof positive that profits alone, which without doubt are vitally important, can never be the only arbiter of success.

Only time will tell how this might affect their business, but what we do know for sure is that organizations are now more than ever being scrutinized and assessed for their values, and this will only increase with time.

Indeed, I do believe we are on the verge of a Renaissance. Those organizations that do not establish their business on appro-

priate human and social values will stumble and ultimately fall. Alternatively, those organizations that have a BE that is grounded in human and social values, will improve prosperity not only for themselves, but also for those around them.

Further, as people increasingly question the very rationale of their existence and focus more on what they want to achieve in their personal lives, organizations will increasingly need to attract and retain employees on the basis of their shared social values.

I will leave the final word on this issue to Drucker, whose influence has been pervasive throughout this book. In an article entitled the Role of the Social Sector, Drucker takes everything a step further, perhaps even unto its logical conclusion.

> *I take a dim view of most of the programs companies create to develop their people. The real development I've seen of people in organizations, especially in big ones, comes from their being volunteers in a non-profit organization -- where you have responsibility, you see results, and you quickly learn what your values are. There is no better way to understand your strengths and discover where you belong than to volunteer in a non-profit. That is probably the great opportunity for the social sector -- and especially in its relationship to business.*

> *We talk today of the social responsibilities of business. I hope we will soon begin to talk about the non-profit organization as the great social opportunity for business. It is the opportunity for business to develop managers far more effectively than any company or university can. It is one of the unique benefits that the social sector can offer -- to provide a place where the knowledge worker can actually discover who he or she is and can actually learn to manage him or herself.*

It is a simple message – capture the heart and everything else will follow. That is the ultimate objective of The Human Asset Organization©.

THE HUMAN ASSET MANIFESTO

Before you move on to THE NEXT STEPS please read the Statement of Affirmation on the next page. It represents a summary of the principles established in this section. I hope that you will also be moved to act on the suggestion that follows.

The Human Asset Manifesto
Statement of Affirmation 4

- *I believe that organizations are at their best when people are at their best*

- *I believe that the greatest prosperity is realized when all stakeholders prosper*

- *I believe that the more worthy the aspiration the more worthy the reward*

- *I believe that liberated & self-actualized individuals can make the greatest contribution*

- *I believe that shared values create a unity of purpose*

- *I believe that organizations that lead social change will be amongst the most competitive*

- *I believe that organizations must recognize the totality of the human experience*

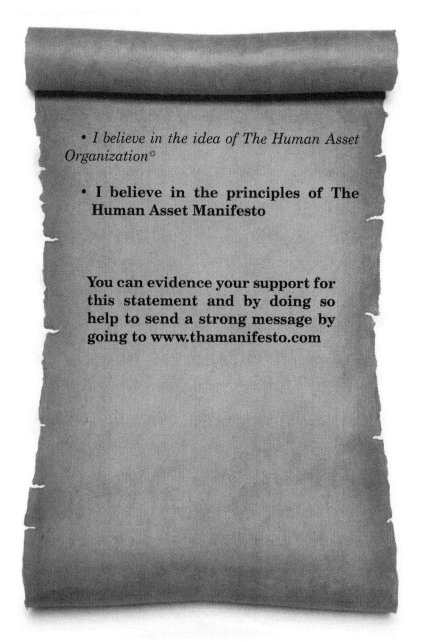

• *I believe in the idea of The Human Asset Organization*©

• I believe in the principles of The Human Asset Manifesto

You can evidence your support for this statement and by doing so help to send a strong message by going to www.thamanifesto.com

THE NEXT STEPS

THE HUMAN ASSET MANIFESTO

CHAPTER

20

WHERE DO WE GO FROM HERE?

THE HUMAN ASSET MANIFESTO

CHAPTER

WHERE DO WE GO FROM HERE?

At the very beginning of this book, I invoked the passion of the mission. If one truly believes in something then to be self-actualized, it should form the basis of one's pursuits. As such, it should not be surprising to you that I have taken The Human Asset Manifesto beyond the writing of this book and made the further and active promotion of its principles into my BE.

It is for that reason that in late 2005 I formed The Human Asset Partners or THAPartners with my friend and colleague Ralph Genang. Our operating philosophy is based entirely on the principles established in The Human Asset Manifesto, and we are totally committed to pursuing our work with the passion and integrity that demands. The objectives of THAPartners, www.thapartners.com, are to provide organizations with an ability to:

1. Improve the level of employee engagement and motivation
2. Better recognize, evaluate and leverage all their human assets
3. Improve innovation, productivity and competitive advantage
4. Further develop knowledge and value-adding capabilities
5. Address risks arising from the divergence in corporate and individual objectives
6. Promote socially responsible business practices
7. Create a more socially harmonious and pleasant working environment
8. Better leverage employee diversity

THAPartners welcome inquiries from corporations, consultancies, HR consultancies, training organizations, or anyone interested in hearing more about our work, including:

THE HUMAN ASSET MANIFESTO

1. Developing The Human Asset Organization©

2. Exchanging ideas and learning more about The Human Asset Organization©

3. Seminars

4. Workshops

5. Speaking Engagements

6. Business Advisory

7. Measuring and assessing of human assets using THAEvaluator©

THAEvaluator© is licensed directly to corporates users as well as consultancies.

Please visit us at www.thapartners.com, email me at jonathan.ledwidge@thapartners.com or ralph.genang@thapartners.com – we would love to hear from you.

ABOUT THE AUTHOR

Jonathan Ledwidge was born in London but grew up in his parents' native Jamaica. He studied Physics and Chemistry at the University of West Indies before joining Price Waterhouse, later qualifying as a Chartered Accountant. He worked for J Wray & Nephew, a manufacturer and distributor of sugar and rum, before migrating to the UK in 1986.

For the next eighteen years, he worked in the City of London for a number of global investment banks, including Continental, CIBC Capital Markets, and ABN AMRO. Much of this time was spent on developing and implementing business strategies for the global capital markets in a range of sophisticated products and services.

Towards the end of his investment banking career, Jonathan focused on learning, knowledge development and cultural change, and devised strategies and approaches for improving output and productivity for product origination and distribution teams in the global financial markets.

Jonathan has combined his extensive knowledge and experience in business, with a lifelong passion for history, politics, and culture. He has read and traveled extensively in pursuit of these interests. It was his recognition of the wider human and social issues within business that ultimately led him to research and write The Human Asset Manifesto (THAManifesto©), develop THAEvaluator©, and launch THAPartners, where he is now the Managing Partner.

Jonathan holds an MBA from Cass Business School in London. His first book, A Mannequin for President, is a critique on US Presidential politics. He describes his overall socio-political philosophy as Equal Lives – the idea that every single human life on this planet is as valuable as any other.

THE HUMAN ASSET MANIFESTO

BIBLIOGRAPHY

The Case For The People

The Wealth of Knowledge, Thomas A. Stewart

Intellectual Capital, Thomas A Stewart

Developing Knowledge Based Client Relationships, Ross Dawson

The Sunday Times Best 100 Companies To Work For, DTI, Investors in People, Best Companies www.bestcompanies.co.uk

People Represent As Much As 80% Of An Organization's Value – What Are They Doing About It?

The Make-Believe World Of The Faddists

The knowledge management puzzle: Human and social factors in knowledge management, by J. C. Thomas, W. A. Kellogg, and T. Erickson IBM Systems Journal, Volume 40, Number 4, 2001, Knowledge Management, http://www.research.ibm.com/journal/sj/404/thomas.html

Is Scientific Management Dead, Patrick D.T. O'Connor

Merger integration: why the 'soft issues' matter most, Till Vestring, Brian King, Ted Rouse and Julian Critchlow, European Business Forum issue 13, http://www.ebfonline.com/main_feat/trends/trends.asp?id=389

Knowledge Is Of The People, For The People, By The People
Guns, Germs And Steel, Jared Diamond

The Wealth of Nations, Adam Smith

The Meiji Era and the Modernization of Japan, Maria Christensen, http://www.samurai-archives.com/tme.html

THE HUMAN ASSET MANIFESTO

The Industrial Revolution: "Myths and Realities," Peter Landry, http://www.blupete.com/Literature/Essays/BluePete/IndustRev.htm

Facts about the "Industrial Revolution" by Ludwig von Mises, September 1993, http://www.fff.org/freedom/0993e.asp

The Inventors of the Industrial Revolution, Peter Landry, http://www.blupete.com/Literature/Biographies/Science/Inventors.htm#Watt

Knowledge Is Important But Corporations Have Been Slow Learners

Historical Background of Organizational Behavior, (prepared by Professor Edward G. Wertheim, College of Business Administration, Northeastern University, Boston, MA 02115) http://web.cba.neu.edu/~ewertheim/introd/history.htm

A History of Corporate Rule and Popular Protest, Extracted from Nexus Magazine, Volume 9, Number 6 (Oct-Nov 2002) by Richard Heinberg © 2002 Editor/Publisher MuseLetter http://www.wealth4freedom.com/truth/corporations.htm

HUMAN RESOURCES AND COMPETENCIES OVER TIME, Mary Felice, Research Directorate, Policy, Research and Communications Branch, Public Service Commission of Canada, 1998 http://www.hrma-agrh.gc.ca/research/personnel/comp_history_e.pdf

Slouching Towards Utopia: The Economic History of the Twentieth Century, by J. Bradford DeLong of the University of California, Berkley

Structural Change and Spatial Dynamics of the U.S. Software Industry, Ted Egan, Ph.D., ICF Kaiser International, Inc. Paper Presented for Sloan Foundation Globalization Workshop Duke University, April 25,1998 http://www.icfconsulting.com/Publications/egan_sw.asp

Management Across Borders, The Transnational Solution, Bartlett and Ghosal

Ever get the feeling you're being watched? Author: Management Issues News Management-Issues at the heart of the workplace, 22 May 2005,http://www.management-issues.com/ display_page.asp?section=research&id=2159

Firms tag workers to improve efficiency, David Hencke, Tuesday June 7, 2005, The Guardian, http://www.guardian.co.uk/uk_news/story/0,3604,1500838,00.html

How Pixar Conquered The Planet, The Guardian, Friday Nov 12, 2004 http://arts.guardian.co.uk/fridayreview/story/0,12102,1348509,00.html

Why The Car In Front Is A Toyota

The Machine That Changed The World, The Story of Lean Production, James Womack, Daniel Jones, Daniel Roos

The Toyota Way, Jeffrey Liker

Toyota vs. GM: The Devil in the Details, by Leonard M Karpen Jr., The Interactive Investor Journal, http://www.yeald.com/Yeald/a/34021/toyota_vs__gm__the_devil_in_the_details.html

General motors: the road ahead; What should GM do to improve? Advice from the outside Automotive Design & Production, Jan, 2005 by Gary S. Vasilash, Chris Sawyer
http://www.findarticles.com/p/articles/mi_m0KJI/is_1_117/ai_n9485226

Japanese auto plants lead in European productivity, News Release from: World Markets Research, Edited by the Manufacturingtalk Editorial Team on 11 July 2003 http://www.manufacturingtalk.com/news/woa/woa101.html

Technology, human resources and international competitiveness in the Korean auto industry: the case of Kia Motors, Russell D. Lansbury, School of Business, Faculty of Economics and Business, University of Sydney, NSW 2006, Australia

Dirty Rotten Standards

In Pursuit of Quality: The Case Against ISO 9000, John Seddon

In Pursuit of Quality: The Case Against ISO 9000, John Seddon, Bristol Business School Teaching and Research Review, Issue 2, Spring 2000, ISSN 1468-4578
http://www.uwe.ac.uk/bbs/trr/Issue2/Is2-1_1.htm

**"You Cannot Hire A Hand, The Whole Person Comes With It."
– Drucker**

Maslow on Management, Abraham H. Maslow

Motivation and Personality, Abraham H. Maslow

The Practice of Management, Peter F. Drucker

Management Challenges for the 21st Century, Peter F. Drucker

Enlightenment Economics, Diane Coyle, MERRILL LYNCH/IMPERIAL COLLEGE LECTURE, 10 NOVEMBER 1999 (With Nick Crafts, Professor Of Economic History, London School Of Economics) http://www.enlightenmenteconomics.com/credo.html

Employee Motivation, The Organizational Environment and Productivity, Cliff F. Grimes, Accel Team, http://www.accel-team.com/, http://www.accel-team.com/scientific/scientific_01.html

Big Dog's Leadership Page - Organizational Behavior, Ronald R Clark, http://www.nwlink.com/~donclark/leader/leadob.html

A Short History of Empowerment, by Robert L Webb
http://www.motivation-tools.com/workplace/history.htm

Leadership Trends, by Robert L Webb
http://www.motivation-tools.com/workplace/leadership_trends.htm

Motivation in the Workplace, by Robert L Webb
http://www.motivation-tools.com/workplace/index.htm

Working on the Panama Canal, by Robert L Webb
http://www.motivation-tools.com/workplace/panama_canal.htm

Basic Operating Rules of Lockheed Skunkworks, From Kelly Johnson, http://www.astech-engineering.com/systems/avionics/aircraft/skunkworks.html

The Good Boss Report 05-06, Andrea Gregory and Lisa Smale, The Good Boss Company

Bait and Switch: The (Futile) Pursuit of the American Dream, Dr Barbara Ehrenreich

The Roots Of Social Dysfunctionality Within Organizations

Geographies of Consumer Society,
http://www.strath.ac.uk/Departments/gs/pdf/33101/33101_L19.pdf

Features of a Consumer Society, McGregor Consulting Group
http://www.consultmcgregor.com/PDFs/features%20of%20consumer%20society.pdf

Modern Lessons In The Human And Social Evolution Of Customers

Technology's Seamier Side: Fates of Pornography and Internet Businesses Are Often Intertwined, by Mike Musgrove, Washington Post Staff Writer, Saturday, January 21, 2006; Page D01
http://www.washingtonpost.com/wp-dyn/content/article/2006/01/20/AR2006012001888.html?referrer=email&referrer=email

Liquid Candy; How Soft Drinks Are Harming America's Health, Centre for Science in the Public Interest, http://www.cspinet.org/liquidcandy/index.html

New Strategies for Consumer Goods, by Peter D. Haden, Olivier Sibony, and Kevin D. Sneader, The McKinsey Quarterly, January 10, 2005, http://www.marketingpower.com/content24540.php

Advocates threaten lawsuits to curb food marketing, Anna Driver, Reuters, Sun Feb 19, 2006pm ET , http://today.reuters.com/news/articlenews.aspx?type=lifeAndLeisureNews&storyid=2006-02-19T160834Z_01_N19146416_RTRUKOC_0_US-BIZFEATURE-OBESITY.xml

The Bling Generation And Why Managers Should Watch MTV

Boomers, Xers and Other Strangers, Dr. Rick and Kathy Hicks

Young Guns, Mature Minds - Generation Gap Threatens Business, Why employers believe companies will fail without young guns and wise guys, 29 September 2004, Vodafone UK
http://www.vodafone.com/article_with_thumbnail/
0,3038,OPCO%253D40018%2526CATEGORY_ID%253D210%2526MT_ID
%253Dpr%2526LANGUAGE_ID%253D0%2526CONTENT_ID%253D252348,00.html

CellFlix Festival for cellular short films, Ithaca College, http://www.cellflixfestival.org/main.html

Ithaca College Student Wins CellFlix Festival for Movies Shot on Cell Phone, School News, 30/01/06 http://www.ithaca.edu/rhp_news.php?news_id=1866

Project Open, Napster & The Music Industry Version 1.4, 4.7.2004, Frank Bergmann, fraber@fraber.de – ESADE, Barcelona
http://www.fraber.de/gem/Napster%20and%20the%20Music%20Industry%20010617.pdf

Crazy Frog Leaps Over Coldplay in British Singles Chart, Digital Music News, May 2005 (52605) http://www.digitalmusicnews.com/results?title=UK

Working Nation, Views From People At Work, Opinion Leader Research and Vodafone
http://www.vodafone.com/article/
0,3029,CATEGORY_ID%253D21416%2526LANGUAGE_ID%
253D0%2526CONTENT_ID%253D251379,00.html?

And On The Sixth Day God Said "Let There Be Woman!"

Aurora, where women want to work, http://www.auroravoice.com/www2wk.asp

Boom for women's spending power, BBC News, Friday, 5 September 2003 http://news.bbc.co.uk/1/hi/business/3083648.stm

The Female FTSE Report 2004, Centre for Developing Women Business Leaders, Cranfield University School of Management
http://www.som.cranfield.ac.uk/som/research/centres/cdwbl/downloads/FT2004FinalReport.pdf

Women's take on business priorities - Female executives say customers, employees come first, by Andrea Coombes, MarketWatch, Dec 6, 2005 http://www.marketwatch.com/News/Story/Story.aspx?guid=%7bBC4D8229-3571-481D-96E5-FEC032212D28%7d&archive=true&siteid=mktw&dist=SignInArchive&returnURL=%2fnews%2fstory.asp%3fguid%3d%7bBC4D8229-3571-481D-96E5-FEC032212D28%7d%26siteid%3dmktw%26dist%3d%26archive%3dtrue%26param%3darchive%26garden%3d%26minisite%3d

The State of the Nation's Housing 2004, Joint Centre for Housing Studies at Harvard University
http://www.jchs.harvard.edu/publications/markets/son2004.pdf

Women and the Glass Ceiling, Leader Values, Helen Peters, Hagberg Consulting Group
http://www.leader-values.com/Content/detail.asp?ContentDetailID=346

Wall St. women fight back, By THOMAS ZAMBITO, DAILY NEWS STAFF WRITER
http://www.nydailynews.com/business/story/382877p-325016c.html

Percentage of women among total graduates, by subject, Statistics Norway http://www.ssb.no/english/magazine/tab-2003-12-04-01-en.html

The Internet and computer games reinforce the gender gap, Lisa Rabasca, Monitor on Psychology, Volume 31, No. 9 October 2000
http://www.apa.org/monitor/oct00/games.html

The Wasted Asset - Japanese women are smart and entrepreneurial, so why is so little effort made to harness their talents? By Hannah Beech, Time Asia, August 22, 2005 http://www.time.com/time/asia/covers/501050829/story.html

The business case for gender diversity, Women to the Top
http://www.women2top.net/uk/facts/tools/Business_Case_Gender_Equality.pdf

Why are there so few women in games? Research for Media Training North West by Lizzie Haines, September 2004
http://www.igda.org/women/MTNW_Women-in-Games_Sep04.pdf

Sara Lee: Wonderbra, Matthew Moberg, Jonathan Siskin, Barry Stern, and Ru Wu (University of Michigan Business School, MBA Class of 1999) http://www-personal.umich.edu/~afuah/cases/case15.html

The Business Case For Gender Diversity, Scottsdale National Gender Institute   http://www.gendertraining.com/Business%20Case%20for%20Gender%20Diversity.pdf

Complexity causes 50% of product returns –scientist, Reuters, Mar 6, 2006 http://today.reuters.com/news/articlenews.aspx?type=technologyNews&storyid=2006-03-06T150309Z_01_L06746423_RTRUKOC_0_US-PRODUCTRETURNS.xml

Re-imagine, Tom Peters

People Don't Get Less Creative At Forty – They Simply Tire of Knocking Their Heads Against Brick Walls

Preserving Knowledge by Ensuring Its Flow, Research Interview with Frank Lekanne Deprez, director of ZeroSpace Advies and senior lecturer, Nyenrode University, the Netherlands, http://www.zerospaceadvies.nl/publicaties/pdf/BD%20Knowledge%20English.pdf

Stemming the Brain Drain, by David W. De Long and Thomas O. Mann,   Accenture   http://www.accenture.com/Global/Services/By_Subject/Workforce_Performance/R_and_I/StemmingTheBrainDrain.htm

IBM Introduces New Consulting Services to Help Employers Prepare for Baby-Boomer Transition, IBM 9/28/2005 10:34:50 AM, Web Wire http://www.webwire.com/ViewPressRel.asp?aId=4423

Making the most of a mature workforce, Source: The Conference Board: Managing the Mature Workforce, 1 November 2005, Human Resources Magazine http://www.humanresourcesmagazine.com.au/articles/D7/0C037CD7.asp?Type=60&Category=1256

Religion, Race & Ethnicity

Lies, Damn Lies, And Management Speak

New Paradigm, New Approach, New Organization

DARPA Grand Challenge Home,
http://www.darpa.mil/grandchallenge/

Employees participatory management — Tata Tea turns a new chapter, C.J. Punnathara, The Hindu Business Line, Sunday Feb 13, 2005
http://www.blonnet.com/2005/02/13/stories/2005021301640100.htm

Tata Tea net zooms 127% on branded tea sales growth, Hindu Business Line, Tuesday January 31, 2006,
http://www.thehindubusinessline.com/bline/2006/01/31/stories/2006013101961400.htm

The Customer Comes Second, Put Your People First And Watch 'Em Kick Butt, Hal Rosenbluth & Diane McFerrin Peters

Oh Yes, We Can Measure Human Assets – Introducing THAEvaluator©

Why Organizations Must Lead Social Change In Order To Survive

US airlines hit turbulence – again, by Simon Wilson, Money Week, Saturday March 4, 2006
http://www.moneyweek.com/file/3142/us-airlines.html

Students Purchasing More Green & Organic Products for Back to School Needs, Sarah Roberts, Center for a New American Dream - www.newdream.org, Aug 16, 2005
http://www.organicconsumers.org/BTC/students081705.cfm

Defining The Soul Of The Human Asset Organization©

SMEs with a social conscience, CORDIS, Euroabstracts, August 2002
http://www.cordis.lu/euroabstracts/en/august02/feature04.htm#footnotes

Bait and Switch: The (Futile) Pursuit of the American Dream, Dr Barbara Ehrenreich

Liberating the Corporate Soul, Building a Visionary Organization, Richard Barrett

Managing Knowledge Means Managing Oneself by Peter F. Drucker, Leader to Leader, No. 16 Spring 2000, http://www.pfdf.org/leaderbooks/l2l/spring2000/drucker.html

JONATHAN LEDWIDGE

THE HUMAN ASSET MANIFESTO

JONATHAN LEDWIDGE

THE HUMAN ASSET MANIFESTO